Aging, Death, and the
Quest for Immortality

A Horizons in Bioethics Series Book from

THE CENTER FOR
BI◉ETHICS
AND HUMAN DIGNITY

The Horizons in Bioethics Series brings together an array of insightful writers to address important bioethical issues from a forward-looking Christian perspective. The introductory volume, *Bioethics and the Future of Medicine,* covers a broad range of topics and foundational matters. Subsequent volumes focus on a particular set of issues, beginning with the end-of-life theme of *Dignity and Dying* and continuing with the genetics focus of *Genetic Ethics,* the economic and patient-caregiver emphases of *The Changing Face of Health Care,* and the reproductive analyses in *The Reproductive Revolution.* The volume on *BioEngagement* develops strategies for tacking such challenging issues.

The series is a project of The Center for Bioethics and Human Dignity, an international center located just north of Chicago, Illinois, in the United States of America. The Center endeavors to bring Christian perspectives to bear on today's many pressing bioethical challenges. It pursues this task by developing two book series, hundreds of audios and videos, numerous conferences in different parts of the world, and a variety of other printed and computer-based resources. Through its donor-member support program, the Center networks and provides resources for people interested in bioethical matters all over the world. Supporters receive the Center's international journal, *Ethics and Medicine,* the Center's newsletter, *Dignity,* the Center's Update Letters, an Internet News Service, and discounts on a wide array of bioethics resources.

For more information on membership in the Center or its various resources, including present or future books in the Horizons in Bioethics Series, contact the Center at:

The Center for Bioethics and Human Dignity
2065 Half Day Road
Bannockburn, IL 60015 USA
Phone: (847) 317-8180
Fax: (847) 317-8101

Information and ordering are also available through the Center's World Wide Web site on the Internet: *www.cbhd.org.*

THE CENTER FOR
BI●ETHICS
AND HUMAN DIGNITY

Aging, Death, and the Quest for Immortality

Edited by

C. BEN MITCHELL

ROBERT D. ORR

&

SUSAN A. SALLADAY

WILLIAM B. EERDMANS PUBLISHING COMPANY
GRAND RAPIDS, MICHIGAN / CAMBRIDGE, U.K.

Published 2004 by
Wm. B. Eerdmans Publishing Co.
255 Jefferson Ave. S.E., Grand Rapids, Michigan 49503 /
P.O. Box 163, Cambridge CB3 9PU U.K.

Printed in the United States of America

09 08 07 06 05 04   7 6 5 4 3 2 1

ISBN 0-8028-2784-5

www.eerdmans.com

Contents

THE EXPERIENCE OF AGING

ETHICAL ISSUES IN AGING

CONTENTS

CARING FOR THE AGING

THE QUEST FOR IMMORTALITY

Contributors

R. Geoffrey Brown, Ph.D., is senior pastor at Fletcher Hills Presbyterian Church, El Cajon, California.

Jackie Cameron, M.D., is an instructor in clinical medicine at Northwestern University School of Medicine in Chicago, Illinois.

William P. Cheshire Jr., M.D., is assistant professor of neurology at the Mayo Clinic, Jacksonville, Florida.

John Dunlop, M.D., is a geriatrician at Zion Clinic in Zion, Illinois, a small Christian group practice where he has been since 1976. He is also on the staff of Victory Memorial Hospital in Waukegan, Illinois.

Robert W. Evans, Ph.D., Ph.D., is senior pastor of Redwood Chapel in Castro Valley, California, and is the president of Veritas Ministries International and the director of the Veritas Institute for the Study of Bioethics and Public Values.

Stephen P. Greggo, Psy.D., is chair of the Pastoral Counseling and Psychology Department and associate professor of pastoral counseling and psychology at Trinity Evangelical Divinity School in Deerfield, Illinois.

Vernon Grounds, Ph.D., is chancellor and Cauwels Professor Emeritus of Pastoral Care and Christian Ethics of Denver Seminary in Denver, Colorado.

John F. Kilner, Ph.D., is president of the Center for Bioethics and Human Dignity, Bannockburn, Illinois.

C. Ben Mitchell, Ph.D., is associate professor of bioethics and contemporary culture at Trinity International University in Deerfield, Illinois, and editor of *Ethics & Medicine: An International Journal of Bioethics.*

Robert D. Orr, M.D., C.M., is Director of Ethics at the Fletcher Allen Health Care/UVM College of Medicine in Burlington, Vermont.

Stephen G. Post, Ph.D., is a professor and Associate Director for Educational Programs, Department of Bioethics, School of Medicine, Case Western Reserve University, Cleveland, Ohio.

Susan A. Salladay, Ph.D., R.N., is director of the Center for Bioethics at BryanLGH Medical Center, Lincoln, Nebraska.

Linda L. Treloar, Ph.D., R.N., C.S., NP-C, is on the faculty of Scottsdale Community College in Scottsdale, Arizona, where she teaches courses in geriatric, psychiatric, and disability nursing.

Gregory Waybright, Ph.D., is president of Trinity International University with campuses in Deerfield, Illinois; Miami, Florida; and Anaheim, California.

Introduction

Let's call her "Betty." She is a 75-year-old, married, mother of four children. Each of her children now is a married adult. She grew up in a small town, had a rather unremarkable childhood and adolescence, and married a man she met on her job. They fell deeply in love and together had what could only be described as a normal, middle-class life. They worked hard, raised their children well, contributed to their community and church, and put aside money for their long-anticipated retirement years.

Like thousands of retired Americans, they bought an RV and started to travel around the country, never straying too far on the tether from their hometown. The children were happy for their parents, though from time to time they worried about them as they traveled. Mom and Dad could never get the hang of a cell phone and forgot to turn it on more often than not. They would be a thousand miles away, and no one knew where they were.

Still living in the general vicinity of their parents, the children popped in and out of their parents' home, dropped off the grandchildren to be watched, and life was nearly idyllic. Birthdays and holidays were wonderful family occasions. In a very real sense, the center around which the family orbited was "Mom and Dad's" place.

One day, one of the daughters noticed that Betty forgot that she was going to babysit one of the grandchildren. No worries. She took the baby with her to the doctor's office and didn't think much about it after that. It was a little inconvenient, but everyone forgets now and again. But over time, everyone noticed that Betty was becoming more and more forgetful. She would not only forget appointments like babysitting. She forgot to take her medicine for her blood pressure. She had developed high blood pressure about ten years previously. She'd been on a special diet, but her internist told her that she really needed to be on drug therapy to be sure that she kept her "high blood" under control.

Betty had an unusually chirpy attitude most of the time. She would work in the kitchen or in the garden, whistling and singing hymns she sang in church the previous Sunday. But the children noticed that more recently she had become less active, more sedate, almost brooding.

Her memory lapses continued to grow more pronounced. One day Betty called one of the daughters in tears to tell her that while she was out shopping she'd gotten lost. She had no idea where she was. The daughter asked Betty to give her a street name. Betty looked for a nearby street sign and gave the daughter the general location. Puzzled, the daughter hopped in her car to see if she could locate her mom. When she got to Betty's location, the daughter was deeply troubled. This was a street Mom had traveled a thousand times before. The daughter did notice that some new buildings had gone up recently and that some of the signs had been changed. Maybe it was just temporary confusion due to a changing urban geography. Or maybe not.

After several incidents of this kind, one of the daughters suggested that Betty see her doctor for a checkup. You know, just to be sure everything's all right. Betty's husband and daughter went with her. Following an explanation of some of Betty's recent lapses, and after a physical examination, while Betty was getting dressed the doctor told her husband and daughter that Betty was likely experiencing the first symptoms of Alzheimer's disease. The doctor said not to say anything to Betty. It would only confuse her more. He prescribed a new drug that he said would probably slow the progression of the disease and sent them home with pamphlets that described the disease and its devastating prognosis. As far as anyone could tell, this was not going to turn out well over time — maybe a long time. And it didn't. Eventually, Betty lost the ability to function normally. After a period of increasing agitation, she became sullen, noncommunicative. When she did speak, her sentences made no sense at all. They were never related to the topic of conversation. She would often awaken in the middle of the night and wander through the house. She would peer longingly outside, as if through the bars of a prison.

One day, she wandered off by herself along the sidewalk outside her house. It couldn't have been more than twenty minutes before she was missed, but she'd manage to get a long way down the road before she was found by her frantic husband.

Eventually, she had to be put in an assisted living center that specialized in Alzheimer's patients. And you can guess the rest of the story.

What causes Alzheimer's? The doctor had to admit that he didn't know, but that it had something to do with the aging brain. Aging: that dreaded nemesis.

Aging is a fact of life. Or is it? For years sociologists have been warning us to prepare for the coming wave of senior adults. In his budget request for fiscal year 2005, the director of the National Institute on Aging, Dr. Richard J. Hodes, observed:

> As a nation, we are in the midst of a demographic shift unprecedented in history. There are currently 35 million Americans over the age of 65 — more than at any other time in history. Of these, over 4 million are over 85, and some 65,000 have attained their hundredth birthday. In the coming years, the ranks of American elders are expected to swell; between now and 2030, the number of individuals age 65 and older likely will double, reaching 70.3 million and comprising a larger proportion of the entire population, up from 13 percent today to 20 percent in 2030. Of great interest is the explosive growth anticipated among those most at risk of disease and disability, people age 85 and older: Their ranks are expected to grow from 4.3 million in 2000 to at least 19.4 million in 2050.[1]

Aging needs a face. Attention to the numbers alone tends to hide the fact that the ethical issues associated with aging and with an aging society are some of the thorniest issues in medicine and public policy — not to mention in the lives of individuals, families, and communities. Betty's experience is not unlike the experience of approximately 4.5 million Americans. Each of those persons has a life, a family, and a story.

Alzheimer's is just one of the faces of aging, however. Epidemiologist David Snowdon's study of nuns demonstrates what many know by personal experience; namely, that Alzheimer's is not necessarily the inevitable experience of all senior adults.[2] Many senior adults live healthy, happy, and fruitful lives until natural death. This reality raises an important question: Should we view aging as a disease?

Increasingly, Western culture — especially American culture — has come to loathe every facet of aging. Mushrooming interest in cosmetic surgery, obsessive consumption of antioxidants, and the genetic quest for immortality are phenomena of a relatively affluent and increasingly ageist society.

---

1. See http:/www.nia.nih.gov.
2. David Snowdon, *Aging with Grace: What the Nun Study Teaches Us about Leading Longer, Healthier, and More Meaningful Lives* (New York: Bantam Press, 2001). See also www.nunstudy.org.

We must resist both ageism and fatalism. Aging itself is not a disease to be conquered. Likewise, we do not have to accept stoically every limitation associated with aging. This book is an effort to steer between what we take to be these unnecessary extremes.

The first section examines the experience of aging from a variety of perspectives: a personal perspective, a theological perspective, and a physician's perspective. The section concludes with some very practical suggestions about how to deal with retirement, disability, healing, and death.

Section two offers an analysis of some of the thorny ethical questions associated with aging. Diminishing competency in decision-making capacity makes medical decisions very difficult for some senior adults. Age-based health care rationing has been suggested as a way to offset skyrocketing medical costs. Is this ageism or common sense? As just illustrated, dementia and Alzheimer's are not uncommon among an aging population. How can we enhance appropriate medical decision making under those circumstances? What are our moral obligations to persons with compromised mental status?

The third section applies a theology of care to ministry to older adults, the counseling of seniors, and the application of palliative care. Care of the aging requires intentional strategies specific to the needs of senior adults. An aging population demands the cultivation of these strategic skills.

Finally, the book concludes with a discussion of some of the emerging technologies and interest groups aimed at conquering mortality. Some, like the transhumanist community, see aging as a transitional problem that can be eliminated through the proper application of technology. But is the elimination of aging really desirable? Is it possible? What are the implications of this way of thinking about what it means to be human? How should we understand and treat persons with age-related disabilities? Are they "subhuman"? Does the Christian faith offer any insight for answering the questions we see reflected in the face of our aging neighbors, and even in our own mirrors?

We hope this volume will help individuals, physicians, clergy, counselors, and family members as they treat and minister to senior adults. We believe that both bioethics and the care of the aging require a multidisciplinary approach. We are, therefore, very grateful to each contributor to the volume, especially for their willingness to offer the incredible insights of their professional experience to readers of this book. There is much more to be said, but we believe this is an important beginning.

C. Ben Mitchell, Ph.D.
Robert D. Orr, M.D., C.M.
Susan A. Salladay, R.N., Ph.D.

THE EXPERIENCE OF AGING

A Personal Perspective

VERNON GROUNDS, PH.D.

A creative friend of ours made a plaque which hangs in our kitchen. It is the picture of an aged couple, husband and wife, sitting side by side on an old-fashioned swing. Underneath the picture are those familiar lines from Robert Browning:

> Grow old along with me
> The best is yet to be.

Was Browning overly optimistic? All of us are aging, of course, second by second, whether we are forty or seventy or eighty. Wherever we find ourselves on the timeline of life, we must acknowledge that we are growing older.

We all need to be reminded that aging is an *inevitable* process. We cannot stop the tide from sweeping in. We cannot stop the sun from setting. We cannot keep flowers from fading. Neither can we arrest the passage of time which second by second is making all of us older. An *inevitable* process, aging is also an *irreversible* process. We may entreat with Henry Wadsworth Longfellow,

> Backward, turn backward, oh time in thy flight,
> Make me a boy again, just for tonight.

But that entreaty will never be granted. As Aldous Huxley put it, "There are no back moves on the chess board of life."

In addition to being inevitable and irreversible, the aging process is *individualistic*. No two humans have precisely the same reaction to the ticking

3

away of the hours. Just as no two snowflakes are identical, no two aspen leaves are identical, and no two fingerprints are identical — so no two human beings are identical. We differ radically in temperaments, endowments, and experiences. We are each of us unique, and our responses to the changes and challenges of life are distinctive and different.

Yet, by and large, as we move through time we discover that growing old is a constrictive process, a process that confronts us with a common problem, one set forth suggestively by Robert Frost in his poem "The Oven Bird." That feathery creature is perched on a stone wall in New England; summer is past and autumn rapidly moving into winter. Before long, freezing weather will set in and the world will be blanketed with snow. Yet the oven bird is singing gallantly, Frost writes, "as if to make the most of a diminished thing." That's the problem we confront as we age; how can we make the most of a diminished thing?

Think with me, then, about the ways that life is diminishing. For one thing, it is diminishing *temporally*. We have less and less time in this world. With David, Israel's poet-king, we exclaim, "Teach us to number our days aright, that we may gain a heart of wisdom" (Ps. 90:12).[1]

Life is also diminishing *physically*. Exercise and diet as we may, our energy is less and less, and our strength is gradually ebbing away. We cannot walk as fast and far as we did earlier on. The tasks that we once performed with the greatest of ease may now be laborious struggles.

Moreover, for many of us, life is diminishing *spatially*. We have sold the sizeable houses in which we formerly lived and moved into an apartment or a retirement community. We may be consigned to a room in the home of our children. Once we may have traveled widely, but now perhaps we are confined to a wheelchair or a bed. We cannot walk or drive or move about as we so freely did in years gone by.

Add to all of this shrinking process the sad truth that life is diminishing *vocationally*. In our society we reach a certain year in our journey, usually sixty-five or seventy, when we are expected to give up our professions and jobs. Even simple tasks may be relinquished. I think of my mother-in-law who lived with us for a quarter of a century following the death of her husband. She had enjoyed being a homemaker and insisted on keeping busy when she moved in with our family. At that time, we had no dishwasher, so one of her self-assigned tasks was to do the dishes. Yet as she was increasingly unable to see clearly and to grasp things firmly, she was even relieved of that assignment, much to her distress.

---

1. All scriptural references in this chapter are taken from the New International Version of the Bible.

Again, for many of us, there is a diminishing *financially*. We may not have as much money as we once earned or controlled. Indeed, we may be eking out our existence on slight pensions, or meager Social Security, or all-too-uncertain investments.

Finally, (and I apologize for this dismal recital), life is diminishing *relationally*. Neighbors, friends, colleagues, and family members are far removed or have preceded us in death. One by one our human ties are being cut. The circle of known and loved people is constricting.

What I have been saying about life as a diminishing process may strike you as being excessively melancholy, and I must emphasize that the specific kinds of constriction do not apply to everyone. Bear in mind that, as I have pointed out, we are all different and thus our experiences will be different as we age. Nevertheless, we have, I must repeat, a common problem. How can we best handle this constrictive process? What will enable us to make the most of our diminishing days? I suggest that we can determine, with God's help, how the autumn and winter years of our lives are going to be spent. We can simply refuse to let circumstances control our attitude. After all, attitude in the whole sweep of our experience, and especially in older age, is the crucial factor. Victor Frankl, the well-known Austrian psychiatrist, was sent to a concentration camp when the Nazis took over his homeland. The situation in which he there found himself was worse than deplorable. It was purgatorial. Many of Frankl's fellow prisoners succumbed to despair and so to death. But Frankl observed that, if anyone had a hope for the future, a reason to struggle on, he was likely to survive. Thus in the book he composed while a prisoner, *Man's Search for Meaning*, he argues that there are varieties of values, and that a person can resolutely decide to hold fast to self-chosen values. There are, he says, *experiential* values. We can experience activities and things that give us pleasure, whether food and drink, married love, a beautiful sunset, magnificent music, any and all of the enriching joys of life. But what if we are in a situation where we have no opportunity to relish a delicious dinner or feel delightful sensations? What if, in short, we are robbed of all opportunities for experiential values?

In the same way, what if there is no opportunity to produce any creative values? And these are not simply the higher reaches of culture like art and literature. Creativity can be exercised in the making of an apple pie, the carving of a piece of wood, the furnishing of a home, and the upbringing of a family. But suppose creative values are impossible? What then?

Frankl argues that there is always the possibility of achieving attitudinal values. We can, as was done by some of his fellow inmates in the concentration camp, decide whether we will succumb to despair, give up any hope for the future, degenerate into mere zombies, or, instead, will to be brave, cheerful, helpful, prayerful, and patient.

Frankl reached that conclusion as the fruit of his almost intolerable imprisonment. The well-known American preacher, Chuck Swindoll, has reached the same conclusion from his study and observation:

> The longer I live, the more I realize the impact of attitude on life. It is more important than the past, than education, than money, than circumstances, than failures, than successes, than what other people think or say or do. It is more important than appearance, giftedness or skill. It will make or break a company . . . a church . . . a home. The remarkable thing is we have a choice every day regarding the attitude we will embrace for that day. We cannot change our past. . . . We cannot change the inevitable. The only thing we can do is play on the one string we have, and that is our attitude. . . . I am convinced that life is 10% what happens to me and 90% how I react to it. And so it is with you . . . we are in charge of our Attitudes.[2]

That may sound like baptized stoicism, but it can be viewed, rather, as the appropriation of divine grace by the Holy Spirit's enablement.

The Benefits of Vital Faith

To face the inevitable process of aging with courage, confidence, and even cheerfulness we need a vital faith, yes, a vital faith; not some religion which, as philosopher William James put it, is merely a dull habit. No, we need a vital faith that provides sustaining resources, and I speak now as an octogenarian who is convinced that the gospel of Jesus Christ is precisely such a faith.

The Comfort of an Abiding Presence

A vital faith in Jesus Christ provides, first of all, the *comfort of an abiding Presence.* We may lose family members and friends, we may be living alone. Human companionship may be limited. Yet the gospel assures us we are not alone. We are not abandoned and forsaken. In God we have that friend who sticks closer than a brother. At this stage of life some of the great biblical texts

---

2. Charles R. Swindoll, *Strengthening Your Grip: How to Live Confidently in an Aimless World* (Word, 1982), p. 204.

can become even more meaningful to us. One is Deuteronomy 31:6-8: "Be strong and courageous. Do not be afraid or terrified . . . for the LORD your God goes with you; he will never leave you nor forsake you. . . . Do not be afraid; do not be discouraged." Another such text is Matthew 28:20, "And surely I am with you always, to the very end of the age." Hebrews 13:5 is a third antidote to depressive loneliness: "God has said, 'Never will I leave you; never will I forsake you.'" Indeed, the aging process can be the translation of these texts from mere verbiage to a sustaining experience. The diminishing of flesh-and-blood relationships can stimulate the development of a deepening friendship with that invisible companion whose name is Immanuel, "God with us."

Before I proceed any further let me pause to insert an explanatory comment. A vital Christian faith can greatly enrich the experience of older people. Many, if not most, of those we endeavor to help are believers in the gospel, once active in church affairs, knowledgeable about biblical doctrine, some even theologically educated. But whether strongly religious or only rather superficially God-oriented, they need to have doctrine become emotionally meaningful. My wife and I conduct a late Sunday afternoon service at the assisted living center where we live. Those attending are by and large educated, many of them ex-professionals. Yet when we started this ministry more than a decade ago, I, a seminary professor, quickly realized that central concepts must be so interpreted as to be personally meaningful. Truth must be communicated with graspable simplicity and illuminating vividness.

Consider, then, the point I have been making. Christian faith provides a sense of divine presence. Actually, therefore, I am referring to the doctrine of divine omnipresence as taught, for example, in Psalm 139. But how do I make the reality of God's pervasive presence personally meaningful? Here is a story of graspable simplicity.

A bed-ridden man was alone in his room at the nursing home except for the necessary visits of his caretakers and a weekly visit by his daughter. When he complained to her of loneliness, she reminded him that as a Christian he believed Jesus has promised to be with those who trust him always and everywhere. Yes, he did believe that, yet it was hard to feel any comforting presence. So his daughter suggested that they put a chair alongside his bed, and he could imagine Jesus sitting there, and talk with Jesus day or night. He could even put his hand on the chair as if he were touching Jesus. That simple technique proved a significant help in making the truth of divine omnipresence meaningful to him. In fact, when the nurse entered his room after he had quietly died, his outstretched hand was resting on that chair.

Our problem, then, in ministering to people in general — but especially, I have found, in ministering to older people — is discovering how can the truth be concretized. And how is this to be done? Not by the use of theological jargon, I can assure you, but (keeping in mind, of course, the individual's background) by expressing truth with graspable simplicity and illuminating vividness.

The Awareness of an Unchanging Self-Worth

For another thing, a vital Christian faith provides the *awareness of an unchanging self-worth*. From a purely human perspective the diminishing process may reduce us to unproductive drones no longer contributing anything to the general welfare. We may become shriveled organisms who have lost their charm and vitality. We may be costly burdens to our families and society. Yet from a faith perspective our self-worth is as high as ever, for what is it that gives us value, an even inestimable value? It is the basic biblical affirmation that we bear the image of God whether vibrantly young or helplessly old.

In the Gospel according to Matthew, for example, we learn from Jesus Christ that, as God's image-bearers, we possess a self-worth age cannot diminish. What does our Savior teach us in chapter 6, verses 28-30? "And why do you worry about clothes? See how the lilies of the field grow. They do not labor or spin. Yet I tell you that not even Solomon in all his splendor was dressed like one of these. If that is how God clothes the grass of the field, which is here today and tomorrow is thrown into the fire, will he not much more clothe you, O you of little faith?" What is Jesus saying? We have a value that exceeds the value of flowers, and that value never diminishes. Chemically we may be worth at best only a few dollars. By contrast there are beautiful orchids that command a price higher than our market value. Yet our worth exceeds that of the most rare and exquisite of flowers because we are made in the image of God.

In that same sixth chapter of Matthew, Jesus urges us to consider another aspect of nature: "Look at the birds of the air; they do not sow or reap or store away in barns, and yet your heavenly Father feeds them. Are you not much more valuable than they?" (v. 26). Again in chapter 10, Jesus emphasizes our value compared to that of the birds: "Are not two sparrows sold for a penny? Yet not one of them will fall to the ground apart from the will of your Father. And even the very hairs of your head are all numbered. So don't be afraid; you are worth more than many sparrows" (vv. 29-31). Sparrows may be next to worthless, but there are gorgeous birds in our pet stores which command a fabulous price. Yet Jesus insists that we are measurelessly more valuable than the most exotic feathered creature because we are God's image-bearers, and they are merely his creatures.

Our Savior's estimation of any person's unchanging value is brought out further in Matthew 12:12: "How much more valuable is a man than a sheep!" We certainly are not worth as much as most animals, especially those lumbering champion steers sold annually at the National Stock Show in Denver. Such a steer may be auctioned for over sixty thousand dollars. But we, no matter how frail, are valued at an incomparably higher value by God because we bear his image.

Climactically, in Matthew 16:26, our Lord offers an incredible estimation of our worth: "What good will it be for a man, if he gains the whole world, yet forfeits his soul?" This means that the value of one human being is greater than whatever might be the value of the entire world and all that is in it. Thus, regardless of how shriveled and useless we may become, we have from God's viewpoint an undiminished value.

A nameless woman in an English home for the aged expressed her emotions in a poem which was found in her meager possessions after she had died. The poem brings out poignantly our common need to be appreciated with understanding and dignity for our unique selfhood.

> What do you see, nurse, what do you see?
> What are you thinking when you look at me —
> A crabbed old woman, not very wise,
> Uncertain of habit with far away eyes,
> Who dribbles her food and makes no reply
> When you say in a loud voice, "I do wish you'd try."
> Who seems not to notice the things that you do
> And forever is losing a stocking or shoe,
> Who, resisting or not, lets you do as you will
> With bathing and feeding, the long day to fill.
> Is that what you're thinking, is that what you see?
> Then open your eyes, nurse. You're not looking at me.
>
> I'll tell you who I am as I sit here so still,
> As I move at your bidding, eat at your will.
> I'm a small child of ten with a father and mother,
> Brothers and sisters who love one another;
> A young girl of sixteen with wings on her feet,
> Dreaming that soon a lover she'll meet;
> A bride at twenty, my heart gives a leap,

Remembering the vows that I promised to keep.
At age twenty-five I have young of my own
Who need me to build a secure, happy home.

A woman of thirty, my children grow fast
Bound together with ties that I'm hoping will last.
At forty, my young sons have grown up and gone,
But my man's still beside me to see I don't mourn.
At fifty once more babies play round my knee,
Again we know children, my loved one and me.
Dark days are upon me; my husband is dead,
I look at the future, I shudder with dread;
For my children are rearing young of their own,
And I think of the years and the love that I've known.

I'm an old woman now, and nature is cruel,
'Tis her jest to make old age look like a fool.
The worn body crumbles, grace and vigor depart,
There now is a stone where I once had a heart.
But inside this carcass a young girl still dwells,
And now and again my embittered heart swells.
I remember the joys, I remember the pain,
And I'm loving and living life over again.
I think of the years, all too few, gone too fast,
And accept the stark fact that nothing can last.
So open your eyes, nurse, open and see
Not a crabbed old woman.
Look closer — see me!

What Christian faith enables our caregivers to see is a person who, as God's image-bearer, has an inestimable value no matter how old or infirm we may be. Christian faith can also enable us to see ourselves from this perspective, not, as Bertrand Russell once put it, as a mere collocation of atoms, but as a person entitled to dignity and self-respect because of bearing the image of God.

The Opportunities of Continued Usefulness

What else can our Christian faith provide to sustain us through the constrictive process? I think realistically it offers *opportunities of continued usefulness*. Let me call attention to some of the inspiring and challenging examples of how, even in old age, individuals have remained remarkably active and productive. I mention these human beings without any concern for their religious beliefs. They illustrate the potential that some members of the geriatric set possess.

- Oliver Wendell Holmes, Jr., served on the United States Supreme Court until he was ninety-one.
- Winston Churchill became Prime Minister of Great Britain for a second time at the age of seventy-seven.
- Grandma Moses began painting at the age of seventy-five and produced her most famous canvas, *Christmas Eve,* when she was one hundred.
- Robert Frost, one of America's best-known poets, continued to write and lecture until his eighty-fifth year.
- Clemenceau was elected Prime Minister of France at the age of sixty-five. When he was seventy-seven he was summoned to lead his nation during World War I.
- Michelangelo reached the peak of his genius in his eighties when he chiseled his famous *Pieta* and constructed the dome of St. Peter's Cathedral.

And these are only a few of the many instances which demonstrate that advancing age does not necessarily mean an inability to be active and creative.

Moving into the sphere of Christian faith, consider this striking example of what can be done as one ages. Paul Brand, the famous missionary-doctor, tells about his mother in the book he co-authored with Philip Yancey, *Fearfully and Wonderfully Made.* She came from an elegant home in suburban London but spent most of her life in India as a missionary.

> When Granny Brand reached 69 she was told by her mission to retire and she did . . . until she found a new range of mountains where no missionary had ever visited. Without mission society support she climbed those mountains, built a little wooden shack, and worked another 26 years. Because of a broken hip and creeping paralysis, she could only walk with the aid of two bamboo sticks, but on the back of an old horse she rode all over the mountains, a medicine box strapped behind her. She sought out the unwanted and the unlovely, the sick, the maimed, and the blind, and brought treatment to them. When she came to settlements who knew her, a great crowd of people would burst out to greet her. My mother died at the age of 95. Poor nutrition and failing health had swollen her joints and made her gaunt and fragile. She had stopped caring about her personal

appearance long ago, even refusing to look in a mirror lest she see the effects of her grueling life. She was part of the advance guard, the front line presenting God's love to deprived people.[3]

Inspiring and challenging as such a life undoubtedly is, it may leave older people of lesser ability and tenacity feeling worthless. They simply cannot exhibit such heroism or match such exploits. But a vital Christian faith enables even garden-variety seniors to embrace personally what is said in Psalm 92:14: "They will still bear fruit in old age, they will stay fresh and green." Even though they may think of themselves as ungifted, older disciples can carry on some helpful ministries.

For one thing, no matter how limited they are, they can pray. They can be like Anna of whom we read, "She was very old; . . . She never left the temple but worshiped night and day, fasting and praying" (Luke 2:36-37). Confined to a chair or even a bed, an intercessor is still able to reach heaven through prayer.

There is also opportunity for a ministry of witness. Without becoming a loquacious bore, an older person can testify of God's faithfulness through the years of life. That is the message of Psalm 71. The older generation can pass on to the next generation, grandparents sharing with grandchildren, the stories of what God has done even in uneventful lives. So David gives thanks to God:

> For you have been my hope, O Sovereign LORD,
>   my confidence since my youth.
> From birth I have relied on you;
>   you brought me forth from my mother's womb.
>   I will ever praise you. . . .
> My mouth is filled with your praise,
>   declaring your splendor all day long.
> Do not cast me away when I am old;
>   do not forsake me when my strength is gone. . . .
> Even when I am old and gray,
>   do not forsake me, O God,
> till I declare your power to the next generation,
>   your might to all who are to come.   (Ps. 71:5-18)

Thus David realized the possibility of transgenerational witness — a possibility that can be actualized by today's seniors. Perhaps a grandparent's congre-

3. David Brand and Philip Yancey, *Fearfully and Wonderfully Made* (Grand Rapids: Zondervan, 1980), pp. 155-56.

gation is one small grandchild, but how important it is that the upcoming generations hear about the spiritual experience of the older generations.

In addition, what about a ministry of informal teaching? There need not be repetitious sermonizing, but why not a casual yet purposeful sharing of insight? After all, in the book of Job we read, "Is not wisdom found among the aged? Does not long life bring understanding?" (Job 12:12). Scripture shows us how this transmission of truth can take place. Recall 2 Timothy 1:5: "I have been reminded of your sincere faith, which first lived in your grandmother Lois and your mother Eunice and, I am persuaded, now lives in you also." In that same letter, Paul urges Timothy to remember from whom he has learned spiritual truth and "how from infancy you have known the holy Scriptures" (2 Tim. 3:15). Consider also Titus 2:3: "Likewise, teach the older women to be reverent in the way they live, not to be slanderers or addicted to much wine, but to teach what is good." Grandparents do not need a theological degree in order to impart this basic knowledge to their grandchildren.

Of course there also can be a ministry of helpfulness, those simple acts of kindness which can be performed regardless of limitation and infirmity. All of us, especially as we age, need to remember that Jesus applauds those who do nothing more than give a cup of cold water in his name.

Finally, there is the ministry of modeling. We can be examples of authentic spirituality, exhibiting steadfast faith, patience, and love. The unwavering trust of an aged Christian proves the truthfulness of God's promise, "Even to your old age and gray hairs I am he, I am he who will sustain you. I have made you and I will carry you; I will sustain you and I will rescue you" (Isa. 46:4). As June Masters Bacher urges, "It is good to pause and count our blessings at every birthday. They pile up with the years. God is changeless. He has work for us here and each milestone shows that he chose to have us remain to give Him a hand."

The Opening of Vistas of Limitless Eternity

Is there anything more a vital Christian faith can provide as we move on inexorably toward the end of our journey? Indeed, there is. Vital Christian faith can push back the confining walls of time and *open up the vista of a limitless eternity.* Death may overtake any one of us at any stage of our experience by illness, accident, violence, or even suicide; but, assuming that an individual is gradually deteriorating with the passage of time, certain aspects of life's termination may cause emotional stress. One may experience the haunting thoughts of death's *inevitability;* as Hebrews 9:27 puts it, "Just as man is destined to die once, and after that to face judgment." The inevitability of death means we are facing an appointment that cannot be canceled.

Besides its inevitability, there is the *unpredictability* of death. Even in lingering illness, the hour of departure cannot be predicted with certainty. As we are told in Ecclesiastes 9:12, "no man knows when his hour will come."

Then, too, accompanying the dying process, there will be sometimes — almost always — a feeling of *indignity* as an individual is helplessly unable to care for himself.

Beyond all this, there looms the factor of *finality,* the impossibility of any further possibility, as the existentialists like to put it. Unfinished projects, unhealed relationships, unforgiven hurts, unlived life — all of these may add to the emotional pressure an individual is undergoing.

Finally, what about the *mystery* of death? What really happens as we expire? Is there a prolonged passage between this world and the next, or is there an instantaneous transition? What awaits us at death? Depending on our theology, we will enter into oblivion, purgatory, judgment, or glory. While it does not eliminate all the mystery, a vital Christian faith does provide a certainty. As that remarkable English woman, one-time missionary to Africa, Florence Allshorn said to a friend who had asked her about any "apprehensions of the dark":

> I can never see why one should fear to die. When I walk into the garden here early in the morning and nearly burst with excitement at this world; and when I realize that it is only a shadow, a pale ghost of what *that* world must be like — then I can only feel a tremendous longing to know more of it and be in it.[4]

And that is what a vital Christian faith provides — certainty with a sort of sanctified curiosity.

Conclusion

Belief in the reality of our Savior's resurrection does not for everyone banish all the mystery and gloom of dying and death. From that empty tomb of Jesus, however, a radiant light shines forth. As earthly horizons contract, as life becomes a more and more diminished thing, opening up before a Christian are the immeasurable horizons of a radiant eternity. So in place of anxiety

4. J. H. Oldham, *Florence Allshorn and the Story of St. Julian's* (London: SCM Press, 1951), p. 162.

and despair, believers can rejoice with John Roberts that in the ultimate sense we are "not growing old." What he wrote is not a distinguished contribution to literature, but it expresses the sustaining confidence that we can have through faith in the gospel.

Not Growing Old

They tell me that I'm growing old.
I've heard them tell it times untold,
Yes, this frail shell in which I dwell
Is growing old, I know full well.

What if my hair is turning grey?
Grey hairs are honorable, they say.
What if my eyesight's growing dim?
I still can see to follow Him
Who sacrificed His life for me
Upon the Cross of Calvary.
Why should I care if time's rough plough
Has left its furrows on my brow?
Another house, not made with hands
Awaits me in the Glory Land.
What though I falter in my walk?
What though my tongue refuse to talk?
I still can tread the Narrow Way,
I still can trust, and praise, and pray.
My hearing now is not as keen
As in the past it may have been;
Still I can hear my Saviour say,
In whispers soft, "This is the way!"
My fleshly frame, do what I can
To lengthen out this life's short span,
Shall perish and return to dust,
As everything in nature must.
But in my soul I'm glad to say,
My faith grows stronger every day.
Then how can I be getting old
When safe within my Saviour's fold?

And soon my soul shall fly away,
And leave its tenement of clay,

This robe of flesh I'll drop, and rise
To seize the "everlasting prize."

I'll meet you on the streets of gold
And prove that I'm not growing old.
I'll join the song through ages sung,
And there I'll be forever young.

Let us be glad that profound truth simply stated is what people need as they pass through the experience of aging. The process that makes life a diminished thing may no doubt be discussed from a number of weighty theological, philosophical, and scientific perspectives, all of which have their own indubitable importance. I am thankful, nevertheless, that at the outset we can as Christians affirm the unique values our faith provides.

A Theologian's Perspective

R. GEOFFREY BROWN, PH.D.

The eighteenth-century New England theologian Jonathan Edwards wrote a little-known treatise entitled *The End for Which God Created the World.*[1] In that essay, Edwards sets forth a theological argument with a very practical conclusion. His first premise is that *God maintains nothing with greater passion than the honor of his own glory.* As the biblical writers put it, God is a "jealous God" (Deut. 4:24; Josh. 24:19; Nah. 1:2). He will not share his glory with another. The second premise is that *God is most glorified in the Christian when he or she is most delighted in him.*

In his second premise, Edwards is setting forth the primacy of the Christian's delight in God over the value of the Christian's mere dutiful obedience to God. Let us take as our example a husband who comes home on Valentine's Day with a bouquet of flowers in one arm and a box of chocolates in the other. Balancing his gifts, he manages to ring the doorbell of his home. When his wife comes to the door, he exclaims, "Happy Valentine's Day, Dear!" She responds, "Oh, honey, you shouldn't have. Why did you?" If he answers blandly, "Because it's my duty as a good husband to do such things," then something is amiss. How much more greatly honored is his wife when the husband answers, "Why did I? I couldn't help myself! I'm so crazy about you that I've made dinner reservations at the Ritz, and we're headed out tonight to celebrate our love. We're going to paint this town red by dancing the night away in each other's arms."[2]

1. Jonathan Edwards, "A Dissertation Concerning the End for Which God Created the World," in *Edwards' Ethical Writings,* ed. Paul Ramsey, vol. 8 of the Works of Jonathan Edwards (New Haven: Yale University Press, 1989), pp. 403-536.
2. This example is adapted from John Piper's presentation of the same point by us-

Clearly, nothing is wrong with duty in and of itself; but the merely dutiful heart in service to God, as with the dutiful husband in service to his wife, does not glorify God in the same way as the Christian's heart that overflows in delightful obedience.

The conclusion of Edwards's argument is simply breathtaking and has huge implications for the Christian's approach to aging and other end-of-life issues. The argument is as follows:

- Premise 1: God maintains nothing with greater passion than the honor of his glory.
- Premise 2: God is most glorified in the Christian when the Christian is most delighted in God.
- Conclusion: Therefore, *God's passion for his own glory is the measure of his commitment to the Christian's joy.*

God of Grace and God of Glory

If God's passion for his own glory is as supreme as Edwards declares, then for the Christian aging, dying, and immortality take on an entirely different meaning. God's supreme passion for his own glory makes the Christian's joy unshakable even in the midst of the unpredictable and sometimes frightening experiences of aging and illness, as well as sustaining him or her through the exact moment of death.

Edwards believed on the basis of Scripture that the aim, the reason, the legitimization, the end for which God created the world and all that is within it — and now still sustains it — is his own glory. Creation, therefore, is the direct result of God's glory intentionally emanating out into the "nothing" so that God's Trinitarian knowledge of himself, love to himself, and holiness within himself (wherein consists his glory, Edwards argues) may be shared with the human creature. As his creatures, we come to know him, love him, and become holy like him, in order to "remanate" (or reflect) celebratively his original divine glory. So, says Edwards, there is an emanation out from God, and a remanation back to him.[3] Not to be trite, but it is in one sense as if

---

ing his own wedding anniversary date and the giving of a dozen roses to his wife under the heading of "Don't mention it; it's my duty." See John Piper, *Desiring God: Meditations of a Christian Hedonist* (Sisters, Ore.: Multnomah, 1996), p. 83.

3. For a thorough discussion of this concept, see Stephen R. Holmes, *God of Grace and God of Glory: An Account of the Theology of Jonathan Edwards* (Grand Rapids: Eerdmans, 2000), pp. 57ff.

Christians are backboards, and the basketball of divine glory is bounced off of them and back into God's divine hands with a certainty and accuracy which Shaquille O'Neal and Michael Jordan could neither dream nor ever hope to achieve.

Perhaps a better (although still deficient) illustration of this truth is to say that if God is like the single primary sun of the entire universe, then Christians are his secondary moons. The secondary moon gains its light only as a reflection of the brightness of the sun. The Christian's purpose is precisely, constantly, and always this reflection of God's divine glory. Of course, the Christian's purpose is much higher and loftier than the moon's. A mere moon may cease to reflect the sun by falling out of gravitational alignment, but in every thought or action, Christians are never to depart from conscious reflection of God's radiant glory. This is the Christian's reason for living, our greatest joy, the purpose for which we are made: *to magnify the glory of God in life, in aging, and in death.*

To pursue the imagery a bit further, we may say that the Scriptures at this point line up like planets orbiting the sun of God's glory. Here are some of those planets:

- Psalm 115:1: "Not unto us, Lord, O not unto us, Lord, but to Thy name be all glory, because of Thy faithfulness, because of Thy truth."
- 1 Corinthians 10:31: "Therefore, whether you eat or drink, or whatever you do, do all to the glory of God."
- 1 Peter 4:11 is likewise all-inclusive: "If anyone speaks, let him speak as the oracles of God. If anyone ministers let him do it as with the ability which God supplies, that *in all things* God may be glorified through Jesus Christ, to whom belong the glory and the sovereignty forever and ever. Amen" (italics added).
- The Pauline apostolic conclusion is equally as comprehensive as Peter's: "For of Him and through Him and to Him are all things, to Whom be glory forever. Amen" (Rom. 11:36). In this lyrical song of consummate praise, the apostle Paul at the end of eleven chapters of theological argumentation now sets forth that God's sovereign *will* ("of Him are all things") and God's sovereign *activity* ("through Him are all things") — that both of these, sovereign *will* and sovereign *activity* — serve one end: the end of God's sovereign *glory* emanating out from himself to remanate back to himself: "*to* Him are all things, *to* Whom be *glory* forever. Amen" (italics added).

The Death of Roy Kuhn

These are lofty concepts of theological grandeur. Examples are always helpful in explaining such glorious truths. Dr. Andrew MacFarlan tells of the death of Roy Kuhn, a death in which we see the perspective of the divine glory.

> As I sit writing this, my father-in-law is 3 feet away, lying in a bed in a coma, in his last hours of life. He is 81 years old and has widespread cancer. He is now passing on right in front of my eyes. His spirit and self are in the process of leaving the house that is his earthly body, soon to inherit a heavenly body unencumbered by poor lungs, oxygen tubes, morphine pump, and Foley catheter. . . . Rarely do family members get to experience death with their loved ones these days. Many are afraid. Many can't let go; many do not know they can or how rich and good and deep an experience it can be. . . . My father-in-law's . . . death in our home was a celebration of relationships. He was aided by a few friends, family members, medical professionals, and Hospice personnel . . . when the hour of his death came we were rewarded rather than shattered.
>
> Jacob's ladder seemed to descend from the heavens as the veil between the material and spiritual worlds parted in our presence. We were in a holy place and we knew it. My father-in-law's eyes gradually closed and his breathing slowed to a stop as he "walked home" into eternal life. He was gone from here; the shell of his body clearly no longer housed him. We sobbed gently in sadness, in relief for him and in celebration of his life. One of our close friends looked over at me and through bright sparkling wet eyes and tear-washed cheeks whispered, "Look what Kevorkian is stealing from people."

Dr. MacFarlan concludes, "The elements that helped to make this death such a deeply fulfilling human experience are available to everyone: faith, forgiveness, family, friends, and the help of professionals, especially hospice."[4]

What else helped? Although Dr. MacFarlan does not state it explicitly, it is implied: God is most glorified in us when we are most trustingly contented in him; God's glory transcends human suffering; and God maintains nothing with greater passion than the honor of his glory. "Precious in the sight of the Lord is the death of His saints" (Ps. 116:15).

---

4. As quoted in Scott B. Rae and Paul M. Cox, *Bioethics: A Christian Approach in a Pluralistic Age* (Grand Rapids: Eerdmans, 1999), p. 252.

Protagoras or Isaiah?

The ancient philosopher Protagoras could be called the father of our contemporary cultural ethos. His phrase, *Homo mensura* ("man, the measure of all things"), certainly reflects our age. Yet, the biblical texts above, as well as accounts like Dr. MacFarlan's, stand in stark contrast to Protagoras's ancient creed. Jonathan Edwards makes it clear, with unmistakable scriptural poignancy, that man is not at all the measure of all things, but rather, the glory of God is the measure of all things in heaven and on earth. God himself, through the prophet Isaiah, reveals the primacy of divine glory with six deft strokes that erase forever Protagorean anthropocentricity:

> *For my name's sake* I defer my anger, *for the sake of my praise* I restrain it from you, that I may not cut you off. Behold, I have refined you, but not like silver; I have tried you in the furnace of affliction. *For my own sake, for my own sake,* I do it, for *how should my name be profaned? My glory I will not give to another.* (Isa. 48:9-11, emphasis added)

These six strokes demand that Christians regard every aspect of their lives — including their aging, dying, and death — as designed ultimately, inescapably, sovereignly, to bring God glory:

1. For *my* name's sake!
2. For the sake of *my* praise!
3. For *my* own sake!
4. For *my* own sake!
5. How should *my* name be profaned?
6. *My* glory I will not give to another!

What Isaiah 48:9-11 "hammers home to us," says John Piper, "is the centrality of God in his own affections."[5] Nobody loves God like God loves God; nobody glorifies God the way God glorifies God. "The most passionate heart for the glorification of God is God's heart. God's ultimate goal is to uphold and display the glory of His name."[6]

---

5. John Piper, *Let the Nations Be Glad! The Supremacy of God in Missions* (Grand Rapids: Baker, 1993), p. 17.
6. Piper, *Let the Nations*, p. 17.

A Host of Questions

For Christians ministering in times of life and death, a host of questions arise. How does the glory of God mediate the DNR (Do Not Resuscitate) directive of an elderly critically ill patient? How does the glory of God relate to suffering and the palliation of the dying? What freedoms do presuppositions about God's glory afford for the living will? For the surrogate decision-maker? For the durable power of attorney for health care (DPAHC)? What does the Christian's conviction that God's supreme passion is for his own glory do for a responsible embrace of death as neither disaster nor dread but qualified delight?[7]

We begin to see answers to these kinds of questions in the experience of Carl Lundquist, who was president of Bethel College and Seminary in St. Paul, Minnesota, for twenty-eight years. In 1988, six years after his retirement, doctors told him that he had a rare form of cancer called mycosis fungoides, a variant of cutaneous T-cell lymphoma that invades the skin over the entire body. He speaks of his experience in a letter to a friend:

> That day in the hospital room, I picked up my Bible when the doctor had left. I turned to the joy verses of Philippians, thinking one might stand out. But what leaped from the page was Paul's testimony in chapter one, "I eagerly expect and hope that I will in no way be ashamed but will have sufficient courage so that now, as always, Christ will be exalted in my body whether by life or by death. [The Greek word here for "will be exalted" is *megalunthesetai,* which means literally "shall be magnified."] For to me to live is Christ and to die is gain." And I discovered that a verse I had lived by in good health also was a verse that I could live by in ill health. To live — Christ; to die — gain. But by life or by death, it's all right either way. . . . So I simply trust that the Great Physician in His own way will carry out for me His will which I know alone is good and acceptable and perfect. By life or by death. Hallelujah![8]

7. See John F. Kilner, *Life on the Line: Ethics, Aging, Ending Patients' Lives, and Allocating Vital Resources* (Grand Rapids: Eerdmans, 1992), pp. 102-3. Dr. Kilner notes that "To refuse to accept physical death as 'normal' or 'good' does not entail embracing another extreme: death as disaster. . . . Death is both enemy and destiny, both penalty and promise, both cross and resurrection. It is necessarily a real evil, the result of rebellion against God, but it is something over which God's love did, does, and will triumph . . . too benign a view of death may lead to too hasty an abandonment of a God-guided commitment to life, while too desperate a view of death may result in too prolonged a dying process."

8. As quoted in John Piper, *The Purifying Power of Living by Faith in . . . Future Grace* (Sisters, Ore.: Multnomah, 1995), pp. 357-58.

Dr. Lundquist died, February 27, 1991, after deterioration of his own skin cells, but with no deterioration in his confidence that God alone is worthy of his own glory.

"Never Shall I Leave Thee . . ."

Why is God's will "good and acceptable and perfect"? The question may be given an Edwardsian answer: "Because God's passion for his glory is the measure of his commitment to the Christian's joy." God's passion for his glory is so invested *ad extra* in the redemptive grace of Jesus Christ bequeathed to his own that once the Christian soul has been captured effectually by the glory of God, that same glory will never leave that soul. Therefore, the divine passion for the preservation of the divine glory becomes a protective covering over all of the Christian life. Christians are thereby freed, both spiritually and psychologically, to affirm the unfolding of life events as part of the "good and acceptable and perfect" will of God.

Likewise, neither shall the Christian die one moment apart from that same omnipotent and omnipresent divine passion for the divine glory. All end-of-life circumstances, then, are enveloped by God's passion for his own glory. "For I am persuaded that neither death nor life, nor angels nor principalities nor powers, nor things present nor things to come, nor height nor depth, [*nor feeding tubes, nor catheters, nor respirators,*] nor any other created thing, shall be able to separate us from the love of God which is in Christ Jesus our Lord" (Rom. 8:37-38). Why will these unpredictable perils not be able to separate the Christian from the hand of Providence? Because nothing can overcome God's sovereign passion for his own glory as the measure of his commitment to the Christian's joy — in life, in dying, and in death itself.

Christian Realism and *A Priori* Reasoning

Admittedly, this orientation may initially appear to be utopian idealism or religious sentimentalism, but it is, instead, Christian realism. This radical faith perspective, grounded in biblical revelation, faces squarely the deadliness of disease, admits openly the rancor of pain, and dares not deny the questioning moments in the silence of the night when anxiety roams the soul.

These great realities made the difference in the death of Roy Kuhn. After speaking of faith, forgiveness, family, friends, and hospice, Dr. MacFarlan said,

These things didn't take away the real, daily details of pain, fear, loneliness, blocked bowels, sleepless nights, yelling out, bedpans, crying fits, fighting kids, medication, side effects or exhaustion. But they did help make them manageable and meaningful, and they have the potential to make death a blessing rather than a curse. We all experienced the blessing. This was the way it was meant to be.[9]

Well, not really! Christianity acknowledges that before the fall of Adam and Eve, it was not at all meant to be this way. Through our first parents' sin, death became a feared enemy. In Jesus Christ, however, it *is* meant to be different or "all right," as Dr. Lundquist indicated. For what both Drs. Lundquist and MacFarlan had learned was what St. Augustine confessed about the operations of divine grace in his life: *"Credu ut intelligum"* ("I believe in order to know"). This is *a priori* reasoning at its finest, for it is a biblically founded proposition. Christian realism requires intentional presuppositional thinking. Some "given" truth is deposited with such strength and certainty in the Christian mind and heart that the interpretation of all of one's life and death is done from its vantage point.

One primary *a priori* principle arising from God's passion for his glory being the measure of his commitment to the Christian's joy is that no matter what happens, the Christian is biblically entitled to an ultimately positive perspective of death and dying.[10] The secular mind is in a forest of wandering ignorance here. Sadly, it knows nothing of this certainty, nor can it (1 Cor. 2:14).

For the Christian mind, however, this is the arena of assurance from divine revelation. This is the arena of divine self-disclosure, as Francis Schaeffer noted long ago by way of his book title: *He Is There and He Is Not Silent.*[11] To knock on the door of the universe is to find Someone home and to find that Someone has also spoken. God's declaration is that the Christian's death is not for one instant outside the providential bounds of his beneficent glory; and he guards and guides all the way through the valley of the shadow of death so that his glory is not defamed. "For my own sake I do this," says the Lord, "for my own sake, for how should my name be profaned? My glory I will not give to another" (Isa. 48:11).

9. As quoted in Rae and Cox, *Bioethics: A Christian Approach*, p. 252.

10. The concept of a legitimate biblical entitlement is cited here not in echo of the culture's unbridled quest for the demands of autonomous individualism, but actually in contradistinction to that excess.

11. Francis Schaeffer, *He Is There and He Is Not Silent* (Wheaton, Ill.: Tyndale, 1972).

The Nature of the God of Glory

How can Christians have such a positive perspective on death and dying? Simply because God is justly zealous for his own glory. Since he will not be untrue to his own character, he will not be unfaithful to his own people.

This is the one true God "who works *all things* after the counsel of His will" (Eph. 1:11 [italics added]). The Christian's death is subsumed and captured by this "all things" — and by the cross of Christ, which Edwards calls "the locus" of God's glory.

This is the God in whom "we live and move and have our *being*" (Acts 17:28 [italics added]). Since the image of God in a Christian is neither annihilated nor absorbed at death, the Christian, therefore, is not for one second extracted from the eternal, sustaining presence of God for the sake of his glory.[12]

This is the one and only God who tells Christians about the comprehensive scope of his benevolence so clearly that they are enabled to say with the apostle Paul, "We know." "We know God causes *all things* to work together for good for those who love Him, for those who are called according to His purposes" (Rom. 8:28 [italics added]), thereby assuring the Christian of the certainty that death is once again compassed within *all things,* and here death itself shall be irresistibly directed to the registry of divine benevolence. Death shall be worked for the Christian's good through aging, through end-of-life issues, through the nano-second of transition from mortal life to eternal life.

But again, why "all" to the good? Edwards would answer thus: because God's passion for his glory is the measure of his commitment to the Christian's joy — which includes the Christian's ultimate good by virtue of God's pursuing that good for the sake of his own glory. In other words, the Christian's well-being rests on God's pursuit of his own glory. Since God always does what redounds to his own glory, the Christian's well-being is secure.

Astounding Theocentric Certainty

Admittedly, this perspective is exclusively theocentric (God-centered), rather than anthropocentric (human-centered). Nevertheless, this perspective should become the anchor holding the Christian mind close to apostolic thinking on

---

12. The Christian doctrines of creation and providence declare on the basis of Scripture that God not only created heaven and earth *ex nihilo* but now sustains second by second his creation. See Louis Berkhof, *Systematic Theology* (Grand Rapids: Eerdmans, 1974 [thirteenth printing]), pp. 132ff.

death and dying, astounding as it is. According to the inspired apostle, then, Christians are people who delight themselves so much in the glory of God that they "overflow for God's glory" (2 Cor. 4:15) — and overflow occurs even in the midst of affliction because of the hope of heaven and the glory of God. This is, after all, the theme of 2 Corinthians 4 and 5.

Note that in 2 Corinthians 4:8-9, 15, 17, Paul says, "We are hard-pressed on every side, but not crushed; perplexed, but not in despair; persecuted, but not abandoned; struck down, but not destroyed. . . . All this is for your benefit, so that the grace that is reaching more and more people may cause thanksgiving to overflow to the glory of God. . . . For our light and momentary afflictions are achieving for us an eternal glory that far outweighs them all." Paul's language underscores the fact that the Christian life is to be lived and evaluated *sub species aeternitatus* (from the perspective of eternity) — from the viewpoint of what is yet to come.

What eternity? It is the eternity of the glory of God manifested, enjoyed, and revealed unendingly in ever greater revelations of bliss as God for all eternity unfolds his glory in an endless, inexhaustible, infinite way. Edwards notes that God is anchored in infinite "aseity." That is, God may be known, but never known exhaustively. Even when glorified in heaven, Christians are still nevertheless creatures, not divinity. Therefore, the unfolding of his perfections and his glory will go on forever; and those in heaven experience the constant joy of discovering more and more about God. Most important, Christians will enjoy God himself, in whose presence is fullness of joy, and pleasures forevermore (Ps. 16:11).[13]

Five Facets of Comfort

The apostle continues in 2 Corinthians 4 and 5 to describe five key ingredients of the eternal perspective that ground Christians in the midst of temporal afflictions and transient discomforts, including the experiences at the end of life. How can Christians endure, even flourish, under the weight of temporal afflictions?

1. By fixing on what is unseen, rather than seen (4:18).
2. By knowing without having (5:1).

---

13. John Piper, *God's Passion for His Glory: Living the Vision of Jonathan Edwards with the Complete Text of "The End for Which God Created the World"* (Wheaton, Ill.: Crossway, 1998), pp. 249-51.

3. By groaning while waiting (5:4).
4. By believing without seeing (5:7).
5. By actually preferring the "then" to the "now" (5:8).

This is the Christian's *summum bonum,* his or her highest reason for being made a disciple of the Lord Jesus Christ: *that Christians should glorify God by making it their supreme aim consciously to please him before and after and, therefore,* through *the moment of death.* Paul expresses it this way in 2 Corinthians 5:9: "So we make it our goal to please Him, whether we are at home in the body or away from it" — remembering that God is most glorified in us when we are most joyfully delighted in him. Moreover, just because God maintains nothing with greater passion than the honor of his glory, Christians are bequeathed a transcendent confidence in pursuing the goal of pleasing him in life and death, knowing that his sovereign passion for his glory is the measure of his commitment to their joy. Thus, Christ's disciples will overflow in confidence so that God's grace may reach more and more people and so that they, too, may join other Christians in glorifying him — even if spurred to do so by witnessing Christians' responses to end-of-life issues, to aging, and to death itself. For when Paul says he doesn't fix on the "seen" but on the "unseen," the "seen" is a reference to his present sufferings, persecutions, and distresses. But the eternal perspective tells him that these are only temporary, only transitory, only fleeting, and soon will pass away. It is the things that are "unseen" which are permanent, abiding, and eternal.

Complete and "Free at Last"

Why fight the good fight of faith to live in light of eternity? Because, frankly, death completes the Christian. The universality of sin is the universality of bondage to moral imperfection this side of the grave. Regarding the redeemed in the Lord Jesus Christ, a contradiction, as John Murray called it, exists within the believer.[14] Hence, because of the inescapable presence of sin in the world and in the believer, death completes the Christian by opening up at long last the consummate fullness of the deepest desired relationship of life and death — a sin-free, face-to-face eternity with Jesus Christ. "Free at last. Free at last. Thank God a'mighty, free at last."

14. John Murray, *The Epistle to the Romans* (Grand Rapids: Eerdmans, 1965), pp. 256ff.

In the movie *Jerry McGuire,* Renee Zellweger stars as sports agent Tom Cruise's love interest, whom he marries but then leaves, thinking he does not really love her. When Cuba Gooding Jr. catches the winning touchdown pass, it seals a lucrative multi-million dollar deal, and Cruise's cell phone rings after the game is over. He thinks it is his wife, but it is not.

He realizes at that moment that his life is incomplete without her. He goes to her at her sister's house, where a divorce group is meeting, and angry women are calling men "the enemy." Zellweger is sitting there alone, feeling rejected by Cruise. She rises defiantly in the room, turns toward the other women and says, "Men may be the enemy, but I love the enemy." Just then, the enemy arrives and says "Hello" to her in a tender scene. Their eyes meet. He walks toward her, expressing how much he missed her at the triumphant moment of the game. He tells her that despite the victory, it was empty without her. Then he says that classic line, "You complete me." And she retorts, "Oh, shut up! You had me at hello."

Christians love the Lord Jesus Christ. Christians adore him. Christians see the unseen. But something still is missing, for a Christian's God-intoxicated and God-saturated life reaches its grandest proportions and deepest hopes only when it knows the revealed presence of the Lord standing, as it were, in the living room of heaven face-to-face. When Christ comes near and the veil of our fallenness is finally removed, Christians know that all previous revelations of him were but theophanies — veiled manifestations of his glory. But then, after the moment of death, Christians shall see him face-to-face. In death and dying, in end-of-life issues, Christians are therefore substantially free from fear, but not perfectly so. For death still is the enemy, albeit conquered. The cross of Jesus Christ has transformed death into a now vanquished beloved enemy. Hence the Christian in his or her own heart stands amidst a million secular voices to declare, "Death may be the enemy, but I love the enemy; Christ had me at the 'hello' of his sovereign regeneration of my soul."

Practical Responses to Aging and End-of-Life Issues

Substantial Freedom from Fear

This brings us then to the Christian's practical response to end-of-life issues in the light of this confidence-giving fact: *God's passion for his glory is the measure of his commitment to our joy.* It sometimes feels as if Christians free-fall into the vast atmosphere of the complexities of end-of-life issues. But unlike the non-Christian, Christians fall with a parachute securely fastened. As the ground quickly rises to meet the Christian, the approach is thereby entirely different from that of a person without a parachute. Whether death approaches fast or slowly, something holds the Christian, preventing him from hitting the earth with annihilating force.

Because of the Christian's security and hope, fear does not reign. Once fear is dethroned, the dark specter of suffering can be addressed. Good care of the dying raises important questions about our theological view of death and dying. But this should begin long before the dying process begins. Thus, biblical instruction is needed in the church. Christians need the believing community's affirmation in the context of connection and fellowship.[15] If support can be offered in the community of Christian love and truth, the Christian may be confirmed in the knowledge that "whether we live or die, we are the Lord's," and so come to understand that the very instant of transition from death to eternal life is never an instant of separation from the constancy of God's goodness, nor is the soul devoid at that moment of the touch of his sustaining hand. The apostle expressed it in the following way: "I desire to depart and to be with Christ, which is better by far . . ." (Phil. 1:23). The Greek word employed by Paul for "depart" *(epithumian)* was the word that was used when construction of a ship had finally been completed. When the ship began its maiden voyage, it was this Greek word that was used to describe this beginning. If the Christian's maiden voyage of departure is a "beginning" of more fully knowing God at the point of death, then fear is replaced with qualified delight to die. The construction work is completed; the Christian now begins at last that for which he or she was originally created in the *imago Dei* — face-to-face fellowship with God.

The End of Sanctification

In a real sense, death is the consummation of the Christian's sanctification. One of the most grievous aspects of our existence prior to death is our incomplete mortification of sin.[16] Death brings an end to sanctification and, at last, Christians are free not only from the power of sin but from its very presence. Death becomes, paradoxically, a beloved enemy, in that through it the Christian's deepest longings to "Be holy as I, the Lord God Almighty, am holy" (Lev. 11:44) are realized.

15. See Larry Crabb, *The Safest Place on Earth: Where People Connect and Are Forever Changed* (Nashville: Word, 1999).
16. Murray, *Epistle to the Romans.*

Face Lift and More

Moreover, since death is never extracted from the hand of divine Providence, then the fear of aging is relieved by the recognition of the glory of God. Even in an age of high-priced cosmetic surgery, bodily deterioration and aging will not be shameful to the well-informed Christian heart. The joke is told of the lady who found herself in heaven ahead of schedule; St. Peter said, "I've checked with God, and sure enough, you aren't due here for another twenty-five years." So she went back to earth and had extensive plastic surgery, lipo-suction, a tummy tuck, and dyed her hair blonde, figuring if she was going to live twenty-five more years, she was going to do it in style. Whereupon walking out of the beauty salon, she was immediately run over by a truck. Appearing once again in heaven, she said, "I thought I had twenty-five more years to live. What happened?" And God replied, "Oh my! I'm sorry, I didn't recognize you!"

Neither should the Christian fear a slow, lingering demise. This is not to deny legitimate trepidation concerning the possibility of pain and suffering. But the testimony of many of God's people has been that the hope of experiencing one's glorification can provide a persevering peace through whatever the experience of death may bring. God is present with us in our dying.

Courage to Speak Ahead of Time

Affirmations of divine immanence should encourage preparation of advance medical directives. A Support Study of 1995 revealed that 50 percent of the doctors did not know the CPR preferences of the irreversibly dying patients' families.[17] Knowledge of God's glory being the measure of his commitment to our joy in death substantiates the freedom and nerve to address these matters in advance and to challenge the cultural ethos of a hide-and-seek silence on these matters.

In this same way, this pastoral outlook will encourage early, rather than last-minute, entrance into hospice care. Bioethicist Scott Rae notes, "Irreversibly dying patients spent at least 10 days of their stays in the ICU. . . . The place for the irreversibly dying patient is not in the ICU but in a hospice which specializes in providing comfort care for the patients for whom aggressive care is no longer desired or effectual."[18]

17. Rae and Cox, *Bioethics: A Christian Approach*, p. 222.
18. Rae and Cox, *Bioethics: A Christian Approach*, p. 222.

Caveats in the Realm of Certainty

Physician-Assisted Suicide

Against the backdrop of these positive affirmations of death, several cautions arise. The evangelical Christian community, rightly informed,[19] will not embrace physician-assisted suicide because it will affirm that in Jesus Christ, it is overall delight to die, that "to be absent from the body is to be at home with the Lord" (2 Cor. 5:8). Rather, the informed confidence that comes from a passion for the theocentric glory is the same informed conscience that equally engenders christocentric obedience and submission to God's sovereign timing over the Christian's moment of death (Heb. 9:27) as also summoning forth godly perseverance via the stunning faith affirmation of divine preservation: God maintains nothing with greater passion than the honor of his glory. He is most glorified in the Christian who like the psalmist of old "delights to do His will" (Ps. 40:8) and says, "Because I love Your commands more than gold, more than pure gold, and because I consider all your precepts right, I hate every wrong path" (Ps. 119:127-28).

The Interconnected Church and the Communion of the Saints

Moreover, it is distinctly the Christian covenantal community that engenders an unabashed hope in death as delight, in spite of tendencies of the culture to read such affirmations as tantamount to neurotic morbidness. Christians do not approach these matters of life and death in either slavish dependency or autonomous independence, but rather community-bonded interdependency. Death, dying, and end-of-life issues are faced as part of a community grounded in the "here and now" with the joyful anticipation of the perfection of joyous reunion in the "then and there." It is the hope of reunion not just with long since deceased grandma and grandpa or wife or husband, but also with Abraham, Isaac, Jacob, Isaiah, and, most of all, Isaiah's suffering servant of Israel, the Lord Jesus Christ himself, that sustains the Christian's hope. Hence, far from American individualism being ratified, just the opposite. Radical community is maintained. Death as delight rises out of earthly com-

---

19. Educating the church to think Christianly is no small task. As historian Mark Noll has so pointedly said, "The scandal of the evangelical mind is that there is not much of an evangelical mind." Mark Noll, *The Scandal of the Evangelical Mind* (Grand Rapids: Eerdmans, 1994), p. 3.

munity with heavenly bonds, heads toward eternal community with earthly bonds (the communion of the saints), and therefore the Holy Spirit and the Word of God wean Christians away from, and defend Christians against, the erroneous autonomous individualistic views of American culture.

Soli Deo Gloria

The only appropriate response of the aging Christian soul is one which is consistent with Edwards's three premises: (1) God maintains nothing with greater passion than the honor of his glory; (2) God is most glorified in the Christian when the Christian is most delighted in him; and therefore (3) God's passion for his glory is the measure of his commitment to the Christian's joy. Ultimately, God's glory is seen in the face of the Lord Jesus Christ. In him, we have hope of life everlasting. To God alone be the glory!

A Geriatrician's Perspective

JOHN DUNLOP, M.D.

The struggle over who will be the center of life dates from the fall of humanity. Adam felt it; Cain and Abel acted it out. Paul expressed it in terms of the struggle between the flesh and the spirit. St. Augustine wrote of the city of God versus the city of man. More recently, Chuck Colson talked about the kingdoms of men and the kingdom of God. Where is the ultimate meaning of life? Is it in the comfort and well-being of our earthly existence? Or are the ultimate answers found only in God? Are we transcendent spiritual beings temporarily tied to space and time, or are we materialist physical beings hoping against hope to find something beyond ourselves? The attitudes we carry into the closing years of our lives, and the decisions that they inform, often express whether or not God is at the center of our lives.

Author Stephen Sapp speaks of "a self-centered, present-oriented approach to life that has been characterized as 'narcissism.'"[1] He quotes the late Christopher Lasch's book *The Culture of Narcissism*: "The 'narcissist needs to be admired for his beauty, charm, celebrity, or power — attributes that usually fade with time.' Thus the 'irrational terror of old age and death' in America today 'is closely associated with the emergence of the narcissistic personality as the dominant type of personality structure.'"[2] Sapp goes on to show how antithetical is this view of self and humankind to a thoroughly Christian view. Such narcissism reflects the kingdom of man. A Christian view should

---

1. Stephen Sapp, *Full of Years: Aging and the Elderly in the Bible and Today* (Nashville: Abingdon, 1987), p. 163.

2. Sapp, *Full of Years*; cf. Christopher Lasch, *The Culture of Narcissism: American Life in an Age of Diminishing Expectations* (New York: W. W. Norton, 1978).

focus not on the self but on God. The passion of the Christian is to see the glory of God accomplished in every aspect of life. A major value in eternity is that God may be glorified. A passion for the glory of God will dictate many of the decisions we make at the end of life.

In this chapter I propose that the major value we promote in our Christian lives is that God may be glorified through very practical decisions. We must repress the values of this world and embrace God himself as our only value. This represents a challenge to the church. A major goal of our churches must be to equip people to live their later days and ultimately to die with a passion for the glory of God.

Sadly, many confessing Christians give only lip service to the glory of God. The choices they make at the end of life reveal their true values. Too often they emphasize their own pleasure and comfort and lose the passion they once affirmed for God's glory.

The Glory of God

Life is to be lived and death is to be experienced to the glory of God. Over the years, many voices have sought to bring us back to our roots with a passion for God's glory. Augustine caught the vision, as did Calvin, and many of the Puritans such as John Owen and Jonathan Edwards.[3] In our generation the writings of J. I. Packer and John Piper revive these truths. Piper echoes Edwards when he tells us that God is most glorified in us when we are most satisfied with him. There is a link between the joy that we find in God and the glory that our lives bring to him.[4] We find our fullness in God and the joy of that fullness overflows to others. In this way God is glorified. The challenge is how to accomplish that in the closing days of life. How do I allow my joy in God to set the tone of my life so strongly that it will overpower many of the factors that could otherwise be seen as difficulties and discouragements? How do I experience a joy in God that allows me not just to survive in spite of the struggles but also to actually find a joy in God through the difficulties that invariably come at the end of life?

It is my conviction that God desires to make our joy in him the center point of our lives. As we learn to enjoy God through our adult years this pas-

3. John Piper has made Edwards very readable in his book *God's Passion for His Glory* (Wheaton, Ill.: Crossway, 1998), in which he includes the text of Edwards's work "The End for Which God Created the World."

4. John Piper, *Desiring God: Meditations of a Christian Hedonist* (Sisters, Ore.: Multnomah, 1996).

sion will ultimately affect our decisions at the end of life. *Our joy in God allows him to be glorified at the end of our lives.*

Practical Aging

Retirement

One of the first major decisions we face as we age is what to do about retirement. Many have worked hard. They gave their energy and loyalty to their employers for many years. They thriftily saved that "nest egg." All of that is commendable. Nevertheless, at this point they may stray. They are tempted to feel entitled to enjoy their "golden years." In our culture this often means disengaging not only from the workplace but from the church and the community, investing instead in recreation and relaxation. The tragedy is that the church often encourages such narcissistic thinking by shielding retirees from responsibilities and leadership.

Instead, churches should challenge their retirees to use their retirement years for the glory of God. After all, in an era when people are retiring earlier and earlier, there may be opportunity for a second career. That career could involve ministry in the church. This mission field provides another venue for glorifying God. If we instill in believers a passion for the glory of God, they can race to retirement with an exuberant joy. This does not mean that there is no room to enjoy the gifts of God or that he cannot be glorified by activities that may not be regarded as productive. It is true that we can glorify him in recreation and relationships. There is a danger, however, that we seek our joy in the gifts and not in the Giver. If we do focus on material things rather than on God, we do it to our great loss. We will not find our greatest joy in the wonderful gifts that God lavishes on us. We will find our greatest joy in him.

As retirement progresses people may be less active. Quieter days open the potential to involvements which have greater spiritual value. Many people in the prime of life err in being so busy that they do not take time for some important spiritual activities. The later years offer opportunity for an increased emphasis on prayer, on relationships, and on encouraging others, activities that might not have been possible in the working years. *God is glorified when our relationship with him can contribute to spiritual fruit in the lives of others.*

Pain, Suffering, and Disability

More often than we are prepared to accept them, pain, suffering, and disability come with the older years. These difficulties can challenge an individual's faith. Health problems also challenge the caretaker or other close friends. Declining health raises several issues. The first is a basic question of practical theology. Can we experience the difficulties in our later years and still affirm that God is strong and loving? The second question is more sociological. Can we find the help and support we need at the end of life within the relationships we have?

We consider first the theological question. The Psalms help us as we struggle with the meaning of the difficulties of life. For instance, Psalm 62 says,

> One thing God has spoken,
> two things have I heard:
> that you, O God, are strong,
> and that you, O Lord, are loving. (vv. 11-12)[5]

There are three options to explain difficulties in life that do not seem right in our perspective. First, there is the possibility that God does not love. He well knows that we are experiencing difficulties but he does not care enough to help. The second possibility is that he is not strong. He might very much like to intervene on our behalf but finds the situation beyond his control. He is not able to help. The psalmist affirms, however, that God is both loving and strong. Therefore, we must choose a third option: that we do not always understand God's purposes perfectly. We must accept by faith that God is fully in control and that he intends our good, even when things, from our point of view, are not going so well.

Job's life beautifully illustrates this truth. Contrast the theology of Job with that of his four friends. The friends believed in a God who was very predictable. They had a *quid pro quo* point of view. If I do such and such, I can predict that God will respond in this way or that. If I am good, I can predict God will be good to me. If I am bad, I can predict that God will be bad to me. Their view was very simple. God is easily knowable, predictable, and, therefore, controllable! Job responded to his friends by accusing them of having a God they could carry around in their hands (Job 12:6). One might say that the friends had a "small God" theology.

---

5. Biblical citations in this chapter are taken from the New International Version of the Bible.

Job, on the other hand, had a very "big God." When he was the victim of great losses, he could bow before God and worship. When he could not understand the cause of the difficulties, he never demanded restoration, but pled for an audience with God. He moved through his losses to a longing for God. In the end he could only confess that the things God had spoken of were "too wonderful for me to know" (Job 42:3). He did not pretend to understand God. Instead, he allowed his wonder to lead him to worship rather than defiance. A "big God" theology is consistent with Scripture. This is the view of God that our churches must sow and cultivate within believers. It is imperative that our churches prepare people in the prime of life for some of the difficulties that will come later. *God is glorified when we can accept the difficulties he allows for our good, being strengthened by them rather than allowing them to discourage our faith.*

There is also, however, a social dimension that our churches must develop in order to equip believers for the difficulties at the end of life. We may call it a "ministry of dependency." Believers are commanded to "Carry each other's burdens, and in this way you will fulfill the law of Christ" (Gal. 6:2). This command to carry burdens is a charge to help others; at the same time, it obligates us to allow others to help us. The older years often teach us how to depend more on others. There is, indeed, a ministry of dependency.

These lessons were illustrated vividly to me in the waiting room of our local hospital. Mr. B had sustained a cerebral hemorrhage after thrombolytic therapy for a myocardial infarction. While it was a tragedy, it was also such a blessing for me. As I went out of his room to tell his wife what had happened, I found a group of Christian friends praying for him and supporting her. The death of another patient during the same week provided a striking contrast: I had spoken to a man immediately after the death of his wife, and his first response was, "now who will take care of me?" If he had had a supporting church, he would have known the answer to his own question.

The church is a community that is to be characterized by true fellowship. We are to participate intimately in each other's lives. Part of the intimacy is sharing each other's sufferings. We often see pain and suffering decrease as it is shared within a caring community. One of the goals of the church must be to develop communities that can feel one another's pain deeply. *God is glorified in his church when the members develop a depth of fellowship adequate to allow them to bear one another's burdens.*

Healing

There are times when we may be called of God to pray for supernatural healing in view of impending death. If this is from the Lord, it is laudable and not to be condemned.

> "Who among the gods is like you, O LORD?
> Who is like you —
> majestic in holiness,
> awesome in glory,
> working wonders?" (Exod. 15:11)

God delights to work wonders and can accomplish his glory by demonstrating his awesome works. Scripture instructs us to pray for healing and, indeed, we should. God may choose to step in directly and accomplish his purposes. At other times he will use the wisdom and technology given to health professionals. We must look to God to work in whatever way he chooses. We must be ready to give him the glory whenever and however he brings healing.

God's control of healing was shown through another patient recently. Mrs. K is a delightful person in her early nineties who was dying of progressive kidney failure. Every time I saw her she would close our visit by simply saying, "please pray for me." I would often put my hand on her shoulder and ask God to help and heal her. She had appropriately declined dialysis, and, once the renal function dropped below 10 percent, was sent home to die with support from hospice. I was quite shocked to see her walk into the office three months later saying she felt great, that God had healed her. A blood test confirmed normal kidney functions. What could I say but "praise God." *God is glorified when the resurrection power of Jesus is expressed in the healing of his people.*

Death

When we approach the end of life we ought to be very conscious that death is a time when God is to be glorified. Paul affirmed this when he wrote, "so that now as always Christ will be exalted in my body, whether by life or by death" (Phil. 1:20). *God is glorified when Christ is exalted.* In today's culture there are many forces that would lead us to focus more on ourselves than on the glory of God at the end of life.

A commonly used phrase these days is "death with dignity." The phrase is often not well defined. In some contexts it means a "nontechnological" death. Others intend by it a quiet surrender to death that is not a "fight to the finish." Others imply a death that is totally free of pain. For still others it is a desire that they be highly regarded and respected by friends and loved ones at the time of their deaths. Those last two interpretations need be challenged. As Christians, our passion should not be for our own comfort or reputations, but that Christ be exalted and God be glorified.

Ethicist Daniel Callahan is on the right track when he speaks of a natural time for the end of life.[6] Resignation to this fact can ring hollow, however. It is more realistic and fulfilling to approach death not merely as the end of this life but as a transition to the next. This is the biblical perspective. In this sense, death is not a natural end of this life but an appropriate beginning of eternal bliss.

Dying for the Glory of God

How are we to approach death in such a way that we glorify God? First, we must adopt several important attitudes. It is imperative that churches teach believers to long for God, to die to self, to trust God, and to accept that, in Christ, death has been defeated.

A Longing for God

We need to keep before us the goal for which we are striving: Christ himself. We are challenged by the writer of the book of Hebrews: "Let us fix our eyes on Jesus, the author and perfecter of our faith" (Heb. 12:2). Christians must emphasize the final goal of their lives, not the road they are traveling. If people long for God's presence early in their Christian experience, their choices will be radically affected. *God is glorified in our longings for him.* The tragedy is that many believers fail to develop this love and longing for God.

Death to Self

From the moment we receive Christ as Savior, we begin to die to this world. Baptism speaks of death to self and new life in Christ. The progress of our

---

6. Daniel Callahan, "Aging and the Ends of Medicine," *Annals of the New York Academy of Science* 530 (1988): 125-32.

Christian lives is measured by the degree to which we are to give up the values of this world and embrace the values of eternity. As the years progress and believers deal with disability, both mentally and physically, the church must help them learn to give up some of their independence. This may be difficult since it often includes giving up such things as the family home, driving, or control of their own finances. In God's providence this may be a critical part of the death to self. We must learn to see dependency as a virtue, and weakness as an opportunity for spiritual strength (2 Cor. 12:10). *God is glorified when we value him more than the things of earth, including our physical strength.*

Trust in God

At the end of life there is a temptation for us to trust medical technology rather than God. We should not use life-sustaining technologies just because they exist. Death can be a deliberate act of God, not a failure of medical technology. Scripture teaches that God has set a limit to our life span (Ps. 139:16 and Job 14:5). He knows the day of our death, and our death is ultimately in his loving hands. Death is not a punishment, but the means to our eventual reward. We must be reminded that "Precious in the sight of the LORD is the death of his saints" (Ps. 116:15). *God is glorified by our trust in him.*

A Proper Theology of Death

Scripture often presents the truth as a tension between two opposites. Human beings are made in the image of God, yet fallen in sin. God is sovereign, but humans are morally responsible. So it is in the case of death. Death is an enemy, yet through Christ death is a defeated enemy. We are neither to embrace death nor to eschew it. There is certainly room for aggressive medical care to resist death; God has given medical science wonderful abilities to prolong meaningful life and, where appropriate, we must accept and use, with gratitude, the gifts he has given to us. Nevertheless, when a poor prognosis makes medical intervention inappropriate, it is time to back off and celebrate the fact that only in Christ, not in modern medicine, do we have victory over death. *God is glorified in the death of his saints.*

Similarly, there are several attitudes that would diminish the perception of God's glory at our deaths.

Fear of Death

The end of life typically removes masks. There are some who have been professing Christians but at the very end of life realize that there is no substance to their confessions and that they are afraid to meet God. This is a wonderful opportunity to affirm the truth of God's word and the promise of salvation to them and invite them to trust Christ who died to save us from the fear of death (Heb. 2:14-15). Others, while not afraid to meet God, fear the process of dying. For many this is very understandable and may not be an indication of spiritual weakness. They fear the farewells, the possibility of pain, and the suffering. They need assurance of God's love and care for them. Christians need to be taught that living by faith gives an ability to hold a deep trust in the love and strength of God up to the last breath. They also need to know that physicians and their fellow believers are going to minister to them in their time of need.

Vitalism

Vitalism is the belief that everything possible should be done to prolong life regardless of the prognosis. Contrary to vitalism, there is a time to live and a time to die. Christians ought to hold loosely to this, preferring the life to come. Vitalism may be evidence of a lack of trust in God. When vitalism is encountered, patients need to be asked what it is that they fear in death.

Do we attempt to resuscitate an elderly patient with end-stage lung disease? Do we put her on a ventilator? What are our motives? Do we glorify God by prolonging a life? Or in attempting to prolong life are we subconsciously seeking to resist the will of God? There are no simple answers. We must sort out our motives as well as our actions. These decisions require prayer, good medical consultation, and the counsel and prayers of the elders of the church. At times we thank God for his gifts of technology and press forward with aggressive care. At other times we need to remind ourselves that to be absent from the body is to be present with the Lord (2 Cor. 5:8).

Challenges for the Church

The end of life can be a glorious transition rather than a tragic defeat. Life can be lived to the glory of God and he can be exalted in our deaths. God desires his own glory, and he empowers his church to bring him glory. At the end of life, however, there are great challenges before believers. Christians must encourage the ministry of the elderly in every way possible and this must cross generational lines. Churches must affirm that the elderly have great value beyond their productive years. The church must challenge those approaching old age to plan for spiritually productive retirement.

The church must teach a "big God" theology — one where the difficulties of life can lead to worship rather than rebellion. The church needs to teach the meaning of suffering. All believers should be taught the lessons of Job, the comfort of the Psalms, and the promise of the resurrection before times of difficulty come. In that way Christians will have a foundation on which to rest when they go through difficult times near the end of life. The church needs to foster deep relationships within itself that will be sustaining at the end of life. This implies building a community whose members can truly bear one another's burdens. Believers need to have relationships intimate enough that they can laugh and shed tears together.

Finally, church leaders need to help people make wise end-of-life decisions. When is it appropriate not to pursue aggressive care to prolong life? The church needs to facilitate families in these discussions and to provide a proper theological basis for decisions. When families choose not to seek aggressive care but to care for their loved ones at home, the church needs to provide practical help and encouragement.

Too often Christians succumb to the myth that God is glorified only when we do great things for him. This attitude limits God and opens the possibility that we are acting only in our own strength. The glory of God can often be seen not in our strength but in our weakness. The greatest example the world has ever seen of God's glory occurred through an agonizing death on a cross. So, as we approach our latter days, may we live and die to the glory of God.

ETHICAL ISSUES IN AGING

Does Gray Hair Cause Gray Answers?
Ethical Issues in an Aging Population

ROBERT D. ORR, M.D., C.M.

Mrs. Wilson is a seventy-eight-year-old widow who lives alone in a "seniors' apartment." I see her in my office infrequently because she remains quite healthy and functional. Her daughter, Beth, lives across town and tries to walk that fine line between allowing her mother to remain independent while giving her whatever assistance or supervision she seems to need. Twice recently she has called me, concerned that her mother was becoming forgetful and occasionally confused. Work-up suggested early dementia. A trial of an antidepressant seemed to make no difference.

Today Beth waited for me outside her mother's examining room and said, "Doctor Orr, I'm worried. Mother got lost driving home from church last Sunday and is more confused and less neat at home. Please tell her she must stop driving. But please don't tell her I told you about getting lost and don't tell her she is getting Alzheimer's Disease. She will be upset with you and mad at me for 'interfering' in her life."

The Dilemma of the Widow's Doctor

Beth's requests are understandable. She is a caring daughter, interested in her mother's safety and welfare. But she is asking her mother's doctor to violate rules about confidentiality and truth-telling. In the process, she is questioning her mother's competence and stepping in as an involuntary surrogate decision-maker in a very familiar parent/child role reversal. By bringing up the issue of her mother's driving privileges, she is causing the doctor to confront a conflict of interests. Should he continue to be a patient advocate, or is he obligated to be an agent of the state?

The demographics of aging are very familiar. U.S. Bureau of Census data show that life expectancy at birth nearly doubled throughout the 1900s. Much of this increase comes from the prevention and treatment of infectious disease, especially in children. The greatest recent change, however, is the dramatic increase in the past forty years in the number of "old old," a designation for those citizens over age eighty-five. In 1960, a woman at age sixty-five could expect to live another 15.8 years, and a man another 12.8 years. By 1998 this had increased to 19.2 and 15.9 years respectively.[1] Even the most conservative projections anticipate that the number of "old old" in the United States will double (from 5,000,000 to 10,000,000) in the next fifty years, and others estimate this figure may quadruple.[2]

This major demographic shift generates many questions beginning with the words, "Should we . . . ?" Should we use scarce medical resources toward the end of life? Should we resuscitate aged patients? Should we provide artificial nutrition and hydration to patients for whom the prognosis of recovery is nil? These questions are about right and wrong; they are questions about values, duties, obligations, principles of conduct, and, ultimately, about doing the right thing.

I would like to draw a fairly sharp distinction between clinical ethics and health policy. Clinical ethics is the identification, analysis, and resolution of ethical dilemmas encountered in the care of an individual patient — "What are we going to do for *this* specific patient?" Clinical ethics tries to draw some boundaries around the tough choices in medicine. There are some decisions that are ethically permissible, and others that are outside the boundaries of acceptable practice. Health policy, on the other hand, addresses "big picture" questions that have to do with family and social obligations, including such issues as the allocation of resources — "What are we going to be able to afford in health care, education, housing, transportation, defense, and so on?" In an ideal world, we would like to say that health policy questions never influence bedside decisions — the good of the individual patient always comes first. But, because of the increasing cost of health care, professionals are increasingly being asked to be good stewards of our resources.[3] Further-

1. M. Moon, "Medicare," *New England Journal of Medicine* 344 (2001): 928-31.

2. J. C. Day, "Population Projections of the U.S. by Age, Sex, Race, & Hispanic Origin 1993-2050," *U.S. Bureau of Census, Current Population Reports* (Washington, D.C.: U.S. Government Printing Office, 1993).

3. R. B. Saltman and O. Ferroussier-Davis, "The Concept of Stewardship in Health Policy," *Bulletin of the World Health Organization* 78 (2000): 732-39.

more, both professionals and families are increasingly encouraged to consider limitation of treatment for older patients when the potential benefits are small and the cost is great.

In this chapter I would like to address two questions in clinical ethics: (1) who decides for the elderly? and (2) what should we decide? I will also address, though much more briefly, two questions in health policy: (1)who pays? and (2) how much?

Who Decides for the Elderly?

Adults should make their own treatment decisions based on their understanding of the facts, the recommendations of their physicians, and their own personal values, which likely are influenced by their cultural and religious beliefs. But what happens when an individual's ability to understand or to decide becomes impaired? Who decides? And how does that surrogate know what the patient would want? What happens to issues of confidentiality and truth-telling when adult children change roles and become guardians of their parents?

Competence and Capacity

We often use the terms "competence" and "capacity" (short for "decision-making capacity") interchangeably. They are not exactly the same, however. "Competence" is a legal term. Competence is presumed unless a court has determined that an individual is *in*competent. A judicial declaration of incompetence may be global, or it may be limited (e.g., to financial matters, personal care, or medical decisions).

"Decision-making capacity," on the other hand, is a clinical term which is task-specific. A physician may determine that a patient does not have the capacity to make a decision for or against surgery for a hip fracture, but she may have the capacity to decide if she wants a sleeping pill or a laxative.

How does a physician make a determination of capacity? We say, only half facetiously, that a generation ago a patient had capacity if he agreed with the doctor and lacked capacity if he disagreed. Today we recognize that this "standard" was incorrect. But we also recognize that there is no easy test to determine capacity.[4]

4. H. R. Searight, "Assessing Patient Competence for Medical Decision Making," *American Family Physician* 45 (1992): 751-59.

In order to make valid treatment decisions, a person must be able to (a) recognize there is a decision to be made, (b) understand the needed information, (c) understand the treatment options, (d) understand the likely consequences of each option (i.e., risks, burdens, and benefits), and (e) rationally manipulate the information to come up with a decision consistent with his or her values.

Surrogate Decision-Making

How do we make treatment decisions for a person who has lost the capacity either permanently (e.g., from dementia, stroke, or head injury) or temporarily (e.g., from acute illness or injury)? In some instances our goal should be to restore their decision-making capacity. When we are unable to do so, or unable to do it quickly enough to make critical decisions, we must rely on a surrogate. Proxy decision-making raises ethical issues.[5]

Traditionally, we have relied on the "next of kin" to make surrogate treatment decisions. This ambiguous designation has allowed health-care professionals some latitude in choosing between a spouse, adult children, siblings, companions, and so on. In the last ten to twelve years, over thirty-five states have eliminated this latitude by passing surrogate decision-making laws which set up a rigid hierarchy of who should be the designated relative to act as surrogate if a patient has not left written instructions. This can often be very helpful when there is disagreement between family members. Sometimes, however, it is not helpful, because appropriate surrogacy is not automatically established by biologic or legal relationship. The appropriate surrogate is one who knows the patient and knows her abilities, wishes, and values.

Once a surrogate is chosen, either by statute or by tradition, what standard does he or she use in making treatment decisions for the patient who has lost the capacity?

Standards for Surrogate Decision-Making

When possible, a surrogate should make a treatment decision using what is called "substituted judgment." That is, they should make the decision the patient would make if he or she were able. This is the ethically correct thing to

---

5. Ezekiel Emanuel and Linda Emanuel, "Proxy Decision Making for Incompetent Patients," *Journal of the American Medical Association* 267 (1992): 2067-71.

do; we should not do something to a patient that he would not want to have done. In addition, this process often relieves the surrogate of the perception that she is making a life or death decision. It is really the patient who is making the decision; the surrogate is merely speaking on his behalf.

How do we know what the patient would want? Sometimes a patient has left written instructions in an advance directive (see below). If not, perhaps he has said to his loved ones what he would want or not want in specific circumstances, or what values are important to him. We must cautiously consider the context of such statements, however; some comments have more moral significance than others. Absent a written advance directive or a meaningful conversation, perhaps those who know him best have some understanding of his values and can judge what he would find acceptable in a given situation.

When it is impossible to make a "substituted judgment" because there is no surrogate or no knowledge of wishes or values, we drop to the lower "best interests" standard. While this may sound like "just do whatever you think is right," it is not quite that simple. In fact, it is not simple at all. A best-interest treatment decision is a difficult attempt to define "what would most people choose in this situation," and it should often involve second or third opinions, and perhaps ethics consultation as well, in an effort to balance potential benefits and burdens while assessing the patient's current and future quality of life.

Advance Directives

An advance directive is a way for a competent person to let others know what she would want or not want if she should lose the capacity to make decisions. Most discussions of advance directives have focused on the documents themselves. The piece of paper, however, is merely intended to document a conversation between the individual and her loved ones or her professional caregivers. Having that conversation is often more important than the document itself.

There are two basic types of advance directive documents, with several variations of each. One type records what a person would want to have done or not done if he were unable to express his wishes at the time. This is often called a Living Will, but may also be called a Terminal Care Document or a Medical Directive. A Jehovah's Witness card indicating the person's wish to avoid blood products is another example of this type of advance directive.

The second type of advance directive designates whom the person would want to make decisions if she became unable. These are commonly called a Durable Power of Attorney for Health Care, but may be called a Proxy Document, Health-care Proxy, Surrogate Document, and so on.

More recent documents, both state-sanctioned and unofficial, include elements of both what the person wants and whom she trusts to make decisions. Some may also include the individual's wishes about organ donation, autopsy, and so forth.

Unfortunately, many individuals complete the document without having the conversation, and family and professionals may be left with the very difficult task of trying to interpret those stark words at some later date in a situation that doesn't exactly fit the one described on the paper.

Professionals should encourage patients to have these conversations and complete these documents. Even with encouragement, some individuals are reluctant to do so for various reasons; but they are almost always willing to have a conversation with their doctor, at least to designate whom they trust to make their decisions. In these situations, the physician should write a detailed dated note about the conversation in the patient's chart. It can then serve as a statement of the patient's wishes, carrying moral if not legal weight.

How closely does the patient want his or her written advance directive followed? Not surprisingly, patients tend to trust their families and physicians. Two large multicentered studies have found that 70.8 percent and 78.0 percent of patients want their family and physician to make resuscitation decisions rather then relying solely on their previously expressed wishes.[6]

Advance directives are an important part of judicious decision-making for patients who have lost the capacity to do so. A patient can, however, change his or her mind, and can change the written document if desired. In addition, there is a legitimate philosophic question raised about the ability of a healthy person to anticipate her wishes for treatment in a future unknown condition. Some maintain that a person who has become disabled (e.g., from a stroke or dementia) is a different person than the one who wrote the instructions, and that this "new person" may have different values.[7]

Privacy and Confidentiality

For twenty-five hundred years it has been an accepted tenet that health-care professionals should keep confidential the information that patients share with them. There are a few recognized situations where this rule may be breached

6. C. M. Puchalski, A. Ahong, M. M. Jacobs, et al., "Patients Who Want Their Family and Physician to Make Resuscitation Decisions for Them: Observations from SUPPORT and HELP," *Journal of the American Geriatrics Society* 48 (2000): S84-S90.

7. Rebecca Dresser, "Dworkin on Dementia: Elegant Theory, Questionable Policy," *Hastings Center Report* 25 (1995): 32-38.

(danger to self or others, legal requirement for reporting, and so on). The most common situation where this is breached, however, is in the care of the older patient. Every day family members ask physicians and nurses for information. And very often that information is shared, even without explicit consent from the patient, because it seems to be in the best interests of the patient.

It is the practice of many physicians caring for geriatric patients to ask before the fact if the patient would give permission for the professional to talk with a designated family member if the need should arise. Some are reluctant to ask, fearing the patient may say no. It would be better, they presume, to not ask and break confidence when it seems best than to ask and be told this would be unacceptable, since they would then — despite their concern for the patient's well-being — be even more uncomfortable breaking confidence. This is a true dilemma. The tenet of confidentiality should be maintained unless the patient gives permission or it seems clear that the patient is putting herself or others at risk by her actions or decisions.

Truth-Telling

The precept of truth-telling is equally important to the trusting patient-professional relationship. It is very difficult to justify complying with a request from a family member (or from the patient) to tell a lie or to not tell the truth. Sometimes such a request can be resolved by a frank discussion with the person making the request about how the professional should respond if the individual should directly ask if this is the whole truth.

In the past, requests for untruth were common in relation to a diagnosis of cancer or other terminal disease. Today they arise more commonly in regard to dementia. But the patient has a right to know her diagnosis and prognosis so she can participate in health-care planning and financial planning, and so she can address any unfinished interpersonal or spiritual issues. The patient should be encouraged to share prognostic information with her family for similar reasons.

What Is Decided?

Not only is the designation of a surrogate an important ethical issue, the actual decision made likewise raises ethical questions. Professionals and surrogates who are making decisions for an older patient often struggle, trying to appropriately balance the ethical principles of non-maleficence (do no harm), beneficence (do good), autonomy (self-determination), and justice (treating like patients alike). They may sometimes feel constrained to override the autonomy of the patient who has lost her decision-making capacity, because she does not seem to recognize or admit problems of functional capacity (mobility, vision, hearing), memory, or judgment. Their concern is that these gradually developing problems may present a danger to the patient or to others.

These concerns may lead them to make decisions that restrict the person's independence, including involuntary admission to assisted living or decisions about driving. These are major decisions that should not be undertaken lightly. Driving restrictions are probably the most contentious of such decisions.

Driving Restrictions

The ability to drive is a powerful symbol of independence, which is often (incorrectly) perceived by an older person as a right rather than as a privilege. But it also has great practical significance. Driving may contribute to the person's health by preventing social isolation, depression, even malnutrition. But if the individual's memory, judgment, or senses are failing, driving can present a significant danger to that individual and to others in the community.

How are these benefits and risks to be balanced? How severe must the deficit be to warrant restriction? Who decides? — family, physician, Department of Motor Vehicles (DMV)? Are there objective measures of the appropriate parameters? Do these deficits pose greater risks than a bad temper or a drinking habit? Could these deficits safely be addressed with only partial restrictions — for instance, limiting a patient to only driving during daylight hours or to only driving with someone else in the car?

Many older individuals recognize and admit these deficits and voluntarily stop driving. When this ideal is not met, the family most often raises the question with the individual's physician. For many reasons, it is very difficult for the family to just "take the keys away," so they are hopeful that the physician will insist the person stop driving. The physician is then in the difficult position of having to make a recommendation based on a clinical judgment in the office. Sometimes this judgment can be bolstered by specific testing, but this too is not always a precise predictor of driving ability or safety. The physician must then decide what to recommend to the patient and whether to report the situation to the DMV. As protectors of the larger society, state officials face difficult decisions about laws and about individuals. But it is the physician who is most often caught in the most significant conflict of interest between seeking what is best for his patient and fulfilling his secondary obligation to society.

Admission to Assisted Living

A decision to move to assisted living may be precipitated by a crisis (e.g., a fracture or a stroke), incontinence, altered behavior (e.g., wandering), poor nutrition, or caregiver fatigue. Occasionally the person recognizes the need and accepts the move. More often, however, the person is very reluctant and must be persuaded by family and professional caregivers. Caution must be exercised that this persuasion doesn't become manipulation (e.g., overstating the benefits or understating the downside) or coercion (e.g., deception, sedation), both of which are ethically problematic.

Use of Restraints

Physical restraints (doors, bedrails, geri-chairs, various types of ties) and chemical restraints (sedation) have often been used in homes and nursing homes to protect patients from falls and to keep them from wandering into danger. They have also been used to prevent confused patients from infringing on the privacy of others, including preventing pilfering of food. Unfortunately, they have also been used, and not infrequently, as a substitute for adequate staffing or as a presumed protection from liability claims.

The ethical problems with restraints are quite clear. Infringement of personal liberty without adequate justification from the safety of the individual or others is not ethically permissible. In addition, there are physical and psychological risks to the individual: de-conditioning, pressure sores, falls (e.g., from trying to climb over bedrails), even death from strangulation, as well as increased agitation, confusion, and depression. Research data suggests that the dangers of restraints often outweigh the benefits.[8] At the very least, restraints should be considered "non-validated" therapy, requiring a high likelihood of benefit before application.

Thus there are many reasons for caregivers to search for alternatives to the use of restraints, such as structural and staffing changes, increased activities, and video surveillance (which raises its own ethical questions).

---

8. W. Marks, "Physical Restraints in the Practice of Medicine," *Archives of Internal Medicine* 152 (1992): 2203-6.

Limitation of Treatment

Among the most difficult decisions faced by surrogates are those about the use or non-use of specific treatment modalities. When an older patient is deteriorating and has a poor prognosis for recovery or survival, it is appropriate to make decisions about the withholding or withdrawing of therapies which might entail increased suffering for the patient with little likelihood for benefit.

The most common limitation of treatment decision is one to not use cardiopulmonary resuscitation (CPR), a so-called DNR (do not resuscitate) decision. CPR was developed to reverse potentially fatal heart rhythms in a person with known heart disease. Its use has gradually expanded so there is a presumption that CPR will be used on anyone whose heart stops unless a DNR decision has been made and documented. This clearly does not make sense when a person is dying rapidly from a terminal illness, and often does not make sense when a person is dying slowly from an irreversible condition. But the default "use CPR" is in place so that we don't miss any opportunities when it might be beneficial.

Many of the lay public perceive CPR as being very successful; it works over 75 percent of the time on television.[9] In fact, it is successful (i.e., the patient survived to hospital discharge) 0-13 percent of the time depending on the setting, the underlying cause, and the rapidity with which CPR is started.[10] It may be tempting to say, "Well, let's just use it and salvage as many as we can." Its use, however, involves trauma for the dying person and his loved ones. In addition, 10-40 percent of initially successful CPR attempts result in only short-term survival in the ICU.[11] Even more tragically, 5-13 percent of those who survive CPR long enough to leave the hospital are left with permanent brain damage from transient lack of oxygen. CPR is strong medicine that should only be used with proper indications.

Many other therapies are optional in seriously ill elderly patients; such things as ICU care, assisted ventilation, dialysis, and chemotherapy are clearly up for discussion. But the benefits and burdens of even less invasive therapies should likewise be weighed in patients who are in the process of dying — such things as blood transfusions, antibiotics, and artificially administered

9. S. Diem, J. D. Lantos, J. Tulsky, "CPR on TV," *New England Journal of Medicine* 334 (1996): 1578-82.

10. A. P. Schneider, D. J. Nelson, D. D. Brown, "In-Hospital CPR: A 30-Year Review," *Journal of the American Board of Family Practice* 6 (1993): 91-101.

11. C. J. von Gunten, "CPR in Hospitalized Patients: When Is It Futile?" *American Family Physician* 44 (1991): 2130-34.

fluids and nutrition. In these situations, all therapies become optional — all, that is, except two: good symptom control and human presence remain ethically obligatory.

End-of-Life Care

Health-care professionals are obligated to provide excellent care at the end of a patient's life. Such palliative care is multidimensional (addressing not only physical needs, but psychological, social, and spiritual), and it is multidisciplinary (involving nurses, physicians, therapists, chaplains, social workers, volunteers). In addition, this care should be directed at both the patient and the family. Hospice care and the expanded concept of palliative care have contributed to achieving this goal and provide an opportunity for ministry for professionals and congregations.

Who Pays and How Much?

These issues in clinical ethics cannot be addressed without consideration of the health policy questions raised above. This chapter does not provide adequate space to fully address the financial issues, but we cannot ignore them.

Almost all medical treatment is expensive. The makers of health policy have looked most critically, however, at costs for older individuals, especially at the end of life, asking, "Is it worth it?" The data show that 25-30 percent of lifetime Medicare expenditures occur in the last year of life.[12] There are several possible explanations for this. The statistic could be interpreted to mean that we are using too many expensive high-tech interventions during the dying process. There is conflicting data about how much could be saved by the increased use of advance directives and other means to make decisions about limiting the use of expensive treatments at the end of life. It does not appear, however, that the potential savings represent a substantial portion of our health-care budget.[13]

Alternatively, this data about the cost of care at the end of life could indicate that we are often faced with clinical uncertainty about the likely benefit of

12. J. D. Lubitz and G. F. Riley, "Trends in Medicare Payments in the Last Year of Life," *New England Journal of Medicine* 328 (1993): 1092-96.

13. Ezekiel Emanuel and Linda Emanuel, "The Economics of Dying: The Illusion of Cost Savings at the End of Life," *New England Journal of Medicine* 330 (1994): 540-44.

a particular treatment, and there is no way to resolve that uncertainty without trying it. Another interpretation is that good multi-disciplinary care is expensive. Or, it could simply mean that people often get sick before they die.

As individuals get older, the greatest rate of increase in health-related expenses is for nursing home care.[14] Seventeen percent of persons who die between ages sixty-five and seventy-four will have spent some time in a nursing home; that figure increases to 60 percent for those who die between the ages of eighty-five and ninety-four.[15] In addition, 55 percent of individuals admitted to a nursing home stay for over one year, and 21 percent stay for over five years. These costs add up. Sadly, our society continues to debate who should be responsible for these huge costs: the patient, the family, the insurance industry, or the taxpayers. Many families care for their loved ones at home, at great personal and financial cost.[16] Others automatically defer to the state and some even abandon their family members in the nursing home. In the meantime, many individuals who could benefit from a nursing home are unable to enter one because of lack of adequate funding.

We must be cautious to not be overly critical of the makers of health policy. Health-care professionals focus on the individual patient who has a name and a face, and we are patient advocates who are concerned about non-maleficence, beneficence, and autonomy. The job of policy-makers, on the other hand, is to be protectors of society by looking at faceless statistics, being concerned primarily with issues of justice, and making decisions based on cost-benefit analysis — the greatest good for the greatest number.

Conclusion

I have tried to address some of the more common questions raised in relation to our aging population — questions of clinical ethics and (briefly) questions of societal ethics. Health-care professionals must confront these issues on a daily basis and must be prepared to address them using ancient and modern precepts and principles. In addition to this professional mandate for caring, Christian health-care professionals have the guidance of Scripture — the teachings and example of Jesus and the letters of his followers — as well as the

14. B. C. Spillman and J. Lubitz, "The Effect of Longevity on Spending for Acute and Long-term Care," *New England Journal of Medicine* 342 (2000): 1409-15.

15. P. Kemper and C. M. Murtaugh, "Lifetime Use of Nursing Home Care," *New England Journal of Medicine* 324 (1991): 595-600.

16. K. E. Covinsky, L. Goldman, E. F. Cook, et al., "The Impact of Serious Illness on Patients' Families," *Journal of the American Medical Association* 272 (1994): 1839-44.

longstanding tradition of the church caring for its own and others. James taught us that "Pure religion and undefiled before God and the Father is this, To visit the fatherless and widows in their affliction, and to keep himself unspotted from the world" (James 1:27 KJV).

Age-Based Rationing of
Life-Sustaining Health Care

JOHN F. KILNER, PH.D.

Thousands of people die annually — even in developed countries like the United States — for lack of access to widely available high-tech treatments such as organ transplantation. Vastly greater numbers die worldwide for lack of access to immunizations, antibiotics, and prenatal care.[1] The inescapable question echoes around the world: When there is not enough for everyone, who gets it and who does not? Who lives and who dies?[2]

Sometimes the problem is that health care becomes very expensive, or that the resources allocated to it become limited by other priorities — perhaps misplaced priorities. So it may be a question of tight money;[3] or it may be a question of other scare resources, such as organs for transplant.[4]

Valiant efforts have been made to save the lives of those who cannot get transplants. The artificial kidney — hemodialysis — was developed to save

---

1. UNICEF, *The State of the World's Children 2002* (New York: UNICEF, 2002).

2. Victor R. Fuchs, *Who Shall Live? Health, Economics, and Social Choice,* expanded edition (River Edge, N.J.: World Scientific, 1998); William D. Frazier, "Rationing of Health Care — Who Determines Who Gets the Cure, When, Where, and Why?" *Annals of Health Law* 2 (1993): 95-99; John F. Kilner, *Who Lives? Who Dies?* (New Haven, Conn.: Yale University Press, 1990).

3. Paul Menzel et al., "Toward a Broader View of Values in Cost-Effectiveness Analysis of Health," *Hastings Center Report* 29 (May-June, 1999): 7-15; Jack W. Snyder, "Making Medical Spending Decisions: The Law, Ethics, and Economics of Rationing Mechanisms," *Journal of Legal Medicine* 19 (March 1998): 143-50.

4. Volker H. Schmidt, "Selection of Recipients for Donor Organs in Transplant Medicine," *Journal of Medicine and Philosophy* 23 (February 1998): 50-74; Thomas Gutmann and Walter Land, "The Ethics of Organ Allocation: The State of the Debate," *Transplantation Reviews* 11 (October 1997): 191-207.

the lives of those who could not have kidney transplants. That development created a new allocation problem: who would get the available dialysis machines? In 1962, *Life* magazine ran a now infamous exposé about how hospitals were deciding who would live and who would be left to die. People who were socially attractive were the winners.[5]

The matter went to the floor of the United States Congress. Congress understandably was not eager to tackle the issue of how to decide who should live and who should die. No Congressional hearings were held on the matter. Less than thirty minutes of debate took place on the Senate floor. Congress was able to escape developing ethical criteria by deciding to fund dialysis for everyone.[6] What was projected to cost a few hundred million dollars at the time skyrocketed to two billion dollars in the first decade, and then well beyond that.[7] Everyone realized then that the next time a major artificial organ developed, it could not simply be given to everyone.[8] Ethical criteria would be unavoidable.

5. Shana Alexander, "They Decide Who Lives, Who Dies," *Life* 53 (November 9, 1962): 102-25. See also David Sanders and Jesse Dukeminier Jr., "Medical Advance and Legal Lag: Hemodialysis and Kidney Transplantation," *UCLA Law Review* 15 (February 1968): 366-80; "Scarce Medical Resources," *Columbia Law Review* 9 (April 1969): 620-92. For additional sources, see Kilner, *Who Lives? Who Dies?* p. 28.

6. The arguments voiced by a majority of the senators during the brief floor debate confirm this interpretation: United States Congress, *Congressional Report* 118 (September 30, 1972): 33007. See also Leonard M. Fleck, "DRGs: Justice and the Invisible Rationing of Health Care Resources," *Journal of Medicine and Philosophy* 12 (May 1987): 184; James F. Childress, "The Gift of Life: Ethical Problems and Policies in Obtaining and Distributing Organs for Transplantation," *Critical Care Clinics* 2 (January 1986): 144-45; George J. Annas, "The Prostitute, the Playboy, and the Poet: Rationing Schemes for Organ Transplantation," *American Journal of Public Health* 75 (February 1985): 187; Lorraine R. Adams, "Medical Coverage for Chronic Renal Disease: Policy Implications," *Health and Social Work* 3 (1978): 42.

7. Eugene L. Meyer, "Tax Money for Transplant Operations: Who Pays?" *Washington Post* (September 12, 1984): 18; Glenn Richards, "Technology Costs and Rationing Issues," *Hospitals* 58 (June 1, 1984): 81; *National Heart Transplantation Study* (Seattle: Battelle Human Affairs Research Centers, 1984): ch. 44:41; R. W. Schmidt et al., "The Dilemmas of Patient Treatment for End-Stage Renal Disease," *American Journal of Kidney Diseases* 3 (July 1983).

8. Ruth Macklin, *Mortal Choices* (New York: Pantheon, 1987), p. 160; Drummond Rennie et al., "Limited Resources in the Treatment of End-stage Renal Failure in Britain and the United States," *Quarterly Journal of Medicine*, n.s., 56 (July 1985): 227; Glenn C. Graber et al., *Ethical Analysis of Clinical Medicine* (Baltimore: Urban and Schwarzenberg, 1985), p. 208; Minnesota Coalition on Health Care Costs, *The Price of Life: Ethics and Economics* (Minneapolis: M.C.H.C.C., 1984), p. 33; Institute of Medicine, *Disease by Disease Toward National Health Insurance? Implications of a Categorical Catastrophic Disease Approach to National Health Insurance* (Washington, D.C.: National Academy of Sciences, 1973), pp. 8-9.

We have now witnessed the use of a totally implantable artificial heart in humans, and huge demand is predictable.[9] Other lifesaving technologies will not be far behind. The pressure to develop ethical allocation criteria will only be escalating in the days ahead.[10]

One approach to this challenge is to bar older people from receiving life-sustaining health care such as organ transplants and implants[11] — or possibly even allowing them only limited intensive care space.[12] There is evidence that similar age considerations affect treatment decisions in many other areas of health care as well.[13] Prominent bioethicists such as Daniel Cal-

9. For a discussion of the development of the artificial heart, including the latest trials regarding the totally implantable artificial heart and the 100,000 or so lives that might be saved annually by it in the United States alone, see www.heartpioneers.com. Cf. Dale Jamieson, "The Artificial Heart: Reevaluating the Investment," in *Organ Substitution Technology,* ed. Deborah Mathieu (Boulder, Colo.: Westview, 1988).

10. Even the provision of dialysis for everyone in the United States — not to mention elsewhere — has come under huge pressure, because of the great costs involved. See John K. McKenzie et al., "Dialysis Decision Making in Canada, the United Kingdom and the United States," *American Journal of Kidney Diseases* 31 (January 1998): 12-18; Gregory W. Rutecki and John F. Kilner, "Dialysis As a Resource Allocation Paradigm: Confronting Tragic Choices Once Again?" *Seminars in Dialysis* 12 (January-February 1999): 38-43; Shahid M. Chanda et al., "Is There a Rationale for Rationing Chronic Dialysis? A Hospital Based Cohort Study of Factors Affecting Survival and Morbidity," *British Medical Journal* 318 (January 23, 1999): 217-23.

11. Schmidt, "Selection of Recipients"; James Neuberger et al., "Assessing Priorities for Allocation of Donor Liver Grafts: Survey of Public and Clinicians," *British Medical Journal* 317 (July 18, 1998): 172-75; Peter A. Ubel and George Loewenstein, "Distributing Scarce Livers: The Moral Reasoning of the General Public," *Social Science and Medicine* 42 (April 1996): 1049-55; Mary C. Corley and Gilda Sneed, "Criteria in the Selection of Organ Transplant Recipients," *Heart and Lung* 23 (November-December 1994): 446-57.

12. John D. Lantos et al., "Resource Allocation in Neonatal and Medical ICUs: Epidemiology and Rationing at the Extremes of Life," *American Journal of Respiratory and Critical Care Medicine* 156 (July 1997): 185-89; William Meadow et al., "Distributive Justice across Generations: Epidemiology of ICU Care for the Very Young and the Very Old," *Clinics in Perinatology* 23 (September 23, 1996): 597-608; Janet Baltz and Judith L. Wilson, "Age-Based Limitation for ICU Care: Is It Ethical?" *Critical Care Nurse* 15 (December 1995): 65-73; P. Frisho-Lima et al., "Rationing Critical Care: What Happens to Patients Who Are Not Admitted," *Theoretical Surgery* 9 (December 1994): 208-11; Society of Critical Care Medicine Ethics Committee, "Attitudes of Critical Care Medicine Professionals Concerning Distribution of Intensive Care Resources," *Critical Care Medicine* 22 (February 1994): 358-62.

13. N. J. Turner et al., "Cancer in Old Age: Is It Inadequately Investigated and Treated?" *British Medical Journal* 319 (July 31, 1999): 309-12; Marshall B. Kapp, "*De Facto* Health-Care Rationing by Age: The Law Has No Remedy," *Journal of Legal Medicine* 19 (September 1998): 223-49; Robert P. Giugliano et al., "Elderly Patients Receive Less Aggressive Medical and Invasive Management of Unstable Angina: Potential Impact of Practice

lahan, Robert Veatch, and Norman Daniels have all expressed support for some form of age-based rationing, as will be discussed shortly. Why this mushrooming interest in age-based rationing of health care? Are the reasons ethically legitimate? What insights does a Christian perspective give us into the present debate?

The Influence of Economy and Utility

The most commonly cited reason for limiting the lifesaving resources available to older people in the United States is the economic impact of the rapidly growing number of elderly persons.[14] The percentage of the American population over age sixty-five has grown from less than 2 percent in 1790 to nearly 12.5 percent in 2000. Particularly fast-growing are the ranks of the oldest persons — those eighty-five years or older. By 2000, their number in the United States had topped 4.2 million, representing 1.5 percent of the population; moreover, this number is projected to increase considerably in the future.[15]

These escalating numbers, particularly of the oldest persons, signal a rapidly growing need for assistance. Those eighty and older have substantially higher rates of illness and disability even when compared only with persons in their seventies and sixties. Moreover, elderly persons who have severe disabilities are more likely to experience chronic disease, to be older and poorer, and to be more dependent than other elderly persons.[16]

Guidelines," *Archives of Internal Medicine* 158 (May 25, 1998): 1113-20; Mary Hamel et al., "Seriously Ill Hospitalized Adults: Do We Spend Less on Older Patients?" *Journal of the American Geriatrics Society* 44 (September 1996): 1043-48. For a large number of additional sources describing age-based rationing criteria in organ transplantation, intensive care, and a wide range of other health-care settings, see John F. Kilner, "Why Now? The Growing Interest in Limiting the Lifesaving Health Care Resources Available to Elderly People," in *Choosing Who's to Live: Ethics and Aging,* ed. James W. Walters (Urbana, Ill.: University of Illinois Press, 1996), pp. 144-47.

14. For a fuller discussion of this economic justification for age-based rationing of health care, see Kilner, "Why Now? The Growing Interest," pp. 122-26.

15. United States Census Bureau, "Profiles of General Demographic Characteristics," *2000 Census of Population and Housing* (Washington, D.C.: U.S. Dept. of Commerce, May 2000); American Medical Association, "Ethical Implications of Age-Based Rationing of Health Care," downloaded from www.ama-assn.org/ama1/upload/mm/369/15b.pdf on July 10, 2001; Jane A. Boyajian, "Sacrificing the Old and Other Health Care Goals," in *Aging and Ethics,* ed. Nancy S. Jecker (Clifton, N.J.: Humana, 1991), p. 320.

16. Robert H. Binstock and Stephen G. Post, "Old Age and the Rationing of Health Care," in *Too Old for Health Care?* ed. Binstock and Post (Baltimore: Johns Hopkins University Press, 1991), pp. 7-8; Boyajian, "Sacrificing the Old," p. 320.

The association of age and cost is an understandable one. As the reasoning goes, health care for elderly persons is costing more and more money, so in order to cut costs it will be necessary to cut back on the health-care resources that will be available to them. Nevertheless, three observations challenge this simple economic rationale for age-based allocation of health care.

First, health-care costs are increasing as a result of a variety of factors, many of which have no special connection to elderly persons. Why are older people as a group singled out to bear the brunt of cutbacks in lifesaving care?[17]

Second, resource constraints are (for the most part) due to the fact that the sum total of individuals' various desires exceeds the total of available resources. In a country that can justify spending $3 billion annually on potato chips, for example, why would people consider preventing a certain group of patients from obtaining lifesaving health care to be one of the best ways to pursue cost savings?[18]

Third, when it is claimed, economically speaking, that elderly persons are receiving a "disproportionate share" of health-care resources, the question must be raised, "disproportionate to what?" They are not receiving disproportionately to their medical need (assuming that medical criteria are being applied equitably to all). Why do those concerned about disproportionate shares so readily assume that the appropriate frame of reference for "proportion" is age?

These three observations suggest that a more complicated economic trend is at work in the United States than merely a concern to reduce health care or other expenditures. There appear to be other reasons for targeting elderly persons in particular for cutbacks. That lifesaving care is an issue even raises the possibility that there is something undesirable about elderly persons *per se*.[19]

The view that health care ought to be rationed for the elderly is attributable, at least in part, to the utilitarian orientation of American culture. Utilitarianism is an outlook that identifies right actions as those producing the

17. For further probing of this question, see Robert H. Binstock, "Another Form of Elderly Bashing," *Journal of Health Politics, Policy, and Law* 17 (summer 1992): 271.

18. This matter is discussed further in Christine K. Cassel, "The Limits of Setting Limits," in *A Good Old Age?* ed. Paul Homer and Martha Holstein (New York: Simon and Schuster, 1990), p. 200.

19. Needless to say, there are a host of other reasons given by proponents of age-based allocation for limiting lifesaving care. The point here is not that the "real reason" is something different, but that there are forces at work in the culture that may well make the reasons offered more intuitively attractive (or less offensive) than they would otherwise seem on their own merits.

greatest good for the greatest number of people. When employed consciously or unconsciously as a means of determining who should receive limited resources, it predisposes one to view people in terms of whatever contributions are valued most highly by the society, with a bias toward contributions most readily quantifiable and thus comparable.

In a market-driven society like the United States, economic productivity is at the top of the list. So it is no surprise that older people, who are less likely to be viewed as economically productive, are not highly valued. They are "retired" — or even more succinctly put, "retirees" — no longer productive in the ways that matter most in contemporary society. Efforts to defend elderly persons by promoting the image of old age as a time of new possibilities and productivity (the slogan "I'm retreaded, not retired," for example) only reinforce this utilitarian perspective. What matters is productivity.[20]

This emphasis on productivity helps explain American society's preoccupation with youth. Youth is the time of greatest productivity and thus possibility — a time most worthy of society's attention and protection. Accordingly, elderly people are commonly referred to in terms of either their distance from youth (e.g., "over the hill") or their decline from youth (e.g., their "sunset years").

The utilitarian way of thinking that sustains the emphasis on youth and productivity in the United States has been criticized harshly. For instance, comparing everyone's social contribution is extremely difficult, since everything potentially of benefit to anyone in society must be considered. Utilitarian thinking has also been castigated for its lack of inherent protections against how badly a person or group can be treated if society finds such treatment to be economically beneficial. Even if, however, a utilitarian way of thinking were workable and theoretically sound, the question of what should count as a "contribution to society" remains. The tendency to focus on economic contributions in the United States is rather different from the perspective of some other societies around the world.

While European and Asian examples could be cited, a particularly good example of an alternative outlook may be found among the Akamba people of Kenya.[21] The great respect accorded to older people there is intimately

20. For further discussion on this point, see p. 83 of Christine K. Cassel and Bernice L. Neugarten, "The Goals of Medicine in an Aging Society," and pp. 165 and 171 of Thomas H. Murray, "Meaning, Aging, and Public Policy," both in *Too Old for Health Care?* ed. Binstock and Post. See also Henry C. Simmons, "Countering Cultural Metaphors of Aging," *Journal of Religious Gerontology* 7 (1990): 156.

21. John F. Kilner, "Who Shall Be Saved? An African Answer," in *Choices and Conflict,* ed. Emily Friedman (Chicago: American Hospital Association, 1992), pp. 22-27.

bound up with their view of the relationship between the individual and the community. Whereas the utilitarian view conceives of the social good atomistically in terms of individual (mainly job-related) contributions summed over the breadth of society, the Akamba view presupposes a social network of interpersonal relations of which one becomes more and more an essential part the older one becomes. The more interwoven a person becomes with others through time, the greater the damage done to the social fabric when that person is torn away by death.

When we look at the economic, especially utilitarian, context of health-care resource allocation in countries like the United States today, it is no wonder that age criteria have such a strong, albeit often unconscious, appeal. But as we have seen, there are indeed viable alternatives to the economic, individualistic, youth-oriented outlook so influential in the United States.

A Biblical Alternative

The utilitarian outlook is not the only major cultural consideration underlying the contemporary openness to age-based rationing of health care in the United States and elsewhere. In recent decades, Americans have witnessed an increasing reluctance to include biblical-Christian perspectives and arguments in public policy discussions, as a result of concerns over "separation of church and state." What difference has that made in how society has come to view its elderly members? To put the same question differently, if one were open to considering the wisdom that a biblical outlook on life offers, what would that outlook tell us about elderly people and how elderly people should be treated? Regarding the distinctive characteristics of older people, two characteristics stand out at various points in the biblical writings: their wisdom and their weakness.[22]

First, older people are generally wise. "Is not wisdom found among the aged?" Job asks rhetorically, and "Does not long life bring understanding?" (Job 12:12 NIV; cf. 15:10; 32:7). The elders (normally elderly) are, therefore, in the best position to give good counsel (e.g., Deut. 32:7); and a family that has lost all of its elderly has been severely punished (1 Sam. 2:31). In fact, a city with men and women of "ripe old age" is considered blessed (Zech. 8:4).

22. An earlier version of portions of the biblical-Christian discussion in this chapter may be found in John F. Kilner, *Life on the Line: Ethics, Aging, Ending Patients' Lives, and Allocating Vital Resources* (Grand Rapids: Eerdmans, 1992), and in John F. Kilner, "The Ethical Legitimacy of Excluding the Elderly When Medical Resources Are Limited," *The Annual of the Society of Christian Ethics* (1988): 179-203.

The difference that the wisdom of elderly counsel can make is nowhere more dramatically illustrated than in 1 Kings 12 (cf. 2 Chron. 10). There, a large assembly of God's people ask King Rehoboam to lighten their harsh workload. The king consults with two groups of counselors — one of old men and one of young men. His failure to heed the wise counsel of the old men leads to the dramatic break-up of God's kingdom into the two antagonistic kingdoms of Israel and Judah! Wisdom, then, is generally presented as a function of the life experience that only elderly persons have. Because, however, it is also the product of righteousness and God's Spirit, it is possible occasionally for young people to have wisdom (Job 32:8-9; Eccles. 4:13) and older people to lack it (Job 12:20).

A second characteristic of many elderly persons — at least at some point — is that they are weak. Old age is acknowledged in the Scriptures as a time of suffering and vulnerability (Eccles. 12:2-5; 2 Sam. 19:35). It is a time of failing eyes (e.g., Gen. 27:1; 48:10; 1 Sam. 4:15; 1 Kings 14:4), failing feet (e.g., 1 Kings 15:23), and declining overall bodily health (e.g., 1 Sam. 4:18; 1 Kings 1:1). Knowing that insensitive people take advantage of the weakness of older people, the psalmist prays, "Do not cast me away when I am old; do not forsake me when my strength is gone" (Ps. 71:9; cf. v. 18).

Such weakness may be a general characteristic but not an absolute characteristic. Elderly people, therefore, should not automatically be written off as mentally or physically incapable simply because of their age. God often breaks through stereotypes. Who would have thought that Sarah and Abraham would have a child in their very old age (Gen. 18:11-14; 21:5-7); or that the Shunammite woman would have a baby with her elderly husband (2 Kings 4:14ff.); or that the elderly Elizabeth, relative to Jesus' mother Mary, would bear a child (Luke 1:36-37)? Who would have expected Jacob to father Joseph at such an old age that Joseph became special for that reason (Gen. 37:3)? While weakness is often present in older people, it must be discovered and documented — never assumed.

Both the wisdom and weakness of elderly people call for appropriate responses, namely, respecting and protecting. We respond appropriately to wisdom by respecting it and those who possess it. Evil peoples are sometimes characterized by their lack of respect for those who are older (Deut. 28:50; 2 Chron. 36:17; Isa. 47:6). It is an evil day when "the young will rise up against the old" (Isa. 3:5 NIV), when elders are shown no respect (Lam. 5:12). The young are to resist the temptation to despise the old (e.g., Prov. 23:22), and instead are to recognize gray hair — i.e., old age — as a crown of splendor (Prov. 20:29). People are to "rise in the presence of the aged," says the Lord. They are to "show respect for the elderly" (Lev. 19:32). This particular command is one of seven commands in Leviticus 19 that ends with something like the words "I am the Lord," thereby underlining their importance by emphasizing God's authority. This command regarding elderly people adds — before those closing words — the call to "revere your God."

It appears here that the connection between God and older people is special. God is not simply saying that this, like all other commands, should be obeyed. The point, instead, is that obedience to this command in particular expresses a special reverence for God. By showing respect for the elderly, we are revering God.

If we rightly respond to wisdom by respecting those who possess it, we appropriately respond to the relative weakness of the elderly by protecting them. God is frequently portrayed in biblical writings as the protector of the weak (Exod. 22:22-27; Ps. 10:14; 35:10; 140:12; Acts 20:35; 1 Cor. 8:9-12; 2 Cor. 12:9-10), and God's people are challenged to be the same (Prov. 31:8-9; 1 Thess. 5:14). So it is not at all surprising to find God affirming that "Even to your old age and gray hairs I am he, I am he who will sustain you" (Isa. 46:4 NIV).

That God says "even" in old age emphasizes that, from a human perspective, it is easy to find reasons to support younger people, and that, in this utilitarian world, it is all too easy to neglect older people. King David observed this phenomenon in his day, which is why he implores God to sustain him, as he puts it, "even when I am old and gray" (Ps. 71:18 NIV). Because God is a sustainer of elderly people, it is natural to expect that godly people will do the same (e.g., Ruth 4:15).

Elderly people are as worthy of staying alive and even receiving lifesaving care as anyone else. In fact, whether a particular society values the wisdom of the elderly or not is ultimately beside the point. All persons are God's creation in God's own image (Gen. 1:27) and are the objects of God's sacrificial love in Christ (John 3:16). God pours out the Spirit on the old as well as on the young (Joel 2:28; Acts 2:17). The equal worth of all persons demands that all be respected and that the weak accordingly receive special protection.

What are the implications of all this for age-based rationing of life-sustaining health care? First and foremost, a straightforward utilitarian exclusion of older people, because they are less productive in some sense, is just as straightforwardly unethical. It misunderstands what is important about a person and it rests on a philosophy that undergirds some of the most oppressive attitudes and episodes in the history of humanity.

Non-Utilitarian Justifications

There are, however, other justifications for age criteria that do not overtly appeal to utilitarian values. What about them? First of all, that the intuitive appeal of such justifications is greatly strengthened by a utilitarian social context is unavoidable. Against such a backdrop, we should be highly skeptical of arguments for age-based rationing of life-sustaining health care, no matter how philosophically pure they may appear. We also need to address such justifications on their own terms.

Medical Benefit

Perhaps the most commonly invoked non-utilitarian justification of age-based rationing criteria in health care involves an appeal to medical benefit: "This patient is elderly, and elderly patients don't live as long or as well as other patients, and treatment is less likely to be successful in elderly patients — so this patient shouldn't receive treatment."[23] If the real concern here is medical, then the medical criteria involved should be invoked as such. Age *per se* is not the issue. We have to be careful how we use language. We should take care to identify as "medical" only those qualities and criteria that are, in fact, medical.

Age *per se* is not a medically relevant factor in determinations about individual patients, since medical problems that make one elderly person a bad candidate for a given treatment may not affect another. We generally cannot even assume that a particular elderly person has a short life expectancy. It is certainly true that many elderly patients are so physically weakened that they make poor candidates for organ transplantation or intensive care; but others bear up fairly well in these circumstances. Similarly, although elderly patients have often been excluded from dialysis treatment, many of those who have received it have done well.

Accordingly, age is best not identified as a separate rationing criterion at all. Rather, its most appropriate role is probably as one of many "symptoms" to be assessed by the physician making the medical assessment required for any treatment decision. Like any observed symptom, age can be an indicator of a possible medical problem. Age serves best as a tool the physician uses in

---

23. For a more in-depth discussion of the ethical issues involved here, see Kilner, *Life on the Line,* chap. 8; and John F. Kilner, "Age Criteria in Medicine: Are the Medical Justifications Ethical?" *Archives of Internal Medicine* 149 (October 1989): 2343-46.

applying a medical criterion, not as a criterion in its own right. From this perspective it is inappropriate to identify age during a discussion of rationing criteria in a way that implies that it is more than just one among many symptoms considered in a medical assessment.

Even in this more restricted role, however, age considerations must be handled carefully to ensure that they are not accorded more influence than is warranted medically. It is easy enough to underestimate the ability of some elderly patients to endure treatment when life is at stake; and technological developments consistently make treatments more endurable. In the end, the only way to know with confidence how elderly people will bear up under a given treatment may well be to treat them in large numbers, as was done during the early days of dialysis in Italy.[24] Whenever possible, a therapeutic trial can be employed to facilitate more individualized assessments.

Three other non-utilitarian justifications for age-based rationing have also been put forward by contemporary bioethicists such as Robert Veatch, Daniel Callahan, and Norman Daniels. They are based on ethical appeals to equal opportunity, natural life span, and prudence.[25] The appeal to equal opportunity contends that the most important equality at issue here is the equal opportunity to live to the same age as others. Some notion of a *prima facie* right to a minimum number of life-years may be involved.[26] The life span justification holds that there is a natural life span (perhaps seventy, perhaps eighty years) — a span which is normative rather than merely a statistical average at the present moment in history. Once people have reached this age, medicine should generally no longer be concerned with extending their lives.[27] The

24. Terrie Wetle, "Age As a Risk Factor for Inadequate Treatment," *Journal of the American Medical Association* 258 (July 24/31, 1987): 516; G. D'Amico, "Treating End-Stage Renal Disease: An Age Equivalence Index," *Annals of Internal Medicine* 96 (April 1982): 417-23.

25. For a more in-depth discussion of the ethical issues involved in these approaches, see Kilner, *Life on the Line,* chap. 9; and John F. Kilner, "Age As a Basis for Allocating Lifesaving Medical Resources: An Ethical Analysis," *Journal of Health Politics, Policy, and Law* 13 (fall 1988): 405-23.

26. This ethical appeal can be traced back to classical formulations put forward by Robert M. Veatch in two settings, among others: "Justice and Valuing Lives," in *Life Span,* ed. Robert M. Veatch (San Francisco: Harper and Row, 1979), p. 218; and "Ethical Foundations for Valuing Lives: Implications for Life-Extending Technologies," in *A Technology Assessment of Life-Extending Technologies,* Supplementary Report, vol. 6 (Glastonbury, Conn.: Futures Group, 1977), p. 232. Cf. Paul T. Menzel, *Medical Costs, Moral Choices* (New Haven, Conn.: Yale University Press, 1983), p. 191.

27. This ethical appeal can be traced back to classical formulations put forward by Daniel Callahan in two settings, among others: *Setting Limits: Medical Goals in an Aging Society* (New York: Simon and Schuster, 1987), pp. 137ff.; and "Aging and the Ends of Medicine," *Annals of the New York Academy of Sciences* 530 (1988): 128-29.

appeal to prudence maintains that people should be treated equally not so much in the present moment as over a lifetime. Health care should be provided in the way that enables all people to live as long as possible. To achieve this end, the resources available must be prudentially distributed throughout each person's lifetime in a way that will protect against early death. Expensive life-sustaining resources, then, might be made available only to young persons, with personal care services enhanced for those who are older.[28] Each of these three justifications warrants a closer look.

Equal Opportunity

Equal-opportunity justifications for age-based rationing support giving people an equal opportunity to live a long time, thereby maximizing the life-years saved. The most dubious aspect of this justification is the way that it values *life-years* rather than *lives* (i.e., persons). People are more than sums of life-years that are accumulated like nickles. Accordingly, murderers are typically not punished less for killing sixty-five-year-olds than for killing twenty-five-year-olds. Life is equally precious at any age. Although it is indeed better, where possible, to preserve someone's life for a longer rather than a shorter time, it is another thing to suggest that we should seek to preserve one person's life for a long time at the price of denying any chance of living to another.

Two problems unrelated to maximizing life-years are also involved in attempting, by means of an age criterion, to equalize the opportunity people have to live a long life. The first of these involves the manner in which we calculate the patient's opportunity to experience life. Say two women need the same scarce lifesaving resource. One of them is thirty-five years old; the other is thirty-six years old but has recently emerged from more than a year spent in a coma. If we are making decisions on the basis of an age criterion, whom do we choose? Usually the younger woman would be the preferable candidate on the grounds that her shorter life has given her less opportunity to experience life. In this case, however, the older woman has had the lesser opportunity. If we concede that it is valid to consider issues like these in making a decision in the matter, we open the door to any number of imprecise qualitative

28. This ethical appeal can be traced back to classical formulations put forward by Norman Daniels in two settings, among others: *Just Health Care* (London: Cambridge University Press, 1985), pp. 96-97; and *Am I My Parents' Keeper?* (New York: Oxford University Press, 1988), pp. 8-9, chap. 5.

considerations in the assessment of who has had the least opportunity to experience life.

One proponent of this approach admits that such assessments would be "an overwhelmingly complicated task," calling it "procedurally and administratively a nightmare."[29] Yet, how would we justify excluding such factors? A patient's socioeconomic or spiritual condition may have much more to do with her or his lifetime experience of well-being than does age. Age provides too rough an approximation of lifetime well-being (or present physical health for that matter) to be determinative when something as important as life is at stake.

The other problem related to equalizing the opportunity to live long concerns past access of patients to resources. Should a younger person who has already received years of life-extending medical care be automatically preferred to an older person who has received very little? A strictly employed age criterion would say so, although it seems less than accurate to suggest that the younger person has not been given as great an opportunity to live as the older person.

Life Span

No less problematic is a variation of the equal-opportunity justification that limits lifesaving care to those who have not yet reached their natural life span. The very notion of a normative life span requires more critical attention. Even if a theoretical biological limit to the human life span is granted, the actual life span has grown through the years as life-extending care for the elderly has improved. An age criterion of the sort envisioned here would hinder medicine from extending even good-quality years at the end of life.

Furthermore, such an age criterion would demean those living beyond the natural life span. One supporter candidly admits this problem, given the world as it presently exists.[30] However, the problem is also intrinsic to the justification. Those who support this justification assume that extending medical care to those beyond the natural life span is not warranted because these people have already "accomplished" and "achieved" everything of signifi-

29. Robert M. Veatch, "Distributive Justice and the Allocation of Technological Resources to the Elderly," Contract Report prepared for the U.S. Congress Office of Technology Assessment, Washington, D.C. (1985), p. 43; Robert M. Veatch, The Foundations of Justice (New York: Oxford University Press, 1986), p. 146.

30. Daniel Callahan, Setting Limits, pp. 184-85.

cance that they can.[31] An implicit productivity orientation is revealed here: what matters is what one succeeds in doing. The significance of life, though, is to be found as much in "being" as in "doing" — as much in relating to others as in completing tasks. Moreover, our life goals change as we grow older. We have different values at different ages. Those who argue that elderly people no longer have any goals left to reach may be thinking only in terms of their own largely productivity-oriented life goals.

While those who support the life-span justification may not be explicit about their productivity bias, they do typically acknowledge a commitment to maximizing quality of life. In fact, this commitment may in the end provide more support for a quality-of-life criterion than for an age criterion. One supporter candidly admits that an age criterion excluding elderly patients from care is not warranted unless their quality of life is low.[32]

Whether either a quality-of-life or age criterion is really in view here, both are riddled with practical difficulties. It is no easier to assess another person's quality of life precisely than it is to determine if people have essentially completed their life goals — at least without relying on the statements of the patients themselves. There is little reason to assume that all older persons will value their continued life less than younger persons value theirs. Moreover, neither group is likely to be forthright about the degree to which they no longer value their lives if what they say could cost them their lives. The alternative is to withhold resources only from those who voluntarily forgo treatment — but that is to impose neither an age nor a quality-of-life criterion.

Prudence

The final justification of an age-based rationing, prudence, is also problematic for multiple reasons. First of all, it is unjust. While it might not be as thoroughly discriminatory as racism or sexism, it is discriminatory nonetheless. It assumes that all persons move through all age categories and will receive the different types of services provided for each age group. The fact is that many people are born with congenital, genetic, or environmental handicaps that will prevent them from living as long as others. What they give up when young, in order to receive when old, may well never be accessible to

31. See, e.g., Daniel Callahan, *Setting Limits*, pp. 16, 172. Accordingly, Callahan does not consider elderly people to be as worthy of attention as younger people; "the primary orientation" of older people, he suggests, "should be to the young" ("Aging and the Ends of Medicine," p. 128).

32. Daniel Callahan, *Setting Limits*, pp. 184-85.

them. In fact, defenses of this justification suggest that the real concern here is precisely what is most needed by older people: personal care services. If that is their primary need, then an age criterion for acute care is not necessary in order to meet their need. Instead, a greater priority could be placed on personal care services when the larger allocation decisions are being made.

What ultimately makes this justification inadequate, however, is that it is hopelessly idealistic. In an ideal world this proposal might be appealing, but even proponents admit that it would be wrong to introduce age criteria in one health-care setting and not in another. They also admit that age criteria may be politically unacceptable in any setting.[33] The potential strength of the proposal lies in its vision of distributing vital resources equitably throughout an individual's lifetime, but in the end elderly people will likely experience the reality of exclusion from treatment more keenly than they will appreciate the theory that lies behind it. The politics of the issue centers on which groups will gain greatest access to the most resources. Moreover, were the proposal applied throughout a nation such as the United States, existing social and economic injustices could cause the application of an age criterion to make things worse. The potential injustice of an age criterion is so compelling that even those who in theory support age-based rationing may be forced to admit, as one of them has frankly acknowledged, that their proposal "is in no way a recommendation for the introduction of such practices in our present world."[34] That is quite a disclaimer, since that's the world we are talking about in the debate over age-based rationing of health care.

A Christian Perspective

While this critique of particular secular justifications for age-based rationing has rarely appealed explicitly to biblical or theological arguments, such a critique is not irrelevant from a Christian perspective. It exposes the internal problems of the justifications themselves. It demonstrates the weaknesses of these justifications on the basis of widely acknowledged human concerns. A Christian perspective also gives us a larger frame of reference from which to evaluate such justifications by giving us a clearer view of what is at stake. Four elements of a Christian perspective will close this chapter.

33. Norman Daniels, *Am I My Parents' Keeper?* pp. 96-97; *Just Health Care,* p. 111.

34. Margaret P. Battin, "Age Rationing and the Just Distribution of Health Care: Is There a Duty to Die?" *Ethics* 97 (January 1987): 340. Cf. Norman Daniels, *Am I My Parents' Keeper?* p. 96; *Just Health Care,* p. 113.

First, as we have already seen, a Christian perspective reminds us that elderly people tend to be wise and weak, relative to others. So we should be inclined to respect and protect those who are older. This outlook fosters an appropriate skepticism about any approach to health-care resource allocation that singles out older people, as a group, to receive less access.

Second, a Christian perspective reminds us of the importance of cross-cultural understanding, so that our views are not shaped unconsciously by the worst values in our own culture. One of the most striking teachings of Christianity is that there is neither Jew nor Greek, barbarian nor Scythian; but all are one in Christ and all peoples are loved and sought by God (see, for example, Col. 3:11; 2 Pet. 3:9). If that is the case, then those of us steeped in the cultural values of North America need to be challenged by alternative values in other cultures such as that of the Akamba of Kenya. We cannot assume that our culture is normative.

A third Christian insight that has important bearing upon age-based rationing is the sinfulness of the world. People as well as the policies and institutions they establish are less than God intends them to be because people are fundamentally self-oriented rather than God-and-other-oriented (Ps. 14:2-3; Jer. 17:9; Rom. 3:10-12, 23). While it is possible to turn from self-centeredness to God and others, experience and the biblical materials alike testify that the majority of people will never truly do so (see Matt. 7:13-14; Luke 13:23-24).

Accordingly, there is a pressing need for social strategies that take this reality into account and seek to promote the best possible policies in light of it. Good intentions and commitment to laudable concerns such as equal opportunity, a natural life span, and prudence are not enough. It is misleading and perhaps even dangerous to propose age criteria that would be immoral if implemented "in our present world."

Lastly, a Christian perspective sensitizes us to make sure that there are not other hidden injustices built into age-based rationing — that other groups besides older people are not victimized by this approach. What we find is that women, in fact, would bear the brunt of age-based allocation. While the ratio of elderly women to elderly men in 1960 was four to five, older women now outnumber older men three to two. More specifically, of those sixty-five to seventy-four, 55 percent are women; of those seventy-five to eighty-four, 61 percent are women; of those eighty-five and over, 71 percent are women. For those ninety and over, the figure rises to 76 percent.[35] So particularly if very elderly people are to be barred from lifesaving health care, it is

---

35. United States Census Bureau, *Census 2000,* Summary File 1, Matrices P13 and PCT12.

predominantly women who are in view. A specific age cut-off for receiving lifesaving health care, then, will likely be set high enough to ensure a "full life" as life is typically experienced by men — implicitly devaluing the years beyond that point, which are primarily years of women's lives.

Age-based victimization, as with the victimization of other vulnerable groups, is contrary to the spirit and teaching of Christianity. The biblical materials identify the female/male distinction with slave/free and racial distinctions as inappropriate categories used by one group to assert superiority over another (e.g., Gal. 3:28). Biblical writings exhort the community to provide special protection and care to older women in particular, who are frequently widows (e.g., Isa. 1:17; James 1:27). If we are really concerned about such matters as equal opportunity and full life span, we will not support age-based rationing of life-sustaining health care.[36]

Conclusion

A Christian perspective, then, can help us to gain a better insight into the current debate over age-based rationing of life-sustaining health care. Utilitarian intuitions, combined with a predisposition against Christian influences in public policy, make openness to age-based rationing quite understandable. Nevertheless, this form of rationing is objectionable on broadly accepted ethical grounds, as well as on Christian theological grounds.

Our elderly and aged deserve our respect and our protection. Rationing their health care because of their age is to treat them with disdain rather than with dignity.

36. For further discussion of age-based rationing, see David C. Thomasma, "Stewardship of the Aged: Meeting the Ethical Challenge of Ageism," *Cambridge Quarterly of Healthcare Ethics* 8 (spring 1999): 148-59; Kenneth Boyd, "Old Age, Something to Look Forward To," in *The Goals of Medicine*, ed. Mark Hanson and Daniel Callahan (Washington, D.C.: Georgetown University Press, 1999), pp. 152-61; Mary Beth Hamel et al., "Patient Age and Decisions to Withhold Life-Sustaining Treatments from Seriously Ill, Hospitalized Adults," *Annals of Internal Medicine* 130 (January 19, 1999): 116-25; Norman G. Levinsky, "Can We Afford Medical Care for Alice C.?" *Lancet* 352 (December 5, 1998): 1849-51; Sara T. Fry, "The Ethics of Health Care Reform: Should Rationing Strategies Target the Elderly?" in *Current Issues in Nursing*, ed. Joanne Comi and Helen Grace, fifth ed. (St. Louis: Mosby, 1997), pp. 626-31; Alan Williams and J. Grimley Evans, "Rationing Health Care by Age: The Case for and the Case Against," *British Medical Journal* 314 (March 15, 1997): 820-25; Eric Rakowski and Stephen G. Post, "Should Health Care Be Rationed by Age? Yes and No," in *Controversial Issues in Aging*, ed. Andrew Scharlach and Lenard Kaye (Boston: Allyn and Bacon, 1997), pp. 103-13.

Neuropsychological Aspects
of Aging and Their Implications
for Decision-Making among the Elderly

ROBERT W. EVANS, PH.D., PH.D.

Over the past thirty years, rapid advancements in medicine and biotechnology have come to confront societies around the globe with unprecedented ethical quandaries that challenge our faith and test our wisdom. Those advancements affecting the quality and duration of life while in its "margins" — namely, that period between conception and birth, and that period between terminal illness and death — have drawn considerable attention. In turn, a host of questions have attended these advancements related to the manner in which bioethical decision-making is to be carried out for those situated at these "margins" of life.

If there is a single quality that is common to nearly all bioethical discussions, it is that of choice.[1] Whether physician or legislator, scholar or family member, it is widely accepted that patients possess the right to make their own decisions concerning treatment. Under many medical circumstances, a patient's right to self-determination in decision-making is desirable and ought to be respected. When, however, decisions concerning end-of-life treatment are exercised by a patient who is suffering from neuro-cognitive difficulties associated with aging, this calls into serious question the appropriateness of self-directed treatment. This situation is often encountered by physicians and family members dealing with an elderly person suffering from one of the various dementive processes that compromise neurocognitive efficiency.

The purpose of this chapter is to examine some of the neurological and psychological aspects of aging, and to draw attention to several of their impli-

1. "Choice" may be rightly located under the rubric of autonomy.

cations for bioethical decision-making among the elderly. Common misconceptions associated with the process of aging will also be discussed. Health professionals will benefit from this chapter's survey of various neuropsychological instruments available to help in the assessment of neurobehavioral changes associated with aging. Finally, this discussion will conclude with an assessment of the various bioethical implications that aging carries for health professionals, family members, and the church.

Neurological Aspects of Aging

Demographics

There are few areas in medicine that are as misunderstood as the psychological and cognitive changes occurring in elderly persons. Even though the medical profession is becoming increasingly aware of the prevalence of non-neurological conditions that can mimic the effects of a dementive process in the elderly, physicians frequently will arbitrarily assign an organic diagnosis to an elderly patient demonstrating disturbances in neurocognitive efficiency. These diagnostic misattributions are not surprising given that dementia is prevalent in old age (as compared with younger adults). The data suggest, however, that dementia is neither "normal" nor as ubiquitous as commonly believed. Approximately 90 percent of those over age sixty-five, and approximately 75 percent of those over age seventy-five are not demented.[2]

Challenges to the assessment and treatment of elderly populations are further complicated by the fact that the number of elderly people is increasing, both in absolute and relative numbers. In one study, data revealed that approximately 26 million persons, or 12 percent of the U.S. population, were over the age of 65.[3] Within this population, approximately 10 percent were demented. The study also demonstrated that those over the age of eighty-five constitute the most rapidly growing segment of our society.

Should current trends continue, the number of elderly persons in the United States would rise dramatically by the year 2030. Estimates hold that by 2030, some 51 million persons (17 percent) will be over the age of sixty-five, and more than 5 million persons will be demented (or at least twice the num-

2. Leonard Berg and John C. Morris, "Aging and Dementia," in *Neurobiology of Disease,* ed. Alan L. Pearlman and Robert C. Collins (New York: Oxford University Press, 1990), p. 300.
3. Berg and Morris, "Aging and Dementia," p. 299.

ber reported in 1986). Their medical care may exceed 60 billion dollars.[4] These statistics underscore the importance of accurate medical diagnosis among elderly patients.

Structural Changes Associated with Aging

Neurologically, several structural changes occur in the brain as a function of aging. These include a decrease in neuronal density and a decrease in the overall weight and volume of the brain.[5] Unfortunately, there is a general tendency within medical practice to assume that these changes are reflective of degenerative or involutional changes. One should keep in mind, however, that the dendritic branching complexity of neurons increases from the fifth to the seventh decade.[6] That is to say, the behavioral relevance of structural changes that are described with age should be cautiously interpreted.

Unfortunately, little is known about the effects of healthy aging on the human brain. We do know that with increasing age, individuals perform less well on tasks designed to measure reaction time, memory, judgment, orientation, planning, cognitive flexibility, and, perhaps, also visuospatial skills.[7] Longitudinal studies examining the effects of normal aging over time reveal that a general decline in neurocognitive efficiency will occur at different rates for different types of neurological functioning. This decline is described as generally mild, and marked by a great deal of individual difference among elderly persons with respect to the domains of neurocognitive decline.[8] In short, the available research on aging has consistently revealed that age-related cognitive changes tend to be relatively minor and do not interfere with the ability to lead an independent existence.

4. Berg and Morris, "Aging and Dementia," pp. 299-300.

5. Sandra Weintraub and M-Marsel Mesulam, "Mental State Assessment of Young and Elderly Adults in Behavioral Neurology," in *Principles of Behavioral Neurology*, ed. M-Marsel Mesulam (Philadelphia: F. A. Davis Company, 1985), p. 111.

6. Weintraub and Mesulam, "Mental State Assessment," p. 111.

7. For example, see Danny Wedding, Arthur MacNeill Horton, and Jeffrey Webster, *The Neuropsychology Handbook: Behavioral and Clinical Perspectives* (New York: Springer, 1986), passim; and, Bryan Kolb and Ian Q. Whishaw, *Fundamentals of Human Neuropsychology*, third ed. (New York: W. H. Freeman, 1990), passim.

8. Weintraub and Mesulam, "Mental State Assessment," p. 111.

Neuropsychological Aspects of Aging

With increasing age, elderly persons experience an attendant increase in general medical conditions that can interfere with neurocognitive abilities. Physicians may find that the apparent neurological disturbance is merely symptomatic of another condition. In cases such as these, a differential diagnosis between a neurological and a non-neurological condition is further complicated by the fact that there is considerable overlap between demented processes and a host of non-neurological conditions that could explain the same symptom profile as dementia. Furthermore, there are very few symptoms that are specific to an individual degenerative dementing illness.

In many instances, a diagnosis of dementia is offered when a more easily treatable cause of a dementia is present. Examples include metabolic encephalopathy, depression, and space-occupying lesions.[9] An accurate differential diagnosis between dementia and depression is also frustrated by the fact that depressed patients often present the same constellation of signs and symptoms on neuropsychological assessment batteries as patients suffering from dementia.

Neuropsychological Assessment of Dementia

Physicians treating elderly persons will find that the assessment of mental state is the single most important phase in the diagnosis of medical conditions. The assessment of the elderly person's mental state is particularly important in arriving at an appropriate diagnosis and treatment scheme for those suffering from dementia. Unfortunately, very few clinicians are skilled in conducting such an assessment.

Differential diagnosis involving suspected dementing processes is substantially enhanced when the physician has augmented the medical evaluation with a neuropsychological examination. Useful, standardized, broad-spectrum, neurocognitive assessments include the Halstead-Reitan Neuropsychological Test and the Wechsler Adult Intelligence Scale. Specialized tests designed to capture specific disturbances of language include the Boston Diagnostic Aphasia Examination, the Boston Naming Test, the Western Aphasia Battery, and the Wechsler Memory Scale.

Assessing non-neurological aspects of the elderly person's functioning also enhances a differential diagnosis between depression and dementia.

9. Berg and Morris, "Aging and Dementia," pp. 300-312.

Among the more popular instruments for this purpose are the Minnesota Multiphasic Personality Inventory, the Rorschach Inkblot Test, and the Beck Depression Scale. Physicians may also benefit from employing one of the numerous short mental status tests that are now widely available. Several of these tests show promise as a useful initial screening measure to capture the hallmark symptoms of a dementive process. Examples include the Mini-Mental State Examination, the Blessed Dementia Scale, and the Mattis Dementia Rating Scale. Physicians should also assess for impairment in activities of daily living. One useful measure that is widely used to assess this domain of functioning is the Instrumental Activities of Daily Living.

Assessing Special Populations

Among the most challenging cases are those involving an elderly person in command of a superior level of intellectual functioning prior to the onset of initial signs and symptoms of dementia. Similarly, patients who possess special talents pose a unique challenge to the evaluation of early dementive processes. These challenges can be heightened when the patient comes to the attention of medical staff with self-perceived deficits in mental functioning — a scenario that often suggests a depressive diagnosis rather than a diagnosis within the dementia spectrum. Clinicians confronting such situations may wish to employ a more cognitively challenging instrument such as the Graduate Record Examination, the Miller Analogies Test, or the Medical College Aptitude Test.

Alzheimer's disease is the most frequently diagnosed type of dementia. In fact, so frequent is the diagnosis of Alzheimer's disease that many people mistakenly exchange the terms "dementia" and "Alzheimer's" with one another. It is important for the treating physician to designate appropriately the type of dementive processes from which the elderly person is suffering. It should be noted, however, that even when the diagnosis of "dementia, Alzheimer's-type" is made on the basis of strict criteria, there tends to be a great degree of clinical variability between individuals, especially in the early stages of disease. Nonetheless, the accurate assessment and diagnosis of the elderly person is critical for both treatment planning and family education.

Implications for Bioethical Decision-Making

Of particular concern are those cases in which an elderly person is participating in making very difficult medical-ethical choices while suffering from the effects of neurocognitive compromise due to cerebral impairment or neuro-psychological sequelae. Examples include elderly persons issuing requests for assistance in dying or insisting on aggressive pain relief protocols.

Mental State and Informed Consent

Informed bioethical choices are the result of a process that involves a multi-plicity of participants. Those involved in the process of decision-making may include the physician, consulting physicians, clergy, ethicists, the patient, and the patient's family. In such cases, decisions concerning treatment are based upon the reasonable contributions that each person is able to make to the decision-making process. When an elderly person is suffering from a disease process that interferes with neurocognitive efficiency, physicians have grounds to question how the cerebral compromise may interfere with the pa-tient's ability to meaningfully participate in his or her own treatment.

Implications for Physician-Assisted Suicide and Euthanasia

Even under the best of circumstances, the dying person is experiencing a host of emotions that are punctuated by a constant interplay of disbelief and hope, itself superimposed on a background of anguish, terror, rage, acquiescence, and surrender. This internal drama is, in turn, being played out on a stage of-ten marked by bewilderment and pain.

Psychologically, it is significant that dying persons appear to swing be-tween the extremes of denial on the one hand and acceptance with respect to his or her own death on the other hand. Denial is a most interesting and powerful psychological dynamic. Like all defense mechanisms, denial serves to protect and insulate the individual against his or her subjective experience of anxiety. For several consecutive days, or even weeks, the dying persons may tell those present — with seeming insight and peaceful resignation — that they have come to accept the inevitability of death. Such statements, however, are frequently followed by periods when dying persons will shock their listeners with unrealistic talk of leaving the hospital the next day, en-gaging in some protracted project such as school or, perhaps, going on a va-cation. It is as if the dying person is constantly experiencing an interplay between acceptance and denial. On the one hand, patients are able to under-stand what is happening to them, but on the other hand, they are magically disbelieving its reality.

In these situations, the dying person may appear to make rational decisions concerning his or her own demise. Should such a "decision" be made while the person is in a transient mental state of temporary acceptance, however, the decision is likely to reflect only the fleeting perceptions of the moment and not necessarily represent the person's informed conclusions concerning his or her suicide. In other words, it is impossible to say that the pendulum of psychological denial will not swing once again following an apparent "informed choice" and the dying person find himself in a different state of mind in which such a decision would not be acceptable.

This picture is complicated when an elderly person who is involved in the decision-making process may be suffering from progressive dementive processes. Impairment in judgment, orientation, and planning may all be heightened in elderly patients suffering from dementive conditions. Accordingly, though while under the best of circumstances it is exceedingly difficult to trust the "informed" decisions of patients making requests for assistance in dying, such is rendered all the more challenging when the patient is an elderly person who is suffering from disturbances in neuropsychological functioning associated with both organic and non-neurological conditions.

It is noteworthy that individuals contemplating suicide will often display a constricted range of perception concerning their options. For example, psychologists and psychiatrists often encounter acutely suicidal patients in emergency room settings who are unable to perceive that they have any options whatsoever. This constriction in perceptual acuity is heightened among elderly patients who are suffering from dementive processes, as a result of the impairment in judgment, orientation, planning, and cognitive flexibility that accompanies their disease.

Elderly people contemplating death may find that their memories and internal resources have become strangely unfamiliar, unavailable, and unreal. The dying elderly person may find that his or her mind has become preoccupied with that which seems unbearable, and intensely focus on one specific, albeit arbitrarily chosen, way to "escape."

In summary, one must seriously question whether an elderly person suffering from a disturbance in neurocognitive functioning could meaningfully participate in decision-making processes involving difficult medical-ethical choices. Should an elderly patient state a wish for assistance in dying, one could never be certain that the request was neither influenced nor colored by the restricted range of affective and cognitive flexibility that normally accompanies the dying process. And for the elderly person experiencing the effects of dementia or depression, it is highly dubious whether such a decision could be considered informed and, hence, voluntary.

Implications for Pain Management Demands

There is a paucity of well-controlled studies examining the problems of pain among elderly patient populations. Nonetheless, there appears to be some evidence to suggest that there is a high prevalence of pain problems experienced among the elderly population. Some studies have suggested that nearly one-quarter of elderly persons may be experiencing mild to moderate pain during much of their waking time.[10] In general, studies have suggested that the subjective experience of pain tends to be positively correlated with subjective levels of psychosocial distress. In short, the higher the pain intensity experienced by elderly patients, the greater the likelihood that they are experiencing somatic concerns, depression, and anxiety.

Furthermore, degenerative changes and pain-related illnesses tend to be present in higher proportions within elderly patient populations. These conditions include disc disease, arthritis, diabetic peripheral neuropathy, cancer, and a host of neurological disorders. Remarkably, fewer than 10 percent of patients seen in pain clinics are aged sixty-five or older.[11] At present, there is little evidence to suggest a precise reason for the underutilization of pain management clinics among the elderly. Under-use may be affected, however, by such factors as limited access, limited referrals, and negative attitudes regarding mental health treatment modalities.

Controversy continues about whether or not elderly patients decrease in their sensitivities to subjective experiences of pain as they continue to age. Furthermore, it is possible that widely accepted societal stereotypes concerning elderly persons having to endure greater levels of subjective distress affect their experience and reporting of pain to health professionals. Moreover, when health professionals adopt this stereotype, it may bias treating providers against the emotional and physical discomfort of their elderly patients, thereby leading to treatment neglect.

Chronic joint disease and other degenerative conditions are common among the elderly. Among the most common pain disorders experienced by elderly patients are osteoarthritis and rheumatoid arthritis. The majority of patients over the age of fifty demonstrate radiological evidence of osteoarthritis, particularly in their weight-bearing joints, including knees and ankles. Few elderly patients with such objective evidence report subjective expe-

10. L. Hyer, I. Gouveia, W. Harrison, J. Warsaw, and D. Coutsouridis, "Depression, Anxiety, Paranoid Reactions, Hypochondriasis, and Cognitive Decline of Later-Life Inpatients," *Journal of Gerontology* 42 (1987): 92-94.

11. J. A. Kwentus, S. W. Harkins, N. Lignon, and J. Silverman, "Current Concepts of Geriatric Pain and Its Treatment," *Geriatrics* 40 (1985): 48-57.

riences of pain, however.[12] Rheumatoid arthritis is a condition present with greater frequency than osteoarthritis, and tends to be more disabling. As such, rheumatoid arthritis represents a significant life impact for the elderly patient.

Various cancers also occur with greater frequency in people over the age of sixty-five than in younger adults. For example, the risk of dying from breast cancer increases dramatically with increasing age.[13] Complaints of pain tend to be a frequent concern among elderly cancer patients. The pain may be caused either directly by the disease itself or incidentally to the entrapment or pressure placed upon nerves by the tumor. Another source of pain among cancer patients is related to the treatment modality that is employed. Certain chemotherapies are known to cause intense discomfort, and there is also a high incidence of postsurgical pain among cancer patients.

Headaches constitute yet another common source of pain among elderly patients. Tension headaches appear to be the most frequent type of head pain experienced in elderly patients, with significant contributing factors including cervical osteoarthritis, psychological stress, and depression.[14]

Psychogenic pain disorders may also be present in elderly patient populations. Psychogenic pain may be a secondary symptom of a psychophysiological disorder, or it may be indicative of a neurotic conversion disorder. In either situation, an underlying psychological conflict, beyond the patient's awareness, is both generating and maintaining the subjective experience of pain.

Psychogenic pain disorders can also develop secondarily to organically based medical conditions, such as peptic ulcer. Though the pain originates with organic damage, the secondary pain that is generated from increased attention and depression may unconsciously sustain the subjective experience of pain and discomfort. In conversion disorders, the pain originates in the unconscious mind of the patient, but is experienced as if it were in the body. Again, unconscious conflicts both generate and maintain the subjective experience of discomfort.

The treatment of various pain complaints among the elderly is compli-

12. E. T. Sturgis, J. J. Dolce, and P. C. Dickerson, "Pain Management in the Elderly," in *Handbook of Clinical Gerontology,* ed. L. L. Carstensen and B. A. Ededstein (New York: Pergamon, 1987), pp. 190-203.

13. C. M. Hassell, A. E. Guiliano, R. W. Thompson, and H. A. Zarem, "Breast Cancer," in *Cancer Treatment,* ed. C. M. Hassell (Philadelphia: W. B. Saunders, 1985), pp. 137-80.

14. Sturgis, Dolce, and Dickerson, "Pain Management in the Elderly," pp. 190-203, and passim.

cated when neurocognitive impairment is present. Specifically, elderly patients may experience failing memory, which may interfere with their ability to give health-care providers an accurate history concerning both the onset and progression of the subjective discomfort that they are experiencing. Furthermore, impairments in judgment, and the higher levels of depression experienced among elderly patients, may unwittingly cause the person to exaggerate or misattribute the source and course of their pain complaints. Moreover, elderly patients may find it more difficult to comply with various treatment regimens due to disturbances in neurocognitive efficiency.

Depression also increases the subjective experience of physical discomfort. In turn, the increase in pain intensity may lead to decreased socialization and behavioral activity, which serves to further reduce the resources that elderly patients have to draw on to deal with their pain, thereby increasing their depression. Some older persons who are neglected by family and friends may find that they can receive the attention that they crave only by presenting diffuse or exaggerated complaints of pain or other medical difficulties to medical personnel.

Yet another problem is the elderly patient's reaction to pain medications. In general, elderly patients tend to be exquisitely sensitive to the pain-relieving effects of narcotics, in contrast to their younger cohorts. This may be due to alterations of the nerve receptors, changes in plasma protein binding, and the longer time it takes for the elderly person's system to clear itself of narcotic medications.[15]

Furthermore, elderly patients appear to experience a heightened side-effect profile to various narcotic medications. It is therefore important to closely monitor elderly patients who are taking medications for pain-related disorders. For example, aspirin is the most commonly used drug for pain among the elderly. Aspirin is also responsible, however, for a large number of adverse drug reactions that can result in hospitalization.[16] Elderly patients suffering from disturbances in judgment related to neuropsychological impairment may unwittingly take large amounts of aspirin, causing subsequent side effects including gastric bleeding, bronchospasm, and difficulties with coagulation.[17]

Finally, various narcotics, as well as some narcotic pain management medications such as Benzodiazepines, can produce depressive symptoma-

---

15. R. F. Kaiko, S. L. Wallenstein, A. G. Rogers, P. Y. Brabinski, and R. W. Houda, "Narcotics in the Elderly," *Medical Clinics of North America* 66 (1982): 1079-89.

16. R. F. Pfeiffer, "Drugs for Pain in the Elderly," *Geriatrics* 37 (1982): 67-76.

17. Sturgis, Dolce, and Dickerson, "Pain Management in the Elderly," pp. 190-203.

tology and drug dependence. In turn, these conditions can have a negative impact on the proper management of elderly patients experiencing pain-related conditions.

Accordingly, bioethical issues of concern readily attend cases where pain is a significant factor. Particularly thorny are those cases in which elderly patients are taking various medications for pain and in which there is an awareness that these drugs may have limited long-term effectiveness and often lead to adverse side effects. This clinical picture is further complicated when the elderly patient is experiencing a dementive process that may interfere with judgment, thereby calling into question the issue of competency as it relates to the elderly patient's participation in directing treatment. In these situations, the primary treating physician may benefit from collaboration with a neuropsychologist or neuropsychiatrist who can more fully assess the neurocognitive capacities of the elderly patient and offer advice about adjusting the relative weight that is afforded to the patient's participation in medical decision-making.

Conclusions

The purpose of this chapter has been to examine the neurological and neuropsychological factors that may compromise an elderly patient's ability to meaningfully participate in his or her own treatment. Specifically, the relationships of impairment in neuropsychological functioning to requests for assistance in dying and requests for aggressive pain management protocols have been examined.

In general, competent patients have the right to participate actively in their own care. This is predicated, however, on the patient's ability to understand treatment decisions that are to be made and to communicate clearly and coherently his or her wishes at the time that a decision is to be made. Among the elderly, neuropsychological impairment may be present to the extent that it compromises the patient's mental capacity to reasonably participate in bioethical decision-making.

Unfortunately, there is no generally accepted unitary standard of requisite mental capacity to participate in medical decisions. Clearly, the severely mentally retarded, comatose, or floridly psychotic patient may well be incompetent for purposes of participating in medical-ethical decision-making. When it comes to the involvement of elderly patients, however, decision-making becomes far more problematic. Indeed, there is no sharp and bright line that separates competency from incompetency and, generally, shades of gradation exist between these two extremes. Under such circumstances, treating providers are well advised to enlist the consulting advice of a clinical neuropsychologist or neuropsychiatrist who can assess the neurocognitive capacities of the elderly patients so situated.

Quite apart from the moral and theological concerns that would call into serious question the appropriateness of physician-assisted suicide and euthanasia under *any* circumstances, it should be clear that elderly persons are frequently suffering from neuropsychological conditions that compromise cognitive skills such as judgment, orientation, planning, or flexibility. And in these cases, physicians are right to place proportionately less weight upon the subjective requests of the patient. Indeed, mediating conditions may well exist among cognitively impaired patients who are seeking assistance in dying or making requests for aggressive pain management treatment protocols.

The upward shift in the world's age distribution and the correlation between age and chronic illness will not only escalate the cost of medical care in the future but will also increase the challenges to the medical profession in the area of bioethical decision-making. Physicians can contribute significantly to the assessment and treatment of the elderly patient when equipped with a more thorough working knowledge of those neuropsychological conditions that frequently are present within elderly patient populations and by understanding the relationship of the same to bioethical decision-making.

Dementia: Inclusive Moral Standing

STEPHEN G. POST, PH.D.

Respect for choice is only a part of care, for caring involves everything from tone of voice to the small offer to provide a family with a few hours of respite. And underlying care is a form of deep affective affirmation that is the core of *agape* love. Because we sometimes fail to get our definitions of love and care clear, I begin with this endeavor and then turn to matters of moral inclusivity, or true ethical universalism for the deeply forgetful — a universalism uncorrupted by what I will term "hypercognitive arrogance."

A First Principle of Affective Affirmation

Altruism (from the Old French *altrui*, meaning "somebody else") is a broad classification for other-regarding actions. The highest human expression of altruism, altruistic love, involves both a judgment of worth and a related "affirmative affection." Altruistic love is an intentional affirmation of the other, grounded in biologically given emotional capacities that are elevated by worldview (including principles, symbol, and myth) and imitation into the sphere of consistency and abiding loyalty. As such, altruistic love is the epitome of human altruism. Altruistic love is closely linked to care, which is love in response to the other in need. It is closely linked to compassion, which is love in response to the other in suffering; to sympathy, which is love in response to the other who suffers unfairly; to beneficence, which is love acting for the well-being of the other; to companionship, which is love attentively present with the other in ordinary moments. Altruistic love is also linked to justice, since the altruistic moral agent can respond in care to only a limited and proximate

87

number of persons; the agent must therefore consider those larger patterns of social and distributive injustice that deny all persons the goods necessary for essential well-being. Hence the notion of "the love that does justice."

Altruistic love does not eclipse care of the self (to be loosely distinguished from self-indulgence), for without this the agent would eventually become unable to perform altruistic acts. Altruistic love does not demand self-immolation, although it can require significant self-sacrifice and even great risk when necessary. The core definition of altruistic love, however, is not sacrifice, but rather an affective, affirming participation in the being of the other. Love is first a response to the "present actuality" of another as he or she is in irrevocable worth, and it is secondarily the encouragement toward fullness of being.

Love can be identified in part because it elicits a sense of joy in the other, who feels inwardly "a home in which it is safe." The other who receives affective affirmation and all its sequelae such as compassion and care will sense a freedom from anxiety, that is, a certain safe-haven in love where the stress of devaluation and isolation is removed. It seems plausible to hypothesize that, emotionally and physiologically, human beings need altruistic love. Attachment theory suggests that the general need for love may derive from infant experience. The human infant requires tremendous love, and this need does not disappear over the course of the life span, however it is modified.

People tend to remember well over the years those from whom they receive warm, generous love; conversely, people also remember those who have shamed and humiliated them. The opposite of love can be observed in episodes of malignant social psychology, which include intimidation, stigmatization, invalidation, objectification, mockery, and disparagement. There are those who convey, with tone of voice and facial expression, the message that the other's very existence rests on a mistake.

This memory of being loved seems important even to those whose cognitive capacities are either undeveloped or diminished. *The first principle of care for persons with dementia is to reveal to them their value by providing attention and tenderness in love.* There is no question in the mind of any experienced caregiver that the person with Alzheimer's disease, however advanced that disease may be, will usually respond better to a caregiver whose affect is affirming in tone.

In human experience, there are certain key life events that force the self to realize that it is not the only center of value. The birth of a child and the realization of the reality of eventual death are two such events that highlight the error of thinking that all others orbit around the self in its egoism. Claims of the self to ontological centrality are set aside. Ethics is not about enlightened self-interest and rational self-interested choice theory. It is about an affective transformation of the self toward a deep, warm, generous, other-regarding way of life. I will add to the key life events above the challenging reality of loving and caring for a person with Alzheimer's disease.

In caring for the person with Alzheimer's, in seeing and responding to such a person, the self must be transformed: it must experience a decentering of the self through the presence of the other as a call to moral life. The other's expression summons me to take another center of meaning into my world. This discovery of the other as other is often the subject of novels and plays that capture the moral transformation of the cold, uncaring egoist into an empathic other-regarding presence.

"Hypercognitive" Values and the Narrowing of "Personhood"

In 1994, I coined the term "hypercognitive" to describe a form of bias that underlies the stigma associated with Alzheimer's disease and the reluctance to love and care for persons with dementia.[1]

Because I was critical of hypercognitive theories of "personhood" that would set aside most or all obligations to those who are unable to conceptualize plans for the future and implement them, certain moral philosophers responded with hostility. I have addressed their narrow hypercognitive views of the "person" in a second edition of *The Moral Challenge of Alzheimer Disease*.[2]

The perils of forgetfulness are especially evident in our culture of independence and economic productivity that so values intellect, memory, and self-control. Alzheimer's disease (AD)[3] is a quantifiable neurological atrophy that objectively assaults normal human functioning;[4] on the other hand, as medical anthropologists highlight, AD is also viewed within the context of socially constructed images of the human self and its fulfillment.[5] A longitu-

---

1. Stephen G. Post, *The Moral Challenge of Alzheimer Disease* (Baltimore: Johns Hopkins University Press, 1995).

2. Stephen G. Post, *The Moral Challenge of Alzheimer Disease: Ethical Issues from Diagnosis to Dying*, revised ed. (Baltimore: Johns Hopkins University Press, 2000).

3. S. Gilman, "Alzheimer's Disease," *Perspectives in Biology and Medicine* 40, no. 1 (1997): 230-43.

4. N. C. Fox, P. A. Freeborough, and M. N. Rossor, "Visualisation and Quantification of Rates of Atrophy in Alzheimer's Disease," *The Lancet* 348 (1996): 94-97.

5. E. Herskovits, "Struggling Over Subjectivity: Debates about the 'self' and Alzheimer's Disease," *Medical Anthropology Quarterly* 9, no. 2 (1995): 146-64.

dinal study carried out in urban China by Charlotte Ikels, for example, indicates that dementia does not evoke the same level of dread there as it does among Americans.[6] Thus, the stigma associated with the mental incapacitation of dementia varies according to culture.[7]

In response to the voices of caregivers across the country, I have grown increasingly critical of those who would diminish the importance of the deeply forgetful. In contrast to narrow personhood theorists, I hold the belief that persons who lack certain empowering cognitive capacities are not nonpersons; rather, they have become the weakest among us and, due to their needfulness, are worthy of care. The hypercognitivist value system that shapes personhood theories of ethics is merely an example of how our culture's criteria of rationality and productivity blind us to other ways of thinking about the meaning of our humanity and the nature of humane care. I remain impressed with the work of anthropologist Charlotte Ikels, who points out that in Chinese culture, the cognitive domain is not taken to be the total sum of the person, nor is the self conceptualized as essentially independent and autonomous. Thus in the eyes of the Chinese family, the person with dementia is still "there." Fortunately, not everyone in the world kowtows before the exclusionary phrase of the error-prone Descartes, "I think, therefore, I am." In Japanese culture, there are some who find in the image of dementia a release from the fetters of everyday cares and occupations.[8] This image may trivialize a disease that is a sort of human development in reverse, but there is value in seeing value in those who are demented. We should replace Descartes's phrase with, "I feel and relate, therefore, I am."

People with AD and their caregivers have convinced me that they do not need the hypercognitive ideology of human worth; they do require more people who are ready to lend a hand in the world of the forgetful. For care to succeed, we must struggle to overcome the problem of stigma. Around the country, in the context of my workshop panels, people with mild AD point to this problem. They complain that old friends do not communicate with them directly, but instead talk around them. They feel that a gap surfaces even in relations with old friends. One autobiographical account of living with the diagnosis and initial decline of AD is the Reverend Robert Davis's *My Journey into Alzheimer's Disease*.[9] As Davis "mourned the loss of old abilities," he nev-

---

6. Charlotte Ikels, "The Experience of Dementia in China," *Culture, Medicine and Psychiatry* 3 (1998): 257-83.

7. Gwen Yeo and Dolores Gallagher-Thompson, eds., *Ethnicity and the Dementias* (Bristol, Pa.: Taylor and Francis, 1996).

8. S. Ariyoshi, *The Twilight Years* (New York: Kodansha International, 1984).

9. Robert Davis, with help from his wife Betty, *My Journey into Alzheimer's Disease:*

ertheless could draw on his faith: "I choose to take things moment by moment, thankful for everything that I have, instead of raging wildly at the
things that I have lost" (p. 57). Even as he struggled to find a degree of peace
through his religious faith, he was also keenly aware of people who "simply
cannot handle being around someone who is mentally and emotionally impaired" (p. 115). As can occur in time of plague, we try to put distance between
ourselves and the afflicted, especially in the case of a dementing disease that
we would just as soon place out of sight and mind. But we must not separate
"them" from "us." Instead, we must support the remaining capacities and enhance the relational well-being of persons with AD using data that indicate
which interventions are most helpful.[10]

AD is among the most unconsidered issues in the field of bioethics, although it has begun to receive serious attention over the last several years.
There appears to be a certain tension between advocacy ethicists such as myself, who are steeped in the voices of the marginalized forgetful, and founda-
tionalist philosophers who struggle to apply ethical theories to the very complex world of dementia.

The image of denying equal moral consideration to people with dementia is nicely illustrated in the 1982 film *Blade Runner,* in which human beings
have created artificial Replicants to take on hazardous work "off-world."
Rachel, a young woman Replicant, has a brain that contains implanted childhood memories (as a means of improving on previous Replicants). The presence of memories convinces Deckard (a Replicant Terminator), who otherwise
had no sympathy for Replicants, that Rachel is not a thing to be terminated. In
future decades, as more people lose their memories, will we find ourselves so
burdened by economic and caregiving pressures that nonvoluntary euthanasia
of the most deeply forgetful becomes commonplace?

I especially worry about the personhood theories of ethicists such as
Princeton University's Peter Singer, and others, who indicate that persons
must have desires for the future (this is somewhat derivative from John
Locke, who receives an appreciative nod in the litany of personhood theorists). Such a view seems to exclude those without ample temporal glue between past, present, and future. The deeply forgetful must then ultimately be
devalued.[11] I certainly believe that those in the persistent vegetative state lack

---

Helpful Insights for Family and Friends (Wheaton, Ill.: Tyndale, 1989). Page numbers for
quotations from this work will be cited parenthetically in the text.

10. S. R. Sabat, "Recognizing and Working with Remaining Abilities: Toward Improving the Care of Alzheimer's Disease Sufferers," *The American Journal of Alzheimer's
Care and Related Disorders and Research* 9, no. 3 (1994): 8-16.

11. Peter Singer, *Practical Ethics* (Cambridge: Cambridge University Press, 1993).

what I prefer to call the essentially human capacities — cognitive, emotional, relational, or aesthetic — because their higher brains have stopped functioning. Those few persons with AD who become vegetative because they have survived infections long enough have lost the essentially human capacities, and therefore enter a category of exclusion. Yet I remain critical of those who apply exclusionary criteria earlier on in the experience of dementia. My inclusive universalism contrasts with the hypercognitivist's oxymoronic exclusive universalism. People with dementia forget about the future and the past, but they can experience many forms of gratification, that is, *if* we are willing to help them.

Love (synonymous with "care," "*chesed*," or "*agape*"), a basic solicitude, can overcome the tendency to exclude the forgetful.[12] This care is usually best expressed in "being with" the forgetful, as opposed to the "doing to" of invasive medical technologies. Many invasive medical interventions, as well as the high-tech environment of a hospital, should be avoided because they are frightening to persons with AD.

The arrogance of the cognitively intact philosopher was evident in the ancient Stoic ethic of universal concern for "all" humanity possessed of the divine spark of reason. Theologian Reinhold Niebuhr concluded that while Stoicism went beyond the narrow bonds of class, community, and race, it included "only the intelligent" in the divine community. An aristocratic condescension, therefore, corrupts Stoic universalism. In the love and care for persons with AD, there is no room for such condescension.

Quality of Life As Love's Creation

Emotional, relational, aesthetic, and spiritual forms of well-being are possible to varying degrees in people with progressive dementia.

Emotional and Relational Well-Being

Tom Kitwood and Kathleen Bredin developed a description of the "culture of dementia" that is useful in appreciating emotional and relational aspects of

---

12. R. J. Martin and S. G. Post, "Human Dignity, Dementia, and the Moral Basis of Caregiving," in *Dementia and Aging: Ethics, Values, and Policy Choices*, ed. R. Binstock, S. G. Post, and P. J. Whitehouse (Baltimore: Johns Hopkins University Press, 1992), pp. 55-68.

quality of life. It provides indicators of well-being in people with severe dementia: the assertion of will or desire, usually in the form of dissent despite various coaxings; the ability to express a range of emotions; initiation of social contact (for instance, a person with dementia has a small toy dog that he treasures and places it before another person with dementia to attract attention); affectional warmth (for instance, a woman wanders back and forth in the facility without much socializing, but when people say hello to her she gives them a kiss on the cheek and continues her wandering).[13]

There is no need to add to the above description, except to state the obvious: if a man mistakes his wife for a hat, fine, no need for corrections. Many a person with dementia has been badgered by those who wish to impose reality long past the point when it is a serious possibility. In the mild stage of AD, there is much to be said for trying to orient a person to reality; at some point in moderate AD, however, it becomes oppressive to impose reality upon them.

Aesthetic and Spiritual Well-Being

The aesthetic well-being available to people with AD is obvious to anyone who has watched art or music therapy sessions. In some cases, a person with advanced AD may still draw the same valued symbol, as though through art a sense of self is retained.[14] The abstract expressionist de Kooning painted his way through much of his struggle with AD. Various art critics commented that his work, while not what it had been, was nevertheless impressive. As Kay Larson, former art critic for *New York* magazine, wrote,

> It would be cruel to suggest that de Kooning needed his disease to free himself. Nonetheless, the erosions of Alzheimer's could not eliminate the effects of a lifetime of discipline and love of craft. When infirmity struck, the artist was prepared. If he didn't know what he was doing, maybe it didn't matter — to him. He knew what he loved best, and it sustained him.[15]

13. Tom Kitwood and Kathleen Bredin, "Towards a Theory of Dementia Care: Personhood and Well-Being," *Aging and Society* 12 (1992): 269-97.

14. A. D. Firlik, "Margo's Logo," *Journal of the American Medical Association* 265 (1991): 201; see also Alicia Ann Clair, *Therapeutic Uses of Music with Older Adults* (Baltimore: Health Professions Press, 1996).

15. Kay Larson, "Willem de Kooning and Alzheimer's," *The World and I* 12, no. 7 (1997): 297-99.

A review of de Kooning's later art indicates, on the one hand, a loss of the sweeping power and command of brush typical of his work in the 1950s; but there is also a quality to the later work that should not be diminished.

The Spirituality of Coping

When informed of a diagnosis of AD, how might a person find meaning and a degree of inner peace in the midst of anxiety? The person must navigate a journey into deep forgetfulness that seems slightly less anxious only when one forgets that one forgets. Caregivers, in turn, may be shaken to their spiritual foundations by unexpected responsibilities. Clinicians in modern industrialized cultures have placed a Jeffersonian wall of separation between the spheres of allopathic practice and religion-spirituality. The wall has blinded some clinicians to the importance of spiritual and religious concerns in the patient's clinical condition.

AD raises the postmodernist question of the dominance of rationality in our conception of the human self. The slow disintegration of components of thought and, eventually, feeling found in AD raises the basic question: what does it mean to be human?

Chaplains should have a significant role in the disclosure of a diagnosis as serious as AD. They must be able to encourage hope despite the perils of forgetfulness. Hope is a multidimensional attribute of an individual that concerns dimensions of possibility and confidence in future outcomes. It can address secular matters such as future plans and relationships, or religious matters of ultimate destiny. Hope is an aspect of "religious" well-being. Preservation of hope can maximize a patient's psychological adjustment to a severe disability such as dementia. Knowing the diagnosis of dementia enables an individual to participate actively in support groups, to consider consenting for AD research projects, and to make known preferences for future levels of medical treatment after the dementia becomes severe. Yet some clinicians still resist telling the patient about his or her diagnosis, often because they do not wish to create despair. But in the effort to retain hope, the whole ethical process of looking toward future choices is undone.

The spiritual history of patients can be very useful in understanding their sources of well-being, and in helping them to identify religious resources in the community. Clinicians should acknowledge the importance of spirituality and religion in diagnosed individuals, refer to clergy, but also respond (if willing) to the patient's requests for spirituality in the physician-

94

patient relationship. Emphatically, this is a possibility only upon patient request, and perhaps such requests will be relatively rare.

People with a diagnosis of AD often pray, for they are thrown back onto
whatever faith they have in the meaningful and beneficent purposes underlying the universe. They pray because the routine and the control have been
taken from their lives, and probably because they fear the future. They are
shaken existentially, and must begin a final phase of their journey in remarkable trust. The person with a diagnosis of AD will often desire to pray with
family members, to pray in religious communities, and to pray alone. The
word "prayer" comes from the Latin *precari*, "to entreat," to ask earnestly. It
comes from the same root as the word "precarious," and it is in the precari-
ousness of emerging forgetfulness that often the person with dementia is
driven to prayer. Prayer is one way of enhancing hope in the future despite
dementia. Chaplains and clinicians should encourage this propensity to gain
strength through prayer in the midst of cognitive decline.

To present the picture of people with dementia as meaning-seeking, I
borrow from an autobiographical account. The following story — only
lightly edited — was told by a woman in her mid forties with dementia, etiol-
ogy unknown. She is conversant, although there are some days when she is
too mentally confused to engage in much dialogue. She has more difficulty
responding to open-ended questions, but does very well if her conversation
partner cues her by mentioning several alternative words from which she
might choose, at which point she can be quite articulate:

> It was just about this time three years ago that I recall laughing with my
> sister while in dance class at my turning the big 40. "Don't worry, life be-
> gins at forty," she exclaimed, and then sweetly advised her younger sister
> of all the wonders in life still to be found. Little did either of us realize
> what a cruel twist life was proceeding to take. It was a fate neither she nor
> I ever imagined someone in our age group could encounter.
>
> Things began to happen that I just couldn't understand. There were
> times I addressed friends by the wrong name. Comprehending conversa-
> tions seemed almost impossible. My attention span became quite short.
> Notes were needed to remind me of things to be done and how to do
> them. I would slur my speech, use inappropriate words, or simply elimi-
> nate one from a sentence. This caused not only frustration for me but also
> a great deal of embarrassment. Then came the times I honestly could not
> remember how to plan a meal or shop for groceries.
>
> One day, while out for a walk on my usual path in a city in which I had

resided for 11 years, nothing looked familiar. It was as if I was lost in a foreign land, yet I had the sense to ask for directions home.

There were more days than not when I was perfectly fine; but to me, they did not make up for the ones that weren't. I knew there was something terribly wrong and after 18 months of undergoing a tremendous amount of tests and countless visits to various doctors, I was proven right.

Dementia is the disease, they say, cause unknown. At this point it no longer mattered to me just what that cause was because the tests eliminated the reversible ones, my hospital coverage was gone, and my spirit was too worn to even care about the name of something irreversible.

I was angry. I was broken and this was something I could not fix, nor to date can anyone fix it for me. How was I to live without myself? I wanted her back!

She was a strong and independent woman. She always tried so hard to be a loving wife, a good mother, a caring friend, and a dedicated employee. She had self-confidence and enjoyed life. She never imagined that by the age of 41 she would be forced into retirement. She had not yet observed even one of her sons graduate from college, nor known the pleasures of a daughter-in-law, or held a grandchild in her arms.

Needless to say, the future did not look bright. The leader must now learn to follow. Adversities in life were once looked upon as a challenge; now they're just confusing situations that someone else must handle. Control of *my life* will slowly be relinquished to others. I must learn to trust — completely.

An intense fear enveloped my entire being as I mourned the loss of what was and the hopes and dreams that might never be. How could this be happening to me? What exactly will become of me? These questions occupied much of my time for far too many days.

Then one day as I fumbled around the kitchen to prepare a pot of coffee, something caught my eye through the window. It had snowed and I had truly forgotten what a beautiful sight a soft, gentle snowfall could be. I eagerly but so slowly dressed and went outside to join my son, who was shoveling our driveway. As I bent down to gather a mass of those radiantly white flakes on my shovel, it seemed as though I could do nothing but marvel at their beauty. Needless to say, he did not share in my enthusiasm; to him it was a job, but to me it was an experience.

Later I realized that for a short period of time, God granted me the ability to see a snowfall through the same innocent eyes of the child I once was, so many years ago. I am still here, I thought, and there will be wonders to be held in each new day; they are just different now. . . . Now my quality of life is feeding the dogs, looking at flowers. My husband says I am more content now than ever before! Love and dignity, those are the keys. This brings you back down to the basics in life; a smile makes you happy.

People with AD as well as their caregivers can benefit remarkably from pastoral care. Sometimes, the patient who has not spoken coherently for several years will suddenly blurt out a prayer or a hymn, for such deeply learned material is the very last to disappear. The beauty of litanies, prayers, and hymns has a certain affective power. I remain open to the idea that as the capacity for technical (means-to-ends) rationality fades, more contemplative and spiritual capacities are elevated. Demented people continue to respond to their faith and inner needs through long-remembered rituals that connect them with the present. Prayers and hymns are still familiar in many cases, especially after several repetitions. Worship in nursing homes can create the awareness of connectedness.

Caregivers often pray for loved ones with dementia. In a study of religion variables in relation to perceived caregiver rewards, African-American women caring for elderly persons with major deficits in activities of daily living perceived greater benefits to caring based on a spiritual-religious reframing of their situation. Religiosity indicators (i.e., "prayer, comfort from religion, self-rated religiosity, attendance at religious services") are especially significant as coping resources in female African-American caregivers.[16] Spirituality is a clear stress deterrent, and therefore also affects depression rates, which are extraordinarily high in AD caregivers. The authors of this study suggest that "if religiosity indicators are shown to enhance a caregiver's perceived rewards, health care professionals could encourage caregivers to use their religiosity to reduce the negative consequences and increase the rewards of caregiving." This seems self-evident.

Other studies indicate that spirituality is an important factor in coping with the sometimes ruthless stress induced by caring for someone with AD.[17] Spirituality among AD caregivers is a central means of coping.[18] In an important study by Peter V. Rabins and his colleagues, thirty-two family caregivers

16. S. J. Picot, S. M. Debanne, K. H. Namazi, and M. L. Wykle, "Religiosity and Perceived Rewards of Black and White Caregivers," *The Gerontologist* 37, no. 1 (1997): 89-101.

17. Cecil B. Murphey, *Day to Day: Spiritual Help When Someone You Love Has Alzheimer's* (Philadelphia: Westminster, 1988).

18. A. M. Whitlatch, D. I. Meddaugh, and K. J. Langhout, "Religiosity among Alzheimer's Disease Caregivers," *The American Journal of Alzheimer's Care and Related Disorders and Research* (1992): 11-20.

of persons with AD and thirty caregivers of persons with cancer were compared cross-sectionally to determine whether the type of illness cared for affected the emotional state of the caregiver and to identify correlates of both undesirable and desirable emotional outcomes. While no prominent differences in negative or positive states were found between the two groups, correlates of negative and positive emotional status were identified. These included caregiver personality variables, number of social supports, and the feeling that one is supported by one's religious faith. Specifically, "emotional distress was predicted by self-reported low or absent religious faith."[19] Moreover, spirituality predicted positive emotional states in caregiving. Interestingly, the study suggests that it was "belief, rather than social contact, that was important."

In another study, the spiritual perspectives of seventeen caregiver wives of dementia victims and twenty-three non-caregiving wives of healthy adults were compared in a pilot study using a convenience sample. Caregiver wives used symbols such as God, and spiritual behaviors such as prayer and forgiveness, as coping mechanisms. Caregivers tended to share the problems and joys of living according to their spiritual belief more often than the non-caregiver wives of healthy adults. Caregivers also engaged in private prayer and sought spiritual guidance in making decisions in their everyday life more often. Both these studies point to the central importance of religiosity in caregiving for many, but surely not all, professional and informal family caregivers.

Health-care professionals must do more than tolerate the meaning-giving belief systems of their patients. It is these belief systems that provide hope, security, meaning, and strength to empower patients to cope with the shattering experience of severe illness. Health-care professionals should be concerned with the social-scientific and historical understanding of the empowering presence of spirituality (often, but not necessarily, embedded in a religious tradition) in the patient's experience of illness, rather than with its essential validity or truth. The importance of patient beliefs is exemplified in historical accounts of healers who possess knowledge of both medicine and spirituality.

The pluralistic and social-scientific study of the impact of patient spirituality is very different from the theological enterprise of the seminary. Growing numbers of studies demonstrate the value of spirituality as a coping mechanism for patients with major illness. The attention given to patient

19. P. V. Rabins, M. D. Fitting, J. Eastham, and J. Fetting, "The Emotional Impact of Caring for the Chronically Ill," *Psychosomatics* 31, no. 3 (1990): 331-36.

spirituality and religious belief in medical education is another indication of clinical relevance.

Spirituality, as I define it, involves a belief in a presence in the universe that is greater than our own, and for whom the deepest and most abiding affirmative love is definitive. Persons with a diagnosis of AD are in situations where they are losing control, where they have reached certain profound existential limits, and here many will turn to whatever high presence in the universe they consider to be in control. Caregivers will often cope with the demands of providing care through the spirituality that associates their other-regarding actions and affect with the very nature of the universe, with the very center of the cosmos.

End of Life

Humane care for persons with advanced dementia can be fairly objectively considered on the moral axis of a burden-benefit analysis with respect to the relative value or disvalue of various potential medical interventions. It is incumbent on health-care professionals to make clear recommendations to patients and their surrogate decision-makers based on such analysis, rather than to abandon commitment to the patient's good. While family surrogate decision-makers do always retain the full right of choice for a loved one, as informed by both his or her prior directives and current best interests, physicians should never merely present treatment options as choices without highlighting their likely burdens and benefits, as well as relevant alternatives.

The case selected here arrived over my e-mail on December 15, 2000, from a caregiver who shall remain anonymous:

Hello Dear Friends:

As many of you know, my father has been suffering from Alzheimer's disease for the past four and a half years. It has been a long and often very hard road for him, for my mom, and for me too. However, as of 7 p.m. last night, my father no longer has to struggle with this disease, which robbed him of every part of his being, except one. He never once stopped recognizing my mom and never, ever stopped reaching out to her and wanting to have a kiss.

No matter how many parts of his personality were lost, no matter how many hospital visits full of needles and catheters, no matter how many diapers, he always retained his kind, gentle sweetness and his European manners as a gentleman.

In the end, things went very quickly for him. He simply closed his eyes and closed his mouth, indicating no more food or water. We struggled to get him back in bed, thinking he was just having a bad day and didn't have much energy. But very quickly, within hours, it was obvious that he had slipped into a coma in his own bed. . . . That is how he died: very gently, very sweetly and very peacefully. I believe we have received a great gift to have been able to have those last few hours and not have to make any drastic decisions about ambulances, hospitals, nursing homes, etc.

Here an old man died in peace, spared all of the technological burdens that too often afflict persons with advanced dementia. He died in his home, surrounded by loving family members, and had no tubes in any bodily orifice, natural or unnatural.

The most immediate response to the possibilities for suicide and assisted suicide is the assurance that no person with AD will be made to endure unwelcome efforts to prolong dying in the advanced stage of the disease, or discomfort caused by the absence of palliative care. It is the fear of burdensome over-treatment that must be eliminated by clinical practices and laws that respect and encourage the choice of a natural dying.

In the advanced stage, AD is roughly delineated by such features as the inability to recognize loved ones, to communicate by speech, to ambulate, or to maintain bowel and/or bladder control. When AD progresses to this stage, weight loss and swallowing difficulties will inevitably emerge. Death can be expected for most patients within a year or two, or even sooner, regardless of medical efforts. One useful consequence of viewing the advanced stage of AD as terminal is that family members will better appreciate the importance of palliative (pain medication) care as an alternative to medical treatments intended to extend the dying process.

All efforts at life extension in this advanced stage create burdens and avoidable suffering for patients who could otherwise live out the remainder of their lives in greater comfort and peace. Cardiopulmonary resuscitation, dialysis, PEG tube feeding, and all other invasive technologies should be avoided. The use of antibiotics usually does not prolong survival, and comfort can be maintained without antibiotic use in patients experiencing infections.

Physicians and other health-care professionals should recommend this less burdensome and therefore more appropriate approach to family members, and to persons with dementia who are competent, ideally soon after initial diagnosis. Early discussions of a peaceful dying should occur between persons with dementia and their families, guided by information from health-care professionals on the relative benefits of a palliative care approach.

Comfort Care and the Avoidance of Hospitalization

Professionals should inform family members of studies indicating the immense value of *a comfort-care approach that avoids hospitalization.* For example, one study indicates that when persons with AD were hospitalized for pneumonia or hip fracture, they were five times more likely to die than cognitively intact patients receiving the same aggressive treatments.[20] In addition, pain was not well treated in the hospital setting. A number of similar studies now conclude that hospitalization is not recommended, given the limited life expectancy of persons with advanced dementia, the significant burdens of aggressive treatment, and the limited attention given to pain control in hospital settings. The most compassionate decision for such persons is to eliminate hospitalization and concentrate on palliation and comfort care in the nursing home. If a person with advanced dementia is at home, family caregivers should call the local home hospice team rather than emergency medical services (911) in moments of crisis.

A Recommendation for Assisted Oral Feeding

Avoiding hospitalization will also decrease the number of persons with advanced AD who receive tube feeding, since many long-term care facilities send residents to hospitals for tube placement, after which they return to the facility. It should be remembered that the practice of long-term tube feeding in persons with advanced dementia began only in the mid 1980s after the development of a new technique called percutaneous endoscopic gastrostomy (PEG). Before then, such persons were cared for through assisted oral feeding. In comparison with assisted oral feeding, however, long-term tube feeding has no advantages, and a number of disadvantages.

Based on new scientific data, assisted oral feeding coupled with hospice care when needed appears to be the compassionate alternative to tube feeding. This recommendation emerged primarily from two major studies published in the nation's leading medical journals, which point out that PEG tube feeding is associated with increased diarrhea and related discomfort.[21] PEG

20. R. S. Morrison and A. L. Sui, "A Survival in End-Stage Dementia Following Acute Illness," *Journal of the American Medical Association* 284 (2000): 47-52.

21. M. Gillick, "Rethinking the Role of Tube Feeding in Patients with Advanced Dementia," *New England Journal of Medicine* 342 (2000): 206-10; and T. E. Finucane et al., "Tube Feeding in Patients with Advanced Dementia: A Review of the Evidence," *Journal of the American Medical Association* 282 (1999): 1365-81.

tube feeding results in greatly increased imposition of physical restraints to prevent patients from pulling the tubes out of their abdomens. Paradoxically, this is occurring in a time when most long-term care facilities recognize the benefits of minimal- or no-restraint policies. Moreover, nutritional status does not usually improve with the use of tube feeding, nor does such use prevent or lower the incidence of aspiration pneumonia. There is no evidence to suggest that tube feeding reduces skin breakdown and the likelihood of pressure sores. Contrary to myth, there is no average difference in longevity between persons in advanced AD who are tube fed and those are provided with assistance in oral feeding as needed.

Furthermore, the use of PEG tube feeding is contrary to the preferences of an overwhelming number of elderly persons. For example, in one study more than 95 percent of cognitively intact respondents sixty-five years and older indicated that should they ever have severe dementia, they would not want cardiopulmonary resuscitation, use of a respirator, or parenteral or enteral tube feeding.

Moreover, most family surrogates who consent to tube feeding for a loved one with advanced AD come to regret the decision.[22]

Persons with advanced AD who survive to the point of being unable to swallow even with assistance, or who have lost all interest in eating and drinking, are in the final phase of the process of dying. Their increasing sleep naturally limits intake. They will usually die comfortably in several days or a week. Some dehydration may occur, and artificial saliva and ice chips can care for dry mucous membranes. The discomfort of natural dying in the absence of nutrition and hydration has been exaggerated. It is likely that the natural palliative mechanisms of the body make this a relatively comfortable dying process. In the absence of nutrition and hydration, the body draws on endorphin (endogenous morphine), its natural opiate, which blunts nerve endings. The physiological responses and probable physical reactions to the cessation of nutrition and hydration have been described in the medical literature. An emerging consensus indicates that this form of natural dying is comfortable. Families need to know that terminal dehydration brings about a natural analgesic effect in the patient, and that this effect can be supplemented with palliative use of morphine to provide absolute certainty of comfort.

With regard to quality of life, the person receiving long-term tube feeding is denied the gratification of tasting preferred foods. The person with advanced dementia has suffered many losses, including the capacity to commu-

---

22. S. L. Mitchell et al., "A Cross National Survey of Decision for Long-term Feeding in Older Persons," *Journal of the American Geriatrics Society* 48 (2000): 391-97.

nicate by speech, to recognize loved ones, to control bowel and bladder, and to enjoy continuity with the past. In such circumstances, small gratifications are all that remain. Tube feeding denies the sensory benefits of assisted oral feeding, as well as the emotional and relational benefits of interacting with a good caregiver who assists in an emotionally affirming manner.

Of course, assisted oral feeding should be available to all persons with advanced AD as needed. Neglect in this area should not be tolerated, and concerted efforts are called for to educate and support professional and family caregivers in techniques of assisted oral feeding.

CARING FOR THE AGING

Local Church Ministry to and through Older Adults

GREGORY WAYBRIGHT, PH.D.

My eyes began to open to the subject of local church ministry through older adults when I first left the United States as a college student in 1973. I was sent to Japan on a summer mission project and participated in a local church in Kofu, a city to the west of Tokyo. My previous church experience had led me to several perspectives:

1. That fresh, innovative thinking belonged to the young. As one gets older (I thought), there is a calcification of viewpoint. Thus, older people are almost always out of touch with a rapidly changing society and committed to the status quo.
2. That true leadership came from younger adults — certainly those in their pre-retirement years. This became clear as board members would receive "honorary" status when they reached a certain age.
3. That service in the church should be done by those who are young. So often, I heard older people say, "I've done my bit. Let the younger people take over." And I would hear younger people say, "Those older people could never connect with today's youth."
4. That pastoral leadership should be provided by younger men. Search committees would often say that they needed a pastor with a young family who could really relate to the young and draw younger people into the church. Older pastors would have to move to a smaller congregation or perhaps assume a role such as visitation pastor or interim pastor when churches looked for younger leadership. The prime years of being a senior pastor seemed to be something like thirty-five to forty-nine.

5. That retirement from active involvement in work, church, and society was the highest good.
6. That "the future of our church is the young people." This was said so often that it seemed to have the authority of Scripture (though I have never found the biblical reference). Anybody else must have been envisioned as too near death to be worthy of much consideration.

I do not believe that any of this was actually said — but it was implied in virtually every part of church life. All this, of course, was simply a part of a larger "youth culture" prevalent in the America of my upbringing. The culture placed high value on youthful appearance and physical vigor and low value on life experience and wrinkles. The summer in the Japanese church forced me to begin thinking about a different worldview — one in which life experience might provide a foundation for better thinking; in which the wisest leaders might usually be those who have seen where decisions have led through many years of decision-making; in which old and young serve and lead together, with those who are older often being the mentors for the young; and so on.

My perspectives on this were transformed further when I assumed my first role as senior pastor on California's beautiful Central Coast in 1984. The community was made up largely of retired people, college students, and the professionals that served those two groups. The church I served when I first arrived had a large group of people over seventy years of age, a smaller group of people under thirty, and very few in between. The idea that "the future of the church is the young" simply was not true. Those in the older category were those who usually stayed in this particular community the longest. And they were healthy, bright, energetic, and longing to serve. I remember so many of the comments made to me as a thirty-three-year-old "senior" pastor. "Pastor Greg, this concept that we should work until we retire and then do nothing for the rest of our lives (even if we have the funds to do it) is absolutely ludicrous." Or, "We are made in the image of God and thus are called upon to have our lives count. Our service doesn't have to be paid all the time. It simply must be important and productive."

I believe I experienced a genuine paradigm shift. Whereas I had been conditioned to view children and young people as the key to the survival of the church and younger adults as the most desirable church leaders, I began to have my eyes opened to the fact that this was neither biblical nor true. I now believe that this youth-centered perspective is a form of American syncretism. Most societies in history have placed greater respect and higher value on the worth of older people. American society sees age as something to be fought, denied, ignored, and avoided at all costs.

I still remember making a conscious change of perspective. As a steward of the lives entrusted to my pastoral care, I made a commitment to working with the leadership God had brought to this local church. "Older people" took the leadership in areas of assimilation, young women's outreach, and corporate worship. Those working even in areas of nursery and children's ministry were made up to a significant degree of those in the over-seventy crowd. I will not try to be naive or "Pollyannaish" about it and say that we never encountered generational challenges. But, in retrospect, the church was built through such intergenerational ministry.

I know that older adult ministry as envisioned by most evangelical churches in the past has consisted of providing services needed by older adults. The goal would be to provide help for church leaders in areas such as shut-in visitation, hospice, nursing home entertainment, care for Alzheimer's victims and their families, and so on. Most certainly, this is a part of senior adult ministry. It is what I call ministry *to* older adults. I am convinced, however, that this is only a small part of the topic. The real issue includes ministry *through* the older adults whom God calls to a congregation. When I think of older adult ministry, I really am thinking of a ministry in which the local church is focused intentionally on building a Christ-centered intergenerational community in which all serve and are served — in which all participate according to the calling and "gifting" by God.

Of course, this is a huge topic and is one that is not addressed by offering cookie cutter programs or easy "how to's." As the first director of the National Institute of Aging, Robert Butler wrote a Pulitzer Prize–winning work, *Why Survive? Being Old in America;* in it, he wrote, "I am concerned . . . with easy solutions. How does a nation alter its own cultural sensibility toward the old?"[1] I share the same concern for the church. What I have chosen to do is to try to identify the most significant sociological considerations in such a church ministry, to identify the formidable challenges in the initiative, and then to offer several introductory practical suggestions.

Sociological Considerations

Demographics

The culture of a society is often influenced simply by the people who make up the larger community. In 1900, there were only 3 million people in the

1. Robert N. Butler, *Why Survive: Being Old in America* (Baltimore: Johns Hopkins University Press, 1976).

United States who were age sixty-five or older, making up 4 percent of the population. In 1990, these numbers had changed to 31.6 million or 12.5 percent of the population — one of every eight in America being sixty-five or older. In 2003, the number is estimated to be 35 million and nearly 15 percent and in 2030 is expected to be 70 million and 22 percent. Already, the percentages of those sixty-five and older are very close to those eighteen and younger. The single greatest factor in this, of course, has been the growth in life expectancy. Butler points out that life expectancy in the United States in 1900 was only forty-seven years, in 1970 was seventy-one years, and is now in the upper seventies. During most of human history, only one in ten lived to age sixty-five. Now, in America, eight of ten live past sixty-five. In fact, American senior adults now outnumber the entire population of Canada.

Much can and should be noted about these statistics. I simply want to make the point, however, that this reality will affect all areas of our society — political elections, social services, issues related to media and entertainment and, yes, the life of the church.

Stereotypes

The ministry of the local church to and through older adults is often handicapped because of inappropriate stereotypes or caricatures of the senior population. Among these are the following:

1. That older people are relatively homogeneous. In reality, those over sixty-five may be the most heterogeneous of all age groupings. Work experiences, changes in family, life encounters, and educational levels all have an ongoing magnifying effect as life goes on.
2. That the majority of older people live below the poverty level. Even though finances are surely a problem for many older adults, the reality is that only about 10 percent of American adults over sixty-five have an income level below the government-determined poverty level
3. That most older adults are in poor health. Although there seems to be a tendency to talk more about health (and particular body parts) as human beings age, over 70 percent of those over sixty-five in the United States describe their health as good, very good.
4. That a majority of older people worry about death (thus leading many pastors or church leaders to talk about heaven or related topics in senior adult gatherings). A recent study indicates that 24 percent of those over

sixty-five worry about death in comparison to 55 percent of those eighteen to twenty-four.

5. That a large percentage of older adults live in nursing homes. The actual figure is 5 percent. Most are in family settings.

6. That the ability to learn decreases with age. No study supports this. This has implications for the church and for the school. One of the major trends in education is the return to school among those recently retired. Some educators foresee that in the near future a majority of college students will be over fifty years old.

7. That Asian American older adults are all independently cared for by their families and thus do not need the attention of the church. The evidence seems to indicate that the longer extended families are in America (whatever the national or ethnic group may be), the more their demographics parallel the majority community. Most certainly, the term "all" here is inaccurate.

8. That older adults want to disengage from work, friends, family, and church and simply move south to retire. This contention is inaccurate.

9. That older adults are always at peace, able to relax, and free from stress. Again, this is clearly not the case.

The obvious implication of these few observations is that those who work with older adults in the church must know their people rather than simply embracing what society has suggested or characterized. The older adult is not primarily a caretaker but a potential growing disciple and contributing member of the congregation.

Changes in Views of Retirement

It used to be the case that many people lived their whole lives dreaming of retirement. Retirement was viewed as an era of life with no work, no hassles, no burdens. People thought of moving to a sunny area, away from former lives, and spending countless hours doing whatever they love to do. With so many people retiring in good health and living one-third of their lives after leaving the workplace, however, views are changing. People are realizing that relationship is more important than climate. Thus, periods as "sun birds" away from former friends, family, church, and familiar settings are growing shorter even among the affluent. A survey done in Arlington Heights, Illinois, while I was pastor there disclosed that over 80 percent of long-time residents wanted to spend most of their retirement years in the areas where they have cherished relationships and familiar environs.

Even more significantly, those avocations or hobbies so much loved when they had to be "fitted in" to family, work, church, and community responsibilities prove not to be as fulfilling when they become the main staple of existence. As a friend told me, "I can only play so much golf and then I want to do something that matters." Increasingly, older adults seek opportunities in which there can be significant productivity and a positive contribution to what they value.

The Reality of Transition

There is hardly a time in life that involves more change than the entry into senior adulthood. The transition often includes the following:

1. move to a new residence;
2. loss of career (or, at least, a new direction);
3. move (for at least a portion of the time) to a new geographical location;
4. more opportunity for choice in use of time;
5. often a time of loss — through diminished opportunity, sense of purpose, friends moving away, or even death.

We have long known that when people are in transition, they are more open to spiritual things. As long as we are in the routine of a career or long-established pattern of life in the community, we do not think deeply about eternal things.

Thus, I would contend that those recently retired are among the most fertile "mission fields" in America. An active, evangelizing, serving church will almost certainly find among the elderly those who are open to the gospel for the first time or are seeking a reality in faith not yet experienced.

Miscellaneous Realities

A recent study was done by Duke University's Endowment for the United Methodist Church focusing on the rural church and older adult ministry. Several observations were made in the executive summary that transcend the rural setting to move us forward in our understanding of the church and older adults.

1. The majority of "elderly" persons in America consider themselves to be religious and want to be involved in the life of a church.
2. Older persons who describe themselves as having positive faith are physically healthier than those without it.
3. The church is reluctant to explore ministry to older adults with any intentionality and diligence.
4. Most clergy are considered to be ill-trained to serve the needs of older adults. When it happens, ministry with older adults almost always expands into a ministry with the entire family and social networks of the older adults. In other words, it is a key to broad based ministry.

"Boomer Factor"

Those who have been placed in the age category called "baby boomer" (born between 1946 and 1964) have been said to have a dominating influence on the priorities of American society. I will certainly not attempt to defend this in the space I have here — except to say that I believe this is indeed true. At this point, boomers are beginning to approach the years in which they will be the emerging older adult population. If the record of the past five decades continues to play out and boomers insist on the cultural spotlight being focused on their life situations, then we must be ready for a time in which ministry to and through older adults will not be an option — it will be an expectation. I believe that the day is approaching when American culture will no longer be described as a youth culture. It will begin to value age and life experience — as most of the world always has throughout history.

Challenges of Older Adult Ministries

I have been a pastor far longer than I have been a college and seminary president. Therefore, I well remember how frustrating it was for me to hear papers dealing with sociological trends and the need to respond, without reference to the enormous difficulties involved in changing and responding to cultural shifts. It is one thing for the Duke Endowment to say that "the church exists as the logical 'one-stop shop' for needs surrounding aging persons and their caregivers" or that "clergy can take leadership roles in organizing ministries for and with the seniors" in their congregations and communities. It is quite another matter actually to engage in that ministry. Because of an awareness of that, I have tried to put on my old pastoral hat and think through the challenges that simply must be faced if evangelical churches are to be more effective in providing ministry to and through older adults.

The Difficulty of Heterogeneity

As previously stated, older adults may be the most heterogeneous category of all age groupings. All the normal differences of race, ethnicity, and economics exist; but other differences have been developing throughout a lifetime of differing life experiences as well. Among the differences in the older adult population are the following broad categories:

1. the healthy and active and ready to serve;
2. those who are healthy and active physically but lukewarm or cold spiritually;
3. the homebound (those earlier labeled as "shut-in");
4. residents of health-care facilities of various kinds;
5. those "transitionally impaired" (possibly through job loss, stroke, death of loved one, etc.);
6. those whose parents are still alive (a sixty-five-year-old older adult might be caring for parents in their nineties; those parents would also be considered senior adults of the church and community);
7. those dying and in need of hospice.

Of course, such a list could continue and become increasingly specific. I make the point simply because it must be acknowledged that any organization or institution finds it easier to function when there are many similarities among its constituencies. The reality is that older adult ministry must face the challenges of communication, of differing tastes, of finding common ground — in fact, the issues faced by older adults are as diverse and complex as any faced in ministry to those who are younger. Anyone who has ever tried to build one Senior Adults Ministry that includes those in their seventies as well as those in their nineties knows exactly what I mean.

The Old among the Young

I have heard it more often from those older than from those younger that "I don't want to be in a church just with old people." The difficulty is that the very things that might draw and hold those who are younger are often distasteful — even offensive — for those who are older.

The Human Tendency to Hold On to Power or to Traditions

One problem many churches face is the failure to utilize the wisdom, experience, and gifts of those who are older. On the opposite side of the pendulum, many churches face power struggles in a church in which those who have had leadership positions will not allow others to come in, or to make any changes. On one side, some who have been in a church a long time complain that no new or young people are coming to the church. On the other, they find it difficult to allow changes to happen that might facilitate that kind of growth.

The Lack of Resources to Provide the Required Breadth of Ministry

The development of ministry always requires resources, money, time, leadership, training, and so on. All of these seem to be under stress in many local churches. Few are professionally trained for older adult ministry. Those who have leadership skills and the ability to grow into the task are deeply involved in other areas. Funds, of course, are always in demand for missions, facility needs, or other ministry development.

The Difficulty of Caregiving

It must be acknowledged that one aspect of older adult ministry is that of caregiving. (Of course, this is true of ministry to any age group. The point is that there are special needs usually involved as people grow older.) According to the Duke Endowment, of those currently serving the physical and emotional needs of those who are older, 97 percent are women. These caregivers frequently suffer from depression caused by stress. In other words, those who give needed care find themselves desperately needing care. One of the most difficult parts of caregiving is the guilt that comes from feeling that inadequate care is being provided, a guilt that often moves quickly to feeling resentment toward the older adult needing care. Simply stated, the job is not easy.

The Issue: Corporate Worship

One of the greatest challenges to intergenerational ministry is that there is such a divergence of musical tastes and tolerance for differing worship styles. The challenge of a church committed to intergenerational ministry is the same as at a Thanksgiving dinner involving extended family. I have sometimes asked one member of each of three generations to pick out a CD (or LP) that they think everyone at the dinner will enjoy. Usually, the decision is simply to have no background music at the dinner. This, of course, is an option not open to the church. Music is an essential part of worship.

Having mentioned these sorts of challenges, I am still convinced that the church is the one place in our fragmented world in which intergenerational ministry and community can be developed. When it happens, the rest of the world can observe God's handiwork. As Jesus said, "By this shall all men know that you are my disciples: if you have love one for the other" (John 13:35). This love is one that must cut across those walls that normally divide human beings, including that of age. The hope we have in the church is that we have a unity of faith in Jesus Christ — thus being fellow recipients of the Spirit of God. We share a common vision related to evangelism and mission. We have shared values that flow from the preaching and teaching of God's Word. Thus, I am convinced that the church is the one place in the world in which diverse people should be able to experience community with one another and live and serve in unity.

Some Practical Suggestions

I believe that the most difficult thing to do with such a broad topic is to make suggestions that might actually prove to be helpful to ministry and practical to implement. Thus, I have asked myself how I would begin to strengthen my church in this arena of intergenerational ministry if I were to step again into the role of pastoral leadership. I believe I would design a plan following several simple steps.

Identify Who You Are

It is necessary first to assess or evaluate the current state of the church's intergenerational ministry, particularly with a focus on its ministry to and through older adults. Several questions might help begin this part of the task:

1. What is the current age make-up of the church? How does this compare to the community as a whole?
2. Is there any intentional strategy to draw in and minister to a breadth of ages? Does that strategy have measurable goals?
3. More specifically, what is the strategy for ministry to older adults? Who

is in leadership — who is primarily responsible for coordinating and reporting the ministry?

4. Is the church free of barriers that might keep older adults from attending and serving?
5. Does the church consciously reach out to older adults through evangelism and seek to "disciple" senior members?
6. Are the concerns and tastes of the older adult population included in the gathered worship, including those related to music and preaching topics?
7. Are there places for age-specific friendship-building, companionship, and fellowship?
8. Are there intergenerational programs that might facilitate relationships among diverse age groups?
9. Is there a wide range of ages represented in the leadership of the church (pastors, elders, worship leaders, and so on)?

Identify Where You Want to Be

Good strategic planning must "begin with the end in mind." This involves a clear vision of the kind of church community God would have your local church to be. Some have been committed to being "homogeneous" local churches in which a specific age, racial, or economic group is targeted. My own notion is that the local church is to be a microcosm of the universal church. Thus, our goal should be to build local churches with make-up and involvement that reflect the make-up of the redeemed people of God. Another similar approach is to look at the demographical components of the geographical community in which the local church is situated. The objective would be to have a local church that is in keeping with the age make-up of those demographics.

Establish a Strategic Plan to Serve As a Guide to Get You to That Destination

This strategic plan will include many elements. Some that occur to me would be the following:

1. Educate yourself through visiting effective multigenerational and intergenerational churches. In humility, observe and learn. Talk with the leadership.

2. Read the material dealing with older adult ministry and intergenerational churches that is beginning to flood the market. Most of the work done up to this point has been produced by mainline denominations. A starting point from an evangelical perspective is Win and Charles Arn's book, *Catch the Age Wave: A Handbook for Effective Ministry with Senior Adults.* In addition, Sandra Kohlmeier has put together an excellent bibliography of available resources that can be accessed at the Lutheran Church Missouri Synod website at http://www.lcms.org.

3. Identify both pastoral and lay leadership to develop, implement, and coordinate the plan.

4. Identify and budget for the resources to launch the ministry. This includes, of course, staff salaries, development, educational funds for leadership, and programmatic funds.

5. Focus on ministry to and through older adults that is consistent with the larger church mission, values, and ministry. In my view, this would mean a focus on evangelism, spiritual growth, fellowship, caregiving, and opportunities for service according to God's call and gifts.

6. Identify the barriers that could thwart the plan. These may include sins such as age discrimination. Whatever those potential barriers may be, address them courageously, objectively, and with patience.

I am not a sociologist but I am seeing a convergence of this fresh emphasis on ministry to and through older adults with the desire among younger adults to receive mentoring from those who have experienced more of life. In my current role as president of Trinity International University, I am constantly brought into contact with eighteen- to twenty-four-year-old adults in our college. The longing for meaningful relationship with older adults is deep and genuine for so many. Broken families, infidelity among political leaders, and even the impersonal nature of so many large churches have left many young people with a desire for a personal touch from people who are sincerely committed to Christ and who will be willing to engage in life-on-life ministry. If this can be facilitated through prayer and planning, vibrant intergenerational churches will be established.

A Further Related Practical Consideration

What kind of local church does the older adult look for? It is hard to generalize about this. I would, however, make several suggestions:

1. one in which the Word of God is taught with clarity and its relevance to their lives is demonstrated;
2. one where the older adult is respected and welcomed as a full participant;
3. one that provides opportunities for older adults to serve and make a contribution to God's kingdom;
4. one that genuinely encourages older adults to function as vital organic parts of the fellowship;
5. one that facilitates corporate worship in spite of differences in musical tastes and worship styles.

Of course, I would argue that this is the kind of church for which all of us long when we know Christ.

Theological Considerations

One of my greatest interests is thinking through a biblical theology of ministry to the aging. Although I do not have space to develop that here, several areas seem to me to be in need of thought and discussion.

Areas Related to Biblical Wisdom

These areas include the importance of reverence and honor for those who are older (in the family, the church, and society), and the role and responsibility of the Christian family.

Areas Related to Eschatology

In the area of eschatology, we must consider life after death as a present experience (the eternal has already come when the Holy Spirit enters our lives, but has not been culminated). The "outer man" wastes away and groans, but the inner is being renewed each day. We must also pay attention to the Christian view of death as being both an ending and a beginning, and remember that in human experience, the act of growing old is often more difficult than dying.

Areas Related to Ecclesiology

The nature of the local church should reflect the make-up, mission, and values of the universal church. Thus, a call for a heterogeneous intergenerational local church effort is necessary. Finally, we must consider the stewardship of spiritual gifts, remembering that all gifts God gives to the body should be utilized in ways consistent with biblical principles and priorities, regardless of the age of the one gifted.

The Virtues of Talk Therapy

STEPHEN P. GREGGO, PSY.D.

The outcry surrounding the underutilization of mental health services by aging and elderly clients has been echoing loudly among advocates for comprehensive geriatric health care. The claim that "depression" is the common cold of the older adult may be disputed. Epidemiological investigations have left little doubt, however, that depression and anxiety-related symptoms occur at rates and at severity levels substantial enough that we can assert with absolute confidence that these mental health concerns are a significant public health issue for late-life adults.[1] There is also widespread recognition that this population is referred to and treated by mental health professionals less than other age population cohorts.[2]

There appears to be general consensus in the literature regarding older adults that

1. psychopathology decreases overall quality of life while increasing functional disability;
2. psychopathology increases recovery time from adverse health incidents while decreasing compliance with medical treatment;

1. B. D. Lebowitz and J. J. Gallo, "The Epidemiology of Common Late-Life Mental Disorders in the Community: Themes for the New Century," *Psychiatric Services* 50 (1999): 1158-66; and B. D. Lebowitz, J. L. Pearson, L. S. Schneider, et al., "Diagnosis and Treatment of Depression in Late Life: Consensus Statement," *Journal of the American Medical Association* 278 (1997): 1186-90.

2. E. M. French, C. B. Weiner, and P. Mosher-Ashley, "Referral Patterns of Elderly Persons to Psychotherapy by Primary Care Providers at a Community Health Center," *Clinical Gerontologist* 21 (2000): 65-71.

3. psychopathology decreases resistance to potential health threats while increasing the utilization of health services, specifically visits to primary care physicians (PCP's) for aches, pains, and other health-related complaints.

Thus, the call to treat mental health concerns within the aging population is being made for *economic* as well as *ethical* concerns.[3] Furthermore, although the rate of attempted suicide in older adults is lower proportionally than in other age groups, the completed suicide rate of 22.8 per 1000 in adults seventy-five to eighty-four is nearly double that of younger adults. Another stunning datum is that "more than 70 percent of suicide victims are seen by their physicians within the month before their death."[4] It is easy to understand the reasons for the call to educate primary care physicians about these concerns. For better or worse, this worthy effort may be facilitated by the pharmaceutical industry as altruist- and profit-motives merge. Studies show the value of psychotropic medication. Efficacy studies are generally supportive and sufficiently extensive to help direct specific applications.[5] This population prefers to consult their primary care physicians when psychological and physical issues intersect; and a prescription is a concrete, efficient, and often a helpful response by a physician to an older patient's complaints. One survey estimated that 25 percent of older adults residing in community settings are taking psychotherapeutic medications regularly.[6]

Talk Therapy and Psychosocial Supports

The benefits of talk therapy and other psychosocial supports for those dealing with the stressors of this developmental period have been noted for over seventy years since Lillien J. Martin founded the San Francisco Old Age Counseling Center in 1929.[7] Remarkably, those early approaches involved a combi-

---

3. G. S. Moak, "Geriatric Psychiatry and Managed Care," *Psychiatric Clinics of North America* 23 (2000): 437-50.

4. E. J. Klausner and G. S. Alexopoulos, "The Future of Psychosocial Treatments for Elderly Patients," *Psychiatric Services* 50 (1999): 1198-1204.

5. M. G. Cole, L. M. Elie, J. McCusker, et al., "Feasibility and Effectiveness of Treatments for Depression in Elderly Medical Inpatients: A Systematic Review," *International Psychogeriatrics* 12 (2000): 453-61.

6. Lebowitz and Gallo, "Epidemiology of Common Late-Life Mental Disorders," pp. 1158-66.

7. T. L. Brink, "Geriatric Psychotherapy," in *Baker Encyclopedia of Psychology and Counseling*, ed. David G. Benner and Peter C. Hill (Grand Rapids: Baker, 1999).

nation of structured interviews, directive psycho-educational techniques, systematic assessment/intervention around daily routine, and social support. There is truly "nothing new under the sun" (Eccles. 1:9). These strategies and techniques are indeed consistent with the approaches considered as "best practice" in the clinician's repertoire today. When the popular psychotherapeutic approaches were more rigidly psychodynamic, behavioral, or nondirective person-centered, this population was *not* the age group of choice among clinicians, perhaps because the diverse techniques that accompany these classic therapeutic schools may not generate the response among senior clients that they do with younger, more malleable patients. Because doing psychotherapy with older clients is indeed *different* from work with other adult clients, there may be a clinician hesitancy to adjust one's therapeutic approach and style to fit the needs and issues of this population. Interestingly, one empirical study of therapist attitudes on therapy with clients over sixty-five indicated that the single best predictor of clinician willingness to engage with these clients is previous experience working with the elderly.[8] From our own perspective, we would acknowledge that the advice "try it, you'll like it" seems to apply nicely here.

The benefits of psychosocial approaches such as cognitive-behavioral, problem-solving, interpersonal, psychodynamic, and reminiscence therapy were reviewed by E. J. Klausner and G. S. Alexopoulos.[9] There was no difficulty demonstrating a robust effect for treatment over nontreatment, and there was conclusive support that psychosocial and psychopharmacological treatments combined were generally more effective than medication alone in studies with this patient population. When addressing the common problems of older clients — namely, coping with pain, disability, and loneliness — the authors concluded that combining "techniques with known therapeutic value to target problems relevant to elderly patients" holds considerable promise for health promotion and improved quality of life. Klausner and Alexopoulos offered the following conclusions based upon their literature review that touts the beneficial advantage or "virtue" of these approaches:

1. Medication interventions carry increased risks with this population due to the propensity for misuse, less tolerance for side effects, adverse interactions with other medications, and so on. Therefore, psychosocial

---

8. S. Zank, "Psychotherapy and Aging: Results of Two Empirical Studies between Psychotherapists and Elderly People," *Psychotherapy* 35 (1998): 531-36.

9. Klausner and Alexopoulos, "The Future of Psychosocial Treatments for Elderly Patients," pp. 1198-1204.

interventions need to increase. These approaches have much potential for helping elderly clients cope with the life adversity that comes with increasing age.

2. Psychotherapy may be useful when there is a specific mental health concern such as depression. It also, however, has the potential to reduce disability, help with pain management, and increase compliance with rehabilitation regimens.

3. Self-help groups and counseling can be used more frequently and routinely for bereavement counseling and to support caregivers since such groups reduce depressive symptoms, reduce medical morbidity, and facilitate adjustment following loss. The virtue of these groups is clear and the cost modest.

4. Treatment with psychosocial supports might best be delivered in an integrated way with primary care services. Patients prefer this and the resulting teamwork may help to ensure that these approaches are more reasonably accessible and utilized long-term.

The Virtues of Talk Therapy to Address Spiritual Life and Vitality

The arguments offered thus far summarize the growing perspective of those in mental health regarding the rationale for and benefits of psychotherapy for those aging patients experiencing clinical symptoms or syndromes as a result of encountering loss, declining health, and reduced social networks. But absent is consideration of attention to the spiritual dimensions of geriatric care. The writer of Ecclesiastes gives us a vivid image of the aging process:

Remember your Creator
　　in the days of your youth,
before the days of trouble come
　　and the years approach when you will say,
"I find no pleasure in them" —
before the sun and the light
　　and the moon and the stars grow dark,
　　and the clouds return after the rain;
when the keepers of the house tremble,
　　and the strong men stoop,
when the grinders cease because they are few,
　　and those looking through the windows grow dim;

> when the doors to the street are closed
>   and the sound of grinding fades;
> when men rise up at the sound of birds,
>   but all their songs grow faint;
> when men are afraid of heights
>   and of dangers in the streets;
> when the almond tree blossoms
>   and the grasshopper drags himself along
>   and desire no longer is stirred.
>
> Then man goes to his eternal home
>   and mourners go about the streets.
> Remember him — before the silver cord is severed,
>   or the golden bowl is broken;
> before the pitcher is shattered at the spring,
>   or the wheel broken at the well,
> and the dust returns to the ground it came from,
>   and the spirit returns to God who gave it.
>
>   (Eccles. 12:1-7 NIV)

Medical technology, growing from the God-given dominion over creation and human society, may postpone or restrict the inevitable end to life's journey toward death, but the purpose of the decline cannot be denied. (One wonders how this passage might have been revised if Solomon had had access to Paxill, Viagra, and other contemporary pharmaceuticals?) Each person must come to terms before the end of life with the life he or she has lived and with his or her relationship with the Creator. Contemporary health technology may mask the symptoms of the effects of sin on the body, but the end of the journey will surely come.

The root cause of the depressive/anxious symptoms in elderly clients may lie in relational struggles, unresolved (unrepented) transgressions, value conflicts, unfulfilled dreams, and related existential dilemmas. The most valuable virtue of psychosocial supports is often the opportunity to process spiritual concerns, regrets, and perspectives while one is able. These certainly can be and are addressed in private reflection, but the nature of human beings as relational creatures makes the relational context of therapy a choice setting for such a life review. There is opportunity not only for the therapeutic approaches already mentioned but also for applied logotherapy, pastoral care, and focused biblical application. It is my contention that decay in our biological domain, losses in our social networks, and notable development transitions are the divinely appointed signposts to alert human beings to assess their spiritual status along life's journey.

Human beings enjoy the autonomy that comes from being created in the image of God; yet developmental challenges are reminders of our multidimensional and multidirectional journey.[10] Developmentalist Erik Erikson noted that in later adulthood and old age individuals use introspection and later social support to fight off troublesome feelings of despair, disdain, and self-doubt. These internal and external relational processes help the individual gain wisdom and an inner confidence in herself and the meaning of life.[11] This process is defined in developmental terms but it is essentially a spiritual matter involving the need for dependence on our Creator. A virtue of psychosocial therapy is the rich relational encounter to confront and conquer, through grace, critical spiritual issues in a way that readies the individual for eternity.

Recall that when Jesus described the ultimate separation of sheep and goats in eternity (Matt. 25:31-46), he commended ministry to the homeless, helpless, and hungry. We must not overlook the fact that he purposefully included the phrase, "I was sick and you looked after me" (v. 36). This was not a mandate for physicians' house calls or administering medical procedures in the name of our Lord, although such work is consistent with other ministry tasks. The injunction here is to have a ministering conversation or a ministering presence. Apparently not all visits to the sick are about a biological intervention for the illness of the body. There are genuine benefits from human relational contact intended for the encouragement and stirring of the soul. Our Lord's words in this powerful section mirror the prophetic instruction of Isaiah, according to which true worship is not simply an orchestrated ritual or rigorous, riotous prayer; it includes acts of justice and ministry to the oppressed and downtrodden in order to "satisfy the afflicted soul" (Isa. 58:10 NKJV).

Case Vignette

Patricia, a sixty-four-year-old woman, first sought therapy at age fifty-seven with her husband, who was seventy at the time of the initial consultation. She reported intense family conflict, severe marital distress, and significant health concerns related to her life stressors. The developmental issues and the pre-

---

10. P. Wong, "Meaning of Life and Meaning of Death in Successful Aging," online at www.twu.ca/cpsy/faculty/wong./meaning/succag.htm.

senting problems were typical of late midlife and of the concerns of the "young old."

The first round of treatment lasted for about fifty sessions, with brief intermittent encounters following the intensive weekly therapy. Rather than present case details, the following verbatim will tell Patricia's story. The therapist's questions and her answers may appear to report retrospective work, relying entirely on recall; her propensity for journaling and writing letters, however, as well as the clinical record, increases the authenticity and accuracy of this review.

> Therapist: Patricia, please talk about what first brought you into counseling.
>
> Patricia: I was desperate. After years of slow improvement in family relationships, an incident at Christmastime threatened to blow the family apart. Neither my husband nor my daughter was willing to take a step toward resolving their differences. I felt I could not stand by and wait for the outcome as a disinterested bystander, because I was intimately involved and the outcome of this standoff would impact *me*. This is the crisis that drove me to seek professional counseling. What I wanted was for the counselor to fix my husband and daughter. I had a lot to learn.
>
> Therapist: What made the schism between your husband and daughter so disturbing?
>
> Patricia: I saw my dreams of an adult relationship with my children and of grandmothering evaporating. I wanted to fix my family so I could enjoy my children and grandchildren without causing a disturbance in my marriage. I was to learn that the only person I can "fix" is myself. This can be a slow and painful process and it would inevitably cause disturbances at home.
>
> Therapist: It doesn't seem like this intense friction was something entirely new.
>
> Patricia: When our children were growing up my husband controlled our family through fits of rage. We were all terrified of him. Although he hardly ever became physical, there was always that threat. For him, it seemed to work. He always got what he wanted . . . until our children were on their own. I learned that I had enabled my husband's behavior by giving in to his wishes when he raged. Often, when he would fly into a rage at some small infringement or at nothing at all, I would tell the children to go to him and say they were sorry. He would accept their apology but he never apologized for his own behavior.

Therapist: Please share more about the family crisis that moved you into counseling.

Patricia: My husband's and daughter's relationship was now broken and both seemed content to let it remain that way. In the meantime, through other events, my husband became estranged from our son, as well. My husband was putting intense pressure on me to break off my relationships with my daughter and son, having convinced himself that this would force them back to himself. I had never stood up to my husband before, but breaking off my relationship with my children was something I could not do. Had I not been in counseling at this time, I am not sure what the outcome would have been. Either I would have eventually given in to his demands or I would have left him. It was only because I had the support and encouragement of a counselor that I was able to stand up under the intense pressure and yet still stay in my marriage. I counseled weekly for almost a year before I felt strong enough to continue on with just occasional outside support. There were times when I felt like a bloodied boxer, taking time out between rounds when I saw my handler/counselor. He would "wipe me off," give me a new assignment, and send me back into the ring for another round. My assignment was usually to confront my husband on some issue, and I would almost always wait until the evening before my next counseling appointment to "do my homework." One time I was so frightened by my husband's reaction — he karate chopped a small table that was between us; it could have been my neck. Before I confronted him the next time, I packed a bag and had it in the car.

Therapist: What or who changed?

Patricia: How often had I heard in church that the only person you could change is yourself. How often had I heard and read that each person is responsible for his own behavior and attitudes, not for those of others. I had this knowledge in my head, but I had not incorporated it into my life. I badly needed an attitude check. My fear had changed to a mixture of fear and anger. As I learned to acknowledge my emotions, I began to see all the faults in my husband, but none in myself. My husband accused me of self-righteousness and I'm sure he had good reason. I had needed to clearly see the wrong in what my husband was doing and to recognize that my own feelings and thoughts had validity. But like the pendulum of a clock, I did not stop at the midpoint, but swung in the other direction.

Therapist: Do you recall a turning point?

Patricia: I decided I would get a divorce. At our meeting, I told my counselor of my decision and spent the hour enumerating all of the injustices in my marriage and rationalizing why I should get a divorce. He listened without saying a word. The next time we met, the counselor talked and I listened. That put an end to my divorce plans. Escape was not the answer. When I married I made a vow before God. Divorce was not an option just because I was experiencing pain in my marriage. This was a turning point in my counseling. With divorce not an option, the only reasonable thing to do was work to make life in my present situation not just tolerable, but fruitful and honoring to God. I came to grips with the likelihood that my husband might never change. If my life were to improve, I was the one who had to change.

Therapist: Patricia, it sounds like you really had to work on yourself.

Patricia: With support, I had learned to stand up in defense of what I believed was right. Some fear was still there. It dies slowly. I was able to overcome it when I was sure of my motives. I had to learn to speak the truth in love. When I was paralyzed by fear, it was hard for me to speak the truth at all. When I did begin to speak up, I usually spoke in anger. In those early days of change, I had to feel very angry in order to be able to tell my husband how I felt. I had to learn how to harness the energy of the anger and use it for good. Slowly, with coaching, I learned how to introduce a subject in such a way that it was received as being spoken in love. It took longer for feelings of love to return.

Therapist: I recall that your health was in jeopardy shortly after the Christmas crisis.

Patricia: When I first sought counseling, I was experiencing frequent, debilitating headaches, chronic jaw pain (TMJ), irritable bowel syndrome, and exhaustion. Looking back from my present vantage point, I can see pain as an ally. The pain from the TMJ was not constant, but rather was triggered by stress. To this day, my first indication that something is building up tension inside me is often the pain caused by a tightening of the jaw muscles. I have learned, when I notice this tightening, to analyze what is causing it. Very often, just identifying the cause of the stress and thinking about it is all that is necessary to bring relaxation. Other times, I realize that there is something I am holding inside that I need to discuss with my husband. Since I have learned how to discuss sensitive issues in a way that does not cause my husband to become defensive, I have become more confident. Our marriage continues to improve as we both practice open communication.

Therapist: What did you do about those headaches and the other health issues?

Patricia: The headaches that had been plaguing me when I first entered counseling decreased in frequency over the first year. I can say now that I probably experience fewer headaches than most people. The exhaustion lasted longer and it is hard to differentiate the exhaustion due to rheumatoid arthritis from that due to depression. I have chosen not to take medication for depression, desiring rather to get to the root of the problem. My desire always has been to grow spiritually. When the pain is deadened by medication it is too easy to avoid growth. Just as physical pain protects us, emotional pain, too, warns us that something is wrong. As long as the pain is there we are motivated to do something about it. The irritable bowel syndrome continues but is under control. It is very likely related to medications I am on for rheumatoid arthritis. There are some things that we simply have to live with.

Therapist: How has your faith and your involvement in a local church helped you?

Patricia: There was a time when I so much wanted to escape the pain and the struggle that I just wanted out of my marriage. It was at that time that my commitment to God's people held me firm. I knew that many people in our church looked to my husband and me as role models. If I were to leave my marriage it would impact many lives negatively. God knew what was going on inside me but he did not put me on the shelf. I have experienced his mercy and grace through times when I struggled to understand what he wanted me to do. I have especially struggled with the area of submission. When my husband wanted me to break off my relationship with my children, I knew in my gut this was wrong. Being passive by nature, it was very difficult for me to justify doing what I felt was right *because* it was what I wanted to do. I am still learning to listen to the still, small voice within me and not allow myself to be steamrollered by others with stronger personalities.

Therapist: Tell us more about your spiritual journey.

Patricia: During these years the Lord taught me a lot about mercy, compassion, and forgiveness. In the early stages of counseling, when I began to be able to acknowledge my anger with my husband, I often prayed to God to execute justice. But as soon as I prayed that prayer, it hit me that I don't want justice. I want mercy. And I found myself praying to God to be merciful to my husband. Similarly, when I stopped focusing on my husband's faults and recognized that I, too, am a sinner whom God has forgiven, I began to feel compassion for him. Compassion for a sinner can lead to only one thing . . . forgiveness. But I had to admit my anger before I could experience the steps that led to forgiveness. Perhaps because I had already worked through this process, in the past two years when the things my children said and did caused me so much pain, I found myself praying from the start for God to be merciful to them. Many times I have prayed, "Father, forgive them. They don't know what they are doing."

God has once again demonstrated his great mercy to me. He has entrusted me with ministries to women that have potential to positively impact lives spiritually. In the midst of much emotional pain, I was given others to care for. God was reminding me that my struggles have a greater purpose. They are designed not only to produce spiritual growth in me; God wants me to use my life experiences and the story of his provision to bring comfort and hope to others. He continues to open doors, and with his help I am walking through them to a life of purpose and meaning.

Therapist: How would you summarize where you are at today?

Patricia: Today, although relationships in our family remain broken, I have a peace that only God can give. My marriage is much improved through open, honest communication. I have learned to listen to my body when it signals me that something is wrong, and more and more I am recognizing problems without the help of TMJ. I have fulfilling ministries that help me to take my eyes off myself and care for others. Most important, my faith has withstood the test, and the trials have brought about spiritual growth. I know that I am right in the center of God's will.

Guidance for Talk Therapy

Guided by a commitment to treat the whole person created in the image of God, these principles inform and focus the application of clinical techniques when serving seniors:

1. *Identify and pursue wisdom.* The prime adaptive-ego quality at this life stage is wisdom, meaning that accumulated skills for living are used to facilitate further coping and growth. Working with seniors, it is reward-

ing to help identify and unpack the wisdom contained in their stories and experience. Not only do the skills and strategies growing from these life lessons guide the approaches to current challenges, but the review conducted in relationship provides a motivational benefit.

2. *Be confident and build confidence.* Working with older clients may activate a detrimental counter-transference that can reduce the confidence of the clinician. This is particularly problematic as the senior seeking therapy is often worn down by life and adversity, and thus acutely in need of an external source of confidence. Whereas many adult clients thrive when a therapist takes a one-down approach, the dynamics of working with clients who are frail or failing requires a firm, energetic, and expert leadership to supplement and rebuild waning client self-confidence.

3. *Assess and address marital conflict.* The longevity of a marriage does not guarantee its quality or even a reasonable level of satisfaction. The divorce rate among seniors is growing. Although one partner may rebound well, the other often suffers terribly. The intimacy and support pressures are intense in today's senior marriages. The strategies that have worked to stabilize the relationship during earlier stages may not be as adaptive in later years. Late-life marriage therapy may be a fruitful area to address health and quality of life concerns. The vow "for better or worse, in sickness and in health . . ." may take on new meaning, and outside intervention may be useful.

4. *Family support is not a given.* The permeable nature of today's families can greatly affect the support system available to seniors. Long-distance family relationships may be loving and vital, but the lack of proximity and frequency of contact may limit the type of support that can be provided. Estrangements, blended systems, and nontraditional arrangements tend to be negative factors in senior support networks.

5. *Confront directly, reasonably soon, and respectfully.* "Speaking the truth in love" (Eph. 4:15 NKJV) may not be easy at any age. In the case of the aged, however, the truth needs to be communicated in a way that honors the status of the elderly person (Lev. 19:32). Letting critical issues wait until the nebulous "someday," however, is a problem with an aging population, as delay usually only protects the speaker and hinders the senior. Get to the hard things honestly, kindly, and candidly.

6. *Medications provide wonderful tools to heal and manage pain.* The message here is not to avoid psychopharmacological advances, but not to allow them to substitute for or subvert psychosocial approaches either. By all means, use these resources to minimize and manage pain. Use pain,

however — whether physical, psychological, existential, or spiritual — to help address, and by grace resolve, critical matters for life and eternity.

7. *Capture and create ministry opportunities.* Nothing is as devastating to the elderly as the sense of a useless and empty life. Even with limitations, the opportunity to model values and minister to others is available. Clinicians aid in the application of 2 Corinthians 1:3-4, which teaches how God comforts us so that we can give comfort to others. Here imaginative and inspirational pastoral care is clinically therapeutic.

Palliative Care:
Suffering and Healing at the End of Life

JACKIE CAMERON, M.D.

In the twenty-third psalm, the psalmist speaks of dying as a journey through the valley of the shadow of death. The images evoked in this psalm are rich, and contain elements of both comfort and danger. In fact, the presence of a shadow implies that this valley through which we will all travel contains both darkness and light. These are apt metaphors to keep in mind as we consider the difficult task of dying.

This chapter focuses on the ideals, goals, and practice of palliative care. Before we begin, we need to examine some of our personal and cultural attitudes toward dying, death, and suffering. Since relief of suffering is the primary goal of palliative care, I will also provide some definitions of suffering and examples of how suffering manifests itself in the lives of patients and of those who care for them.

I will then attempt to define "palliative care" and "hospice" — and this is no easy task, as there is considerable disagreement and confusion over the distinction between these terms. I will then address specific issues such as pain management (and barriers that impede good pain management), as well as emotional, relational, and spiritual distress. I will conclude with practical suggestions for patients, families, and health-care, psychological, and pastoral professionals.

The Problem of Dying

Before we proceed, I would like to make a confession. My confession is this: I hate death. By death I mean not merely the stark fact that our lives will someday end, but also the struggles and losses that accompany the process of decline and death. This may sound rather strange coming from a palliative care and hospice physician (and a Christian one at that), but let me explain further.

I first began thinking about this after telling one of our oncologists that I had just been to a hospice conference. "A *hospice* conference?" he said. "Oh, *that* sounds like fun — hanging around with a bunch of people who like death!" From his tone of voice, it was clear that he regarded our activities to be somewhat less abhorrent than, for example, cannibalism, but that in his opinion, they definitely fell on the bizarre end of the human behavioral spectrum.

So I did what any red-blooded professional who had just been insulted by an insensitive colleague would do: I got defensive . . . after he left. "We do *not* like death," I silently fumed. "*I* don't like death. In fact, I hate death. I hate the pain. I hate the grief. I hate the fear, the anxiety, and the loneliness that dying people and their loved ones must often struggle with." In short, what I hate most is the suffering that frequently accompanies the dying process — and which, unfortunately, is frequently ignored or forgotten not only by medical professionals but also by much of society, and, sometimes, by the church.

But I also believe that death *itself* is inherently bad and must be seen as such if we are to avoid an overly simplistic or glib approach to caring for those who are coming to the end of their lives. I believe this is an essential fact for all of us to face as we seek to care for those who are dying (and as we contemplate the finitude of our own lives).

"But," you may be thinking, "death is natural. It's inevitable. It leads to something better, and good can even come from it." These statements are all true, but they do not mean that death is inherently good or that the dying process is — or should be expected to be — easy. Let us consider them individually.

First, death *is* natural. This is obviously true. There is currently a tendency, however, to equate *natural* with *good*. We have natural vitamins, natural dishwasher soap, and natural pesticides (with which we kill natural insects) — and the list goes on. In the world of marketing, *natural is good* (and it sells). But natural is not necessarily good. After all, anthrax is natural. HIV is natural. Pain is natural. While some natural materials or processes can be good, they can also be very bad.

A second observation is that death is *inevitable* and that we should accept this as an inescapable fact of human existence. This statement is also true. Death *is* inevitable, and it is only wise (and healthy) to accept the fact that our lives — as we now know them — will end. Acceptance of death's reality, however, does not mean that death is inherently good, or that it is merely a minor annoyance along the journey to something better. Acceptance should never lead us to remain oblivious to another's suffering, nor should we assume that a cognitive acceptance of death's inevitability should — in and of itself — lessen suffering.

A third common observation — particularly among Christians — is that death *leads to something better.* After all, St. Paul claimed that "to live is Christ but to die is gain" and he longed "to be absent from the body but present with the Lord" (Phil. 1:21-23). As Christians we trust that God's love for us endures beyond this life, and that God demonstrated this love most clearly through the life, death, and resurrection of Jesus Christ. Clearly, then, death is an evil through which good *can* be birthed. But when the topic of death and dying comes up, we are sometimes too quick to speak of resurrection or to assert that death is merely the gateway to eternal life. We sometimes jump immediately to our future hope without being willing to face the difficult realities of the present.

We should remember that even from a Christian perspective, death is inherently bad. Death results in the loss of something valuable and irretrievable. Through the creation narratives and through the incarnation, we understand that God delights not only in human life but in the earth and *all* of its inhabitants. It follows, then, that if God delights in his creation, so should we. In John's Gospel, Jesus said, "I came that they would have life, and have it more abundantly" (John 10:10), and I do not believe that he was speaking only about the life to come. All of this points to the fact that life on earth is valuable and that our lives *here and now* are a gift to be relished and to be offered back to God. Death brings an end to this unique part of our existence, and that ending is a very real loss — a loss that should be mourned. A lack of willingness to face this devalues the present.

Facing the Darkness

Why is this so important to remember? Why is it important to take a long and unflinching look straight into the depths of human suffering and perhaps into our own darkest fears? I believe that if we do not, we risk ignoring or minimizing the profound suffering of those around us and among us — those for whom we are called to care. We risk a lack of sensitivity. We risk inaction.

The questions we must then ask are these: What type of action should we undertake? Toward what ends should these actions be directed? These are questions that palliative care seeks to address.

Death and Medical Culture

How, then, should we respond to death's insistent and inevitable presence in our lives? The answers to this question will spring from our faith, our experiences, our relationships, values, hopes, dreams, and fears. My purpose here is to focus on how this question is addressed in the context of health care. Much of modern medicine seems to be focused primarily on death prevention while ignoring the plainly obvious fact that every single patient (and every single doctor and every single nurse and every single researcher) will eventually die. Death is often viewed as an enemy to be battled with all of our most powerful weapons for as long as possible. In one *New Yorker* cartoon, a senior physician and a medical student are standing at the bedside of a patient who has just died. The physician turns to the student and says, "Shows you how much *I* know." In our technology-saturated medical culture, death is frequently seen as a failure. Unfortunately, the patient's values, wishes, and quality of life can get lost completely in the struggle to keep him alive for as long as possible. We find ourselves once again in the midst of paradox: we should not treat death and dying as insignificant, but neither should we struggle so violently against the inevitable that we fail to see when ameliorating suffering — not avoiding death — may become our most important task.

Palliative Care

Death is bad, loss is real, and dying is difficult. That is the bad news. But there is also good news. Where there is suffering, there is also an opportunity for healing. There is much that can be done to help decrease the suffering of dying people and the suffering of those who love them. This is where good palliative care can make a powerful difference. But what is palliative care? How does it relate to hospice?

The World Health Organization defines palliative care as

> The active total care of patients whose disease is not responsive to curative treatment. Control of pain, of other symptoms, and of psychological, social and spiritual problems, is paramount. The goal of palliative care is achievement of the best quality of life for patients and their families. . . . Palliative care . . . affirms life and regards dying as a normal process . . . neither hastens nor postpones death . . . integrates the psychological and the spiritual aspects of care . . . offers a support system to help patients live as actively as possible until death . . . offers a support

system to help the family cope during the patient's illness and in their own bereavement.[1]

As we can see from this rather lengthy definition, the focus of palliative care is quite broad. All aspects of the patient's life are important, and the needs of the family are also addressed.

What, then, is hospice? In the United States, hospice is palliative care focused specifically on patients who have an estimated life span of six months or less, and who have declined further treatment aimed primarily at prolonging life. Patients who meet these criteria are eligible for the Medicare hospice benefit. The six-month rule can be problematic since doctors are not very good at predicting how long someone is likely to live, and are often reluctant to do so even when they do have a fairly accurate estimate of survival.[2] In the United States, hospice care is usually provided in the home, although many nursing homes now work together with hospices in an effort to provide more comprehensive care for their dying residents.

As mentioned earlier, there is considerable confusion about the distinction between palliative care and hospice. In general, palliative care is a broader concept, and its goals are applicable in a wide variety of situations. The WHO definitions are very helpful, but focus exclusively on dying patients. I would argue that *any* intervention that aims to relieve suffering — whether the patient is dying or is expected to recover — is palliative care.

In general, palliation, or relief of symptoms and maximizing quality of life, is an important part of everyday medical practice. It is a very broad concept, but many health-care practitioners equate palliative care with hospice. Unfortunately, some also believe that hospice means "giving up" on their patient (or family member), and subsequently feel that if patients are not imminently dying, they do not need palliative care. I believe this is a mistake.

Let's look more closely at some of these barriers to palliative care. While some of the attitudinal barriers originate in patients or family members, many medical professionals have a very poor understanding of the importance of palliative or comfort-oriented interventions — interventions that

1. *Cancer Pain Relief and Palliative Care*, Technical Report Series 804 (Geneva: World Health Organization, 1990).

2. N. Christakis, "Timing of Referral of Terminally Ill Patients to an Outpatient Hospice," *Journal of General Internal Medicine* 9 (1994): 314-20; J. Hofmann, N. Wenger, R. Davis, et al., for the SUPPORT Investigators, "Patient Preferences for Communication with Physicians about End-of-life Decisions," *Annals of Internal Medicine* 127 (1997): 1-12; J. Tulsky, G. Fischer, M. Rose, and R. Arnold, "Opening the Black Box: How Do Physicians Communicate about Advance Directives?" *Annals of Internal Medicine* 129 (1998): 441-49.

can and should be implemented *while* patients are still receiving intensive, life-prolonging therapies.

For example, the palliative care team was consulted to see Ms. A, a seventy-five-year-old woman with lung cancer who was receiving chemotherapy but who was also experiencing pain, confusion, and severe anxiety. As it turned out, we had been consulted by a physician who was covering for her usual oncologist (cancer doctor). When we arrived to see her later in the day, her original doctor had returned and was surprised (and not at all pleased) to see us. "Who consulted you?!" he demanded. "Well, it must have been Dr. X, because it certainly wasn't me! I am treating her aggressively. That's what she wanted. She's getting chemo. Eventually, she will need you guys, but not yet." He paused and then continued, "You can go ahead and see her if you want, but remember, I am being aggressive."

Unfortunately, the perception that chemotherapy or other treatments designed to combat disease and prolong life are aggressive, courageous, and worthwhile, whereas pain and symptom management are passive, cowardly, or of minimal importance is widespread. Palliative care and hospice are, as I have noted, sometimes viewed as "giving up." This is simply not true. Aggressive chemotherapy *must* be accompanied by aggressive pain and symptom management *and* careful psychosocial and spiritual support. Studies have shown that patients who are physically comfortable and whose emotional and spiritual needs are addressed have a better quality of life, are more satisfied with their care, and are more likely to be able to cooperate with other therapies.[3]

Exploring Suffering

Palliative care focuses on the relief of suffering. As noted above, suffering is a complex interaction of physical, psychological, social, and spiritual pain and

3. J. Holland et al., NCCN, *Oncology* 13 (1999): 459-50; T. Oxman et al., "Lack of Social Participation or Religious Strength and Comfort As Risk Factors for Death After Cardiac Surgery in the Elderly," *Psychosomatic Medicine* 57 (1995): 5-15; G. Fitchett, B. Rybarczyk, and G. DeMarco, "The Role of Religion in Medical Rehabilitation Outcomes: A Longitudinal Study," *Rehabilitation Psychology* 44 (1999): 333-53; H. Koenig, K. Pargament, J. Nielsen, "Religious Coping and Health Status in Medically Ill Hospitalized Older Adults," *The Journal of Nervous and Mental Disease* 186 (1998): 513-21; J. Holland et al., "The Role of Religious and Spiritual Beliefs in Coping with Malignant Melanoma," *Psycho-oncology* 8 (1999): 14-26; International Association for the Study of Pain, "Classification of Chronic Pain," *Pain* 3, supplement (1986): 51-226.

loss that severely and adversely affects the lives of patients and families. Financial problems and moral dilemmas may also contribute to suffering, which is sometimes referred to as "total pain," meaning that it encompasses all aspects of one's life. One of the most widely cited authors to write about suffering is Eric Cassell. Cassell maintains that suffering occurs when one's integrity or intrinsic unity as a person is threatened and a sense of disintegration and fragmentation takes over.[4]

This integrity can be threatened in a variety of ways. For example, serious illness can cause changes in physical appearance like weight gain, weight loss, or hair loss. Complex abilities such as driving, or more basic abilities such as walking or eating, may be lost. Relationships and roles change. It is not uncommon for those who saw themselves as the provider of care to be very distressed by the realization that they are now primarily the *recipient* of care. Memory and thinking may be impaired. Events or people from the past may be forgotten, and the future that once seemed promising may suddenly seem alarmingly short.

One of our recent patients, Ms. N., was an eighty-eight-year-old woman with advanced cancer whose disease had spread to her bones and lungs. She had been living independently, but, as a result of pain, weakness, and shortness of breath, she could no longer care for herself as she once had. She had many friends, but several had died recently, and her husband had died twenty years earlier. As she struggled to come to terms with her own illness and impending death, she said, "I can't *believe* I'm dying. I mean, I knew I was sick, but I always thought I'd get better. Some of my friends have died, but I guess I never really thought that would happen to me. I don't know what I was thinking." Later, she also said, "I was always the one who helped other people to be positive and hopeful, and now I can't even do that for myself." Her physical pain was quite intense, but her sadness, fear, spiritual unease, and changing relationships also contributed to her suffering. Pain medications helped but were not enough. All members of the palliative care team — the social worker, volunteers, nurses, chaplains, and physicians — worked together to listen, ask questions, and provide care and support.

Even things that appear to be relatively insignificant can contribute to suffering. One seventy-two-year-old writer who was dying of lung cancer repeatedly told us, "I am a person who gets up every morning, drinks a cup of coffee, and reads the *New York Times*. Now I don't have any taste for coffee and I don't have any interest in reading the paper. This is not *me!*" Though she suf-

4. Eric Cassell, "The Nature of Suffering and the Goals of Medicine," *The New England Journal of Medicine* 306 (1982): 639-45.

fered from depression, nondepressed individuals commonly experience a similar sense of loss when daily routines become disrupted. The loss of the familiar can be a source of intense suffering, and should never be disregarded.

If suffering results from loss and a sense of fragmentation, then healing — in the sense of restoring at least some measure of wholeness — is needed. It is for this reason that palliative care seeks a comprehensive and integrating approach.

Specific Issues for Special Attention

Though palliative care seeks a broad vision of human healing, some issues deserve special attention. The first is (physical) pain. I will also briefly address anxiety and depression, forgiveness and closure in relationships, and spiritual concerns commonly encountered in dying patients. It is only by remaining aware of the importance of all of these factors that we can help patients to begin to recover at least some sense of wholeness.

Pain

The International Association for the Study of Pain (IASP) defines pain as "an unpleasant sensory and emotional experience associated with actual or potential tissue injury or described in terms of such damage."[5] (This means that people often describe their pain as "gnawing," "pressing," "stretching," "burning," "crushing," and so on.) Another definition states it more simply: "pain is whatever the experiencing person says it is, existing whenever he/she says it does."[6]

Note that pain is a sensory *and* emotional experience. Even when we try to focus on what we think is a purely physical problem, we discover that it, too, is much more complex than we might have expected. Another important question to ask is what does this pain *mean* to the person experiencing it? It may mean the disease is getting worse. It may mean that it will be more difficult to get out of bed or out of the house, making the person more dependent and, possibly, socially isolated. It may mean a loss of dignity.

Pain may increase anxiety and depression. It may cause sleep distur-

5. International Association for the Study of Pain, "Classification of Chronic Pain," *Pain* 3, supplement (1986): 51-226.
6. International Association for the Study of Pain, "Classification of Chronic Pain."

bances, loss of appetite, and fatigue. Decreased activity and altered posture may place the patient at increased risk for pressure sores (bedsores), muscle pain, blood clots, and lung problems. Relationships become strained. Sometimes pain becomes so severe that some people consider suicide. Finally, there is reason to believe that unrelieved pain may even shorten overall survival.

"Well," you may be thinking, "this is thoroughly depressing!" But please know that there *is* good news. Pain *can* be treated. The vast majority of persons who have acute pain or cancer-related pain are able to experience significant relief when the proper combinations of medication and other therapies are used. Chronic pain not caused by cancer is more challenging to treat. It almost always requires a combination of medications, psychological support, physical therapy, and other interventions. Sometimes massage or acupuncture also help. With appropriate interventions, most people are able to experience enough pain relief that their quality of life improves significantly — even if pain is not eradicated completely.

Unfortunately, despite the devastating impact of pain on human lives and despite our increasing ability to provide significant relief, far too many people continue to suffer from unrelieved pain. In one study of nearly two thousand oncologists, 86 percent agreed that cancer pain was under-treated, but only 51 percent felt that patients in *their* care had under-treated pain.[7] Another study found that in a group of patients with advanced cancer, even though two thirds had pain medications prescribed, 42 percent felt that the medication was inadequate and 36 percent felt that pain prevented them from engaging in daily activities.[8]

Pain is also very common in elderly people who do not have cancer. It has been estimated that 45 to 80 percent of nursing home residents and 25 to 50 percent of elderly persons living at home experience pain that is inadequately treated.[9] This is a serious problem, particularly as we have already seen pain's devastating effects on human lives.

What are some of the barriers to pain management? Why is this problem so widespread? The answers are as complex as the problem itself. Patients and their families, physicians and nurses, institutions and even state and federal regulatory agencies may all impede the proper assessment and treatment of pain.[10]

7. International Association for the Study of Pain, "Classification of Chronic Pain."

8. International Association for the Study of Pain, "Classification of Chronic Pain."

9. AGS Panel on Chronic Pain in Older Persons, Clinical Practice Guidelines, "The Management of Chronic Pain in Older Persons," *Journal of the American Geriatrics Society* 46 (1998): 635-51.

10. J. Von Roenn et al., "Physicians' Attitudes and Practice in Cancer Pain Manage-

Patients are often reluctant to tell their physicians or nurses that they have pain. Some fear that doing so might "distract" the doctor from fighting the disease (especially in cancer). Some worry that if they talk about their pain, they might be viewed as a "complainer" or a bad patient. Others believe that nothing can be done about pain and that they must therefore suffer in silence. Some patients have lost their ability to communicate their pain (such as those with dementia or who have had a severe stroke).

The burden then falls on the health-care professional. Doctors and nurses must ask patients about pain — and then *listen to* and *believe* what patients tell them. We must take pain seriously and let our patients know that pain management is an important part of their total care.[11]

When pain is severe enough to warrant the use of opioids (that is, morphine and morphine-like medications), many more problems arise.[12] Fear of addiction is very common among patients and physicians.[13] If patients have severe pain, however, they need strong pain medicine. If they have continuous pain, then they need continuous pain treatment. We use similar approaches when prescribing insulin regimens for persons with diabetes — yet we do not accuse diabetics of being insulin addicts.

We live in a nation obsessed with avoiding dependence. I commonly hear people proudly proclaim that they have "gone off" sugar or salt or caffeine or chocolate. As a firm believer in moderation, my first response is to wonder (usually silently), "Now why would you go and do a thing like that?!" If I am feeling especially perverse, I'll mention that I know that I am dependent on caffeine because when I do not get it first thing in the morning, I will develop a splitting headache by ten or eleven o'clock. More than one person has responded with a slightly scandalized, "so what are you going to do about that?" to which I reply, "make sure I get coffee!"

ment: A Survey from the Eastern Cooperative Oncology Group, *Annals of Internal Medicine* 119 (1993): 121-26; C. Cleeland, "Barriers to the Management of Cancer Pain," *Oncology* 2, supplement (1987): 19-26.

11. K. Foley, "Pain Assessment and Cancer Pain Syndromes," in *Oxford Textbook of Palliative Medicine*, ed. D. Doyle, G. Hanks, and N. MacDonald, second ed. (Oxford: Oxford University Press, 1998), pp. 310-31.

12. N. Cherny and R. Catane, "Professional Negligence in the Management of Cancer Pain," *Cancer* 76 (1995): 2181-84; S. Ward et al., "Patient-Related Barriers to Management of Cancer Pain," *Pain* 52 (1993): 319-24; T. Elliott et al., "Physician Knowledge and Attitudes about Cancer Pain Management: A Survey from the Minnesota Cancer Pain Project," *Journal of Pain and Symptom Management* 10 (1995): 494-504; M. Zenz and A. Willweber-Strumpf, "Opiophobia and Cancer Pain in Europe," *Lancet* 341 (1993): 1075-76.

13. J. Paice, C. Toy, and S. Shott, "Barriers to Cancer Pain Relief: Fear of Tolerance and Addiction," *Journal of Pain and Symptom Management* 16 (1998): 1-9.

My headache is a manifestation of physical (physiological) dependence. Steroids, morphine, anti-anxiety medications, and some blood pressure–lowering medicines can all produce a physiological dependence. For practical purposes, this means that they should not be stopped abruptly or a withdrawal reaction will occur. Such medications must be reduced gradually before stopping. Dependence (in this sense) is a physiological phenomenon, *not* a moral one.

Addiction is entirely different. Addiction is defined as (1) taking a substance you do not need or in quantities that are neither warranted nor safe; (2) continuing to take/use the substance despite *harm* to yourself and others; (3) engaging in harmful and immoral or illegal *behaviors* such as lying, stealing, forging prescriptions, etc., in order to maintain the habit.[14]

Opioid addiction is very uncommon in cancer patients with pain.[15] In addition, a recent study has found that although prescriptions for morphine-like pain medications (opioid analgesics) have increased dramatically, the rates of opioid abuse have not increased proportionately, and the abuse of some medications seems to have decreased.[16]

Even though the risk of addiction is low (particularly for patients with terminal cancer), some risk of abuse does exist. This does *not* mean we should not use these medications, however. It *does* mean that we must pay close attention to our patients' histories and daily lives. We should not be afraid to ask how things are going at work and at home, since pain affects and is affected by every aspect of one's life.

Another barrier to pain management is the fear that high doses of opioids might hasten death. This fear is particularly prevalent among medical professionals, but has found its way into ethical discourse as well as recent legislation. I will not go into detail, but scientific evidence and clinical experience clearly demonstrate that these medications are very safe when used properly. Unfortunately, until very recently, medical schools and residency programs have not emphasized the importance of learning how to manage pain — and some have not taught it at all. Misunderstanding, fear, and lack of experience have combined to produce generations of physicians who not only do a poor job of managing pain, but who are also incapable of advocating for patients by encouraging more enlightened legislation and regulatory oversight.

14. G. Hanks and N. Cherny, "Opioid Analgesic Therapy," in *Oxford Textbook of Palliative Medicine*, ed. D. Doyle, G. Hanks, and N. MacDonald, pp. 331-55.

15. R. Kanner and K. Foley, "Patterns of Narcotic Drug Use in a Cancer Pain Clinic," *Annals of the New York Academy of Science* 362 (1981): 161-72.

16. D. Joranson et al., "Trends in Medical Use and Abuse of Opioid Analgesics," *Journal of the American Medical Association* 283 (2000): 1710-14.

Fortunately, this is beginning to change. The hospice and palliative care movement has helped to raise awareness about inadequate pain management. The American Geriatrics Society has produced guidelines on managing pain in the elderly. Just over a year ago, the state of Illinois simplified revised documentation requirements in an effort to make opioid medications more accessible for patients. In January 2001, the Joint Commission on Accreditation of Health Care Organizations (the organization that inspects and certifies most hospitals and nursing homes in the United States) required all accredited institutions to assess pain and to provide appropriate interventions for pain relief for *all* patients. Change is occurring.

Other Sources of Physical and Emotional Distress

Emotional and psychological distress are also very common in patients nearing the end of their lives. In our recent survey of hospitalized cancer patients, I and my colleagues found that 44 percent felt distressed by pain, 41 percent by fatigue, and 37 percent by worry. Nearly a third felt nervous and 24 percent felt depressed.[17] It is important to remember that these symptoms do not occur in isolation. Physical symptoms can increase emotional distress and vice versa.

One day during morning hospital rounds, we asked an elderly patient with congestive heart failure whether or not he had felt short of breath overnight. His response was sobering. "You always ask me if I am short of breath. I never really knew what that meant, but now I know. Last night, I felt so short of breath that I was afraid I would die. Then it got worse, and I was afraid that I would *not* die." Not surprisingly, his fear and anxiety increased as his breathing difficulties increased, and the combination made him long for a more rapid death. Fortunately, medications and breathing treatments decreased his shortness of breath, and his fear and anxiety decreased as well. His suffering had a very profound, if brief, impact on his hopes and goals for the immediate future. Though this patient did not have to make any important decisions while in great distress, it is easy to see how unrelieved suffering might significantly impact decision-making. This, I believe, underscores the importance of aggressive palliative care.

17. J. Cameron, J. Paice, and T. Buchanan, "Spiritual and Psychosocial Distress in Oncology Inpatients," *The Journal of Palliative Medicine* 4 (2001): p. 261. Presented at the American Academy of Hospice and Palliative Medicine, Phoenix, Arizona, June 22, 2001.

Relationships

Tensions and changes in relationships can increase and can be increased by physical and emotional distress. Many of our dying patients struggle with feelings of isolation and loneliness. They may feel abandoned as family, friends, and even physicians feel uneasy in their presence and visit less frequently or stay away altogether. Some even feel abandoned by God.

As I mentioned earlier, role reversals and changes can also contribute to suffering. Many of us are more comfortable when we are giving than when we are receiving. Mothers and fathers, pastors and nurses, doctors, teachers, and others whose lives revolve largely around caring for others may have their sense of identity and worth seriously undermined as they lose their ability to function in these roles, and become the recipients rather than the providers of care.

Our social workers and chaplains spend a considerable amount of time trying to help patients discover new ways in which they can give to their families and find value and meaning in their rapidly changing lives.

Spiritual Distress

In recent years, there has been an upsurge of interest in the relationship between spirituality, religion, and health. Much of the research in this area has attempted to demonstrate that religious beliefs and practices may have beneficial effects on physical and emotional health and may be manifested by lowered blood pressure, decreased likelihood of depression, decreased mortality, or better quality of life.

While it seems obvious that spiritual well-being is an important part of total health, spiritual dis-ease or distress can definitely increase suffering. I have seen many patients who feel that they have been betrayed by God: "What did I do to deserve this? I have been faithful. I trusted God to protect me and look what happened!" Job was not the only one to harbor such thoughts. Theological musings about the meaning and purpose of suffering are rich and often illuminating, but may not prove terribly helpful in the midst of a pastoral crisis. (Patients may, however, get to the point where they *are* ready to undertake this type of reflection, and it can be very healing.)

Often, people simply need permission to express such thoughts without the threat of judgment or condemnation. They need to know that such feelings are normal, and that this represents another area in their life that needs healing — healing which may or may not occur on this side of death. In the novel *Naked Before God: The Return of a Broken Disciple,* Jesus' disciple Nathaniel has a terminal lung disease and struggles with feelings of anger and bitterness as his health deteriorates and death nears even as he watches Jesus heal strangers. Nathaniel constantly worries that his questioning and rage make him an unworthy candidate for God's healing love — on earth and in heaven. Jesus is aware of Nathaniel's concerns and repeatedly insists that Nathaniel's doubts are not sins that make him unworthy, but wounds that require healing. Jesus then reminds Nathaniel that heaven is not a reward for those who have already attained perfection, but is instead "the place where your healing will be complete."[18]

Recently, a friend told me of a colleague who had just died of cancer. Our friend said that this gentleman was amazing in that he never seemed to be afraid and his faith remained strong and unwavering. This is a powerful and inspiring testimony, and many people face death with remarkable courage and trust. But not everyone is able to do this. Even persons with strong faith may find themselves anxious and confused by the turns their lives take. When faced with uncertainty and change, particularly when confronted with the possibility of imminent death, most of us become uneasy. Fear is a normal part of human life.

Christian faith is not a vaccination against fear. It is a commitment to persevering in a relationship with God that is sometimes joyful and comforting yet at other times baffling. At times we have a strong sense of God's presence, and at others there is a maddening silence.

A recent issue of *Christianity Today* included a passage by Gardner Taylor that reflects the experience of many dying people (and of most of us, I think): "There are days when we can bring before God a deep and glad laughter of joy and gratitude. There will be other days when we can only muster a bitter, angry complaint. If it is honest, be confident that God will accept whatever it is we truly have to lift up before him, and he will make it serve his purpose and our good."[19] These are truly words of comfort that may bring healing to another's parched and aching soul.

18. B. Williams, *Naked Before God: The Return of a Broken Disciple* (Harrisburg, Pa.: Morehouse, 1998), p. 20.

19. G. Taylor, *Christianity Today,* 5 February 2000, p. 70.

Practical Suggestions

For Patients and Families

Communicate with health-care professionals:

- Tell them about pain and other symptoms.
- Tell them about feelings of depression and worry; ask for recommendations or referrals to appropriate professionals.
- If your faith is important to you and impacts your medical decision-making, tell them that too.
- If they are not willing to listen, find someone else.
- Ask about palliative care and hospice (and prognosis) — they may not bring it up.
- Learn to receive with gratitude; it may be more blessed to give than to receive, but it is certainly *not* blessed to be incapable of receiving.
- Seek and grant forgiveness.

Communicate with those you love:

- Discuss your hopes and values with your loved ones.
- Begin (or continue) to have the difficult conversations about what you would or would not want in the event that you become unable to make your own decisions.
- Designate a health-care power of attorney and review your wishes regularly.

For Health-Care, Psychological, and Pastoral Professionals

- We should ask and listen. If we ask about pain, sadness, worry, relationships, or spiritual concerns, it lets patients know that we think these are important too. I like to think of this as respectful curiosity. They may tell you to back off, but you may also open a door and allow them to express their pain.
- We must ask ourselves whether our need to "fix" the people in our care renders us unable to see or hear what they really need. We need to try to remain aware of *whose* needs we are really addressing. For example, in palliative care, we commonly encourage patients to openly discuss their concerns about dying with us and with their family or friends. Some-

times we may push a little too hard in an effort to get patients to express understanding of their prognoses to a degree where we feel confident that they are not "in denial." Whose needs are taking precedence?

Conclusion

Dying can be a time of courage, generosity, forgiveness, reflection, and hope. But unrelieved suffering can be a major impediment. Palliative care makes the relief of suffering a high priority — as much a priority as shrinking tumors or fighting infection — and strives to maintain a broad vision of human health and healing.

I believe that palliative care is about helping people to *live* as comfortably and as fully as possible for whatever time they have left. Or, as a seminary student who had done clinical pastoral education at a hospital for the dying in New York said, "it's not about simply staying alive, it's about living."

If we return to Psalm 23, we should note what it does *not* say about the valley of the shadow of death. It does not say that God's presence will cause the sun to come out, the shadows to melt away, and the birds to begin a cheery song. There will still be darkness and shadow, but God will be with us, and even in the darkness, there will also be light. It does not say that things will not be difficult. It says that we will not be alone. In fact, it doesn't even say that we will *feel* God's presence, but that despite the shadows that may temporarily obscure our vision, God walks with us — now, during and through our dying, and for all eternity.

THE QUEST FOR IMMORTALITY

The Quest for Immortality

C. BEN MITCHELL, PH.D.

Contemporary futurists have made a fascinating find: humans are immortal!
Dr. Ben Bova, author of *Immortality: How Science Is Extending Our Life-Span
and Changing the World,* states triumphalistically, "Physical immortality is
within sight. There are people living today who may extend their life spans indefinitely."[1] Or even more intriguingly, he says, "The first immortal human
beings are probably living among us today. You might be one of them. There
are men and women who may well be able to live for centuries, perhaps even
extend their life spans indefinitely. For them, death will not be inevitable."[2]

"You may be one of the immortals. Particularly if you are less than 50
years old, in reasonably good health, and live a moderate lifestyle, you may
live for centuries or longer."[3]

What are we to make of these claims? Should we rewrite our wills?
Should we go ahead and buy that hundred year watch? Should we rethink retirement?

This revolution in longevity has resulted in a mega-shift in our thinking
about aging and ethics. Remember the pessimistic titles of the old standards?
Ethics in an Aging Society by Harry R. Moody. *Too Old for Healthcare? Contro-
versies in Medicine, Law, Economics, and Ethics* by Binstock and Post. Or, *A
Good Old Age? The Paradox of Setting Limits* by Homer and Holstein. These
sound so dull and lifeless when compared to IMMORTALITY! Not that long

---

1. Ben Bova, *Immortality: How Science Is Extending Our Life-Span and Changing the
World* (New York: Avon Books, 1998), p. xiii.

2. Bova, *Immortality,* p. 3.

3. Bova, *Immortality,* p. 3.

ago former Colorado governor Richard Lamm declared that after 70 years individuals had used enough of the nation's health care dollars and needed to get out of the way so the younger generation could take advantage of scarce medical resources. But if you may live to 100 or 150, that is a long time without healthcare. We seem to have moved from an era of "limiting healthcare" to the threshold of "limitless health."

One of the fastest growing cottage industries in the world is aging research. But unlike a past generation — which assiduously studied the effects of aging — this generation of scientists is set on nothing less than eradicating aging. These new "prolongevists," as they like to be called, are trying to prove Shakespeare wrong when he said, "We owe God a death."[4] Instead they are trying to make Woody Allen a prophet who quipped in his typically Woody Allen way: "I don't want to achieve immortality through my work. . . . I want to achieve it through not dying." Allen also famously said, "It's not that I'm afraid to die. I just don't want to be there when it happens."

If you are really convinced that you might live 100 more years, 250 more years, or centuries, there is even a Life Extension Foundation. Once you become a member, "you'll have access to a toll-free phone line where knowledgeable advisors can answer your questions and assist you in setting up an affordable life extension program designed to reduce your risk of degenerative diseases and slow the rate at which you age" (www.LEF.org).

What are the life extension technologists promising? How should we respond? Do we "catch the age wave" and enjoy our final-though-feeble last days or do we "board the techno-shuttle to endless days"?

Revolutionary Longevity

One of the starkest features of aging — its hallmark, in fact — is that the risk of falling ill and dying increases inexorably as we get older. This unwelcome principle was first cast into mathematical form in 1825 by Benjamin Gompertz, a pioneer in actuarial science. What Gompertz found was that, like compound interest, adult mortality rates increase exponentially with age. In effect, your risk of dying doubles with every eight additional years that you live. If Gompertz were alive today, he would find that this fundamental property has not been altered but that the overall level of death rates has fallen. The most significant trends affecting longevity today are the unexpected and continuing decline in the death rates of older people.

4. William Shakespeare, *King Henry IV,* Part II.

As recently as 1900, life expectancy at birth for the average American male was only 48.3 years; for the average female, 51.1. And life expectancy in America was about as good as anywhere on Earth. Childhood diseases, a lack of sanitation, and the accompanying infectious diseases like cholera and tuberculosis took the lives of many of our early-twentieth-century kin.

By the middle of the last century, life expectancy at birth had increased to 66 for males and 71.7 for females, representing a gain of twenty years increased life expectancy. By the end of the century, life expectancy at birth had risen to 75.7 years for the average American male and 82.7 for the average American female. Or to put it in even more grandiose-sounding terms, men live nearly 28,000 days and women live nearly 30,000 days.

In the United States, Great Britain, and other developed countries, life expectancy actually improves with age. It is likely, barring some major environmental catastrophe, that average life expectancy will continue to rise.

In their helpful study, *The Quest for Immortality: Science at the Frontiers of Aging,* University of Chicago researchers Jay Olshansky and Bruce Carnes point out that these sanguine data did not occur by happenstance, but are the result of revolutions: "longevity revolutions," as they call them.[5]

The last longevity revolution, as just mentioned, occurred at the turn of the twentieth century. In 1900, 10 to 15 percent of all babies born in the United States died before reaching their first birthday — mostly from infectious diseases. And when life expectancy is 45, someone who dies at 50 brings the average up a little bit, and the death of an infant brings it down. If 10-15 percent of the population die as infants, life expectancy averages come down significantly.

Say Olshansky and Carnes, "Adding 33 years to the life expectancy of the U.S. population over the course of the twentieth century by saving the young was an achievement of monumental proportions. This achievement would, however, pale in comparison to the biomedical progress that would be required to make the same gain in life expectancy over the next century by extending the lives of older people."[6]

How precisely might this revolution be brought about, according the the prolongevists?

5. S. Jay Olshansky and Bruce A. Carnes, *The Quest for Immortality: Science at the Frontiers of Aging* (New York: W. W. Norton & Company).

6. Olshansky and Carnes, *The Quest for Immortality,* pp. 87-88.

The Genomic Revolution

The 2001 prestigious and popular BBC Reith Lectures were given by gerontologist Tom Kirkwood, professor of medicine and head of gerontology at the University of Newcastle upon Tyne and author of the 1999 volume, *Time of Our Lives: The Science of Human Aging.*[7] Interestingly enough, the venue of the lectures changed so that the second lecture was not delivered in London, but at Cold Spring Harbor Labs, the Long Island, New York, research facility where James Watson has been doing genetic research for decades. Kirkwood reminds us that on 26 June 2000, the day the first draft of the map of the human genome[8] was announced, then President Bill Clinton telephoned Prime Minister Tony Blair to congratulate him on the birth of his son Leo and to celebrate that "Leo had, at a stroke, gained 25 years in life expectancy." That is to say, that advances in genetics are destined to multiply life expectancy.

The bad news, says Kirkwood, is that your DNA is in trouble. The DNA in your body is taking damaging blows as you read this. The attack rate on DNA has been estimated at 10,000 damaging hits per cell per day. Since your body is composed of several trillion cells, "the carnage is considerable." In fact, during a single evening of watching television or reading, you will use up about one ten thousandth part of one percent of your life expectancy. Do not panic, however. That is not a lot, and you probably will not feel it (except on one part of your body); but another grain of sand has passed through the hourglass of our lives.

The major culprit doing damage to our DNA is, we are told, nothing less than oxygen. Those so-called "free radicals" (no doubt a term hippies coined in the 1960s) damage our cells from within. Of course toxins from without, like tobacco smoke and sunlight, are taking their toll too.

To make matters worse, we all suffer from genetic anomalies, some of them worse than others. Diabetes, cancers, and other diseases are linked to mutant genes. Not only might gene therapy one day be used to treat these conditions, but some researchers believe that through genetic screening and careful mate selection, we can extend human life beyond our present imaginations.

Geneticist Michael Rose, for instance, hypothesized that longevity could be increased through selectively breeding offspring. Using fruit flies to

7. Tom Kirkwood, *The Time of Our Lives: The Science of Human Aging* (New York: Oxford University Press, 1999).
8. The human genome is all the genetic information contained in the 23 pairs of chromosomes in the cells of a human being.

test his theory, Rose used only those fruit fly females that produced eggs later in their lifespan to contribute eggs for the next generation. "In human terms, he said, this would be like selecting human females aged twenty-five and older to be mothers and then only permitting the daughters who were fertile after age twenty-six to reproduce, and so on for many generations until only women capable of producing babies near the maximum recorded age of menopause would be permitted to be mothers for the next generation."[9]

His experiment was a success. Each generation of fruit flies lived a little longer than the previous one. Now, that is great news for fruit flies! And, as you might imagine, the media dubbed Rose, "Lord of the Flies."[10] Nevertheless, if we followed the same process in humans, a measurable increase in life expectancy would be observable within about two and a half centuries, according to Rose's research.

Embryonic Stem Cells and the Human Cloning Revolution

President and CEO of Advance Cell Technology, Michael West, hopes that human embryonic stem cell research, combined with cloning technology, will lead to the next longevity revolution. West and his colleagues reported in the journal *Science* that cloning technology may reverse cellular aging. Through so-called therapeutic cloning, West believes our decrepit cells can be replaced by more youthful cells. Cloning those cells would avoid the problem of tissue rejection which presents such a formidable challenge to other forms of transplantation. Of course, the research subjects in these experiments are human embryos, whose stem cells must be harvested for the research. The extraction of stem cells results in death to the embryo.

In an interview published by the Life Extension Foundation, West was asked about the moral status of the early human embryo. When asked about therapeutic cloning and whether or not it was morally problematic, West said, "What we are proposing as an ethical and moral use of cloning technology in the arena of human medicine is the creation of microscopic balls of cells, called blastocysts. These are aggregates of about 100 cells that exist up to about 14 days of development [West underestimates the cellular size of the embryo at this stage]. At 14 days, small aggregations of cells begin to individualize. By that, we mean the cells begin to become the various cells and tissues of the body, or that they've committed themselves to become an individual

9. Olshansky and Carnes, *The Quest for Immortality*, p. 108.
10. Olshansky and Carnes, *The Quest for Immortality*, p. 108.

human being. Prior to day 14, the small ball of cells can still become two individual human beings. They can become identical twins, and indeed that is how identical twins form: the small ball of cells divides into two. So, prior to day 14, this small ball of cells has not individualized, it has not decided to become one individual or two individuals."

He goes on: "So, because they have not individualized, they have not committed to becoming a person. And because there is no person there and there are no differentiated cells of any kind, the blastocyst is often called a pre-embryo to distinguish it from an embryo which is committed to becoming a given individual."

Dr. West's rather optimistic characterization of human cloning, and his stereotypical certainty about the moral status of the human embryo, are unconvincing. First, just because we cannot tell yet that the early blastocyst is not being directed to become an individual, does not mean that the blastocyst is not being so directed. It only means that, if it is, we have not yet identified the cellular mechanism. Second, just because by our lights we cannot tell whether the blastocyst will produce one or two persons through twinning, does not mean that there is "no person there." There is *at least* one person there, perhaps more. Double homicide doesn't seem to be a helpful way to make his argument work. Finally, Dr. West is increasingly being left behind by his colleagues in developmental embryology who have ceased to use the term "pre-embryo" because they recognize it as more politically than biologically accurate.

Then Dr. West turns theologian. "There is nothing in the Bible," he says, "that you could bring as evidence that life begins with a fertilized egg. It is more an aesthetic preference, the sense that life should begin with a compassionate and loving act of making love, not with some stranger inserting a sperm head through the zona pelucida into an oocyte [egg cell] under a microscope and culturing in a CO_2 incubator." He goes on to add: "What I think we need to do as a society is to grow up. We are living in an age where it is in our power to do good, to alleviate human suffering, and we need to be mature and use our discoveries to make the world a better place." Even if that means cannibalizing our offspring? one might ask.

Other technologies of regenerative medicine that are championed to increase longevity are melatonin therapy, human growth hormone, robotics and prostheses, nanotechnology, and, if all else fails, cryonics. Cryonics is a means of buying time by freezing persons in liquid nitrogen until we can sort out all of this aging stuff.

Tom Kirkwood said in his Reith Lectures: "It is fortunate, but by no means coincidental, that the revolution in longevity is accompanied by an equally unprecedented revolution in the life sciences." Life extension technology is one with the biotechnology revolution, not only in part on the merits of the technology itself, but also because baby boomers fear growing old more than nearly anything.

Not the Way It Used to Be

At this point I should mention that there have been exceptions to today's average human life span. Moses, the author of Psalm 90, declared, "The length of our days is seventy years — or eighty, if we have the strength; yet their span is but trouble and sorrow, for they quickly pass, and we fly away." But Moses never meant to say that no one ever lived longer than eighty years. Moses himself lived to be 120. Methuselah's age is given as 969 years; Noah's 950. Even if, as some suggest, those numbers were really to be measured in months, the lifespan is remarkable. Methuselah would have been 81, Noah slightly over 79. In an age when most people did not live to see 30, those are astonishing life spans. In 1997, the world record for reliably documented life span was extended spectacularly by Jeanne Calment, a French woman who died at the remarkable age of 122 years and 5 months.

All these facts argue that attempts to extend one's life or to extend the lives of the entire human community are not intrinsically wrong. The question is a means/ends question. What are the appropriate means to extend human life span? Are there ethical boundaries to be protected? Moreover, there is an important *telos* or purpose question. It is fairly clear to me that while there is nothing intrinsically wrong with extending human life span, there is nothing intrinsically right about it either. Especially in a narcissistic, avaricious, and acquisitive age such as ours, why would we want some people to live longer? To live better, yes! But not necessarily to live longer. In fact, living better may help you live longer.

The Nun Study

In *Aging with Grace: What the Nun Study Teaches Us about Leading Longer, Healthier, and More Meaningful Lives,* David Snowdon chronicles a twenty-five-year longitudinal Alzheimer's study of 678 Catholic Sisters of Notre Dame.[11] Snowdon and colleagues found, for example, that a history of stroke

11. David Snowdon, *Aging with Grace: What the Nun Study Teaches Us About Leading Longer, Healthier, and More Meaningful Lives* (New York: Bantam Books 2001).

and head trauma can boost your chances of coming down with Alzheimer's later in life. They found that a college education and an active intellectual life may actually protect you from the disease. Even more interesting is their finding that the sisters who had expressed the most positive emotions in their writing as girls ended up living the longest, and that those on the road to Alzheimer's expressed fewer and fewer positive emotions as their mental functions declined. Snowdon and colleagues are under no illusion; the mechanisms behind these findings are notoriously difficult to tease out. But they may be onto something very important for meaningful longevity. There may, in fact, be ways to extend our lives meaningfully. But for how long? And how long is too long?

Life and Its Limits

In a remarkable essay, "*L'Chaim* and Its Limits: Why Not Immortality?"[12] Leon Kass, a physician, classical humanist, and chair of President Bush's bioethics advisory commission, asks whether limitless life is a good to be pursued. He puts the question this way: "If life is good and more is better, should we not regard death as a disease and try to cure it?"[13]

Kass considers the possibility that, contrary to our contemporary ethos, mortality might not simply be an evil, but it might, in fact, be a blessing. He attempts in his essay to make a case for what he calls "the virtues of mortality." In other words, he argues that death may not be all bad. His method for addressing this possibility is to use a series of very interesting Socratic questions. He asks us to reflect on these questions:

1. If the human life span were increased even by only twenty years, would the pleasures of life increase proportionately?
2. Could life be serious or meaningful without the limit of mortality?
3. Would our perception of the beautiful be tarnished by the experience of physical immortality? Is beauty recognized because it is fleeting.
4. Could immortal human beings be noble? "To suffer, to endure, to trouble oneself for the sake of home, family, community, and genuine friendship, is truly to live, and is the clear choice of this exemplary mor-

---

12. Leon R. Kass, "*L'Chaim* and Its Limits: Why Not Immortality?" in *Life, Liberty, and the Defense of Dignity: The Challenge for Bioethics* (San Francisco: Encounter Books, 2002), pp. 257-74.
13. Kass, "*L'Chaim* and Its Limits," p. 259.

tal. This choice is both the mark of excellence and the basis for the visible display of his excellence in deeds noble and just. Immortality is a kind of oblivion — like death itself."[14]

Human beings long not so much for the eradication of death, says Kass, but for a wholeness, wisdom, goodness, godliness, and shalom that cannot be satisfied by our earthly existence. Mere continuance of life will not purchase fulfillment in life. "The implication for human life," Kass maintains, "is hardly nihilistic: once we acknowledge and accept our finitude, we can concern ourselves with living well, and care first and most for the *well-being* of our souls, and not so much for their mere existence."[15]

This truth seems to be part of what the apostle Paul wrestled with in 2 Corinthians. He himself found the limitations of our fallen humanity bothersome. But his hope did not rest in finding a way to extend existence in a fallen world, but in the hope of a resurrected body, free from the ravages of the cosmic consequences of sin. In 2 Corinthians 4 and 5 he *groans* about this earthly body, this "tent." He longs to be freed from the suffering, the pain, and the finitude. Yet, he does not aim to transcend his humanity, but anticipates God's power to transform his humanity through redemption. He is confident that his mortality shall put on immortality — that he will have a future existence not made with human hands, but one that is eternal and heavenly.

> But we have this treasure in jars of clay to show that this all-surpassing power is from God and not from us. We are hard pressed on every side, but not crushed; perplexed, but not in despair; persecuted, but not abandoned; struck down, but not destroyed. We always carry around in our body the death of Jesus, so that the life of Jesus may also be revealed in our body. For we who are alive are always being given over to death for Jesus' sake, so that his life may be revealed in our mortal body. . . .
>
> Therefore, we do not lose heart. Though outwardly we are wasting away, yet inwardly we are being renewed day by day. For our light and momentary troubles are achieving for us an eternal glory that far outweighs them all. So we fix our eyes not on what is seen, but on what is unseen. For what is seen is temporary, but what is unseen is eternal.
>
> Now we know that if the earthly tent we live in is destroyed, we have a building from God, an eternal house in heaven, not built by human hands. Meanwhile we groan, longing to be clothed with our heavenly

14. Kass, "*L'Chaim* and Its Limits," p. 268.
15. Kass, "*L'Chaim* and Its Limits," p. 270.

dwelling, because when we are clothed, we will not be found naked. For while we are in this tent, we groan and are burdened, because we do not wish to be unclothed but to be clothed with our heavenly dwelling, so that what is mortal may be swallowed up by life. Now it is God who has made us for this very purpose and has given us the Spirit as a deposit, guaranteeing what is to come. (2 Corinthians 4:7-11, 16-18; 5:1-5)

The impulse for immortality is a deeply human impulse. Thus, the desire to extend human life through technology is not, in itself, wrong. The means, however, must meet high ethical standards. The sanctity and dignity of human life, made in God's image, are at stake. The end, too, must not be for merely "more of the same." That is, mere continuance of life is not a good worth pursuing. The near end must be to serve God and neighbor more completely, to love more faithfully, and to share the benefits of longevity, whatever they may be, with others. An extended life of selfish narcissism would be hellish.

The ultimate end of longevity must be the glory of the sovereign God. That end can only be fully realized when Christians are loosed from the very presence of sin and its consequences. The experience of sinless glorification is reserved for a future which is so far above and beyond our own daily experience that it makes us long expectantly for what we shall one day experience forever. And that is a very long time!

Reflections on Disability, Life, and God

LINDA L. TRELOAR, PH.D., R.N., C.S., NP-C

After awakening a few hours after going to sleep, I had begun to pray and read Scripture when I sensed God speak to me: "I want you to begin telling others what you've learned through the care of Joy." At various times over the years I felt God's leading in this area of my life but shoved it aside. I was immediately convicted by God's clear answer to my prayers seeking direction for my life; then terror flooded through me. Like Moses (Exod. 3:11), I objected: "Yes, Lord, I know I should do that. But what do I know about disability except my own experience?"

My background as a nurse enabled me to care for others who were ill, but did little to prepare me for disability as the mother of a young adult daughter with neuromuscular disease. God's response to my midlife questions occurred a few weeks following Joy's near brush with death in 1996, an experience that resulted from medical errors in decision-making and difficulties in accessing follow-up medical treatment.[1] Joy is now twenty-six years of age, and she and others with disabilities have changed my views on health and wellness. According to Jürgen Moltmann, "True health is the strength to live, the strength to suffer, and the strength to die. Health is not a condition of my body; it is the power of my soul to cope with the varying condition of that body."[2]

Although I felt inadequate to do what God directed, I believed that I understood disability. In truth, I did not understand the perspectives of people

1. See Linda L. Treloar, "Lessons from Joy: Living with Disability," *Journal of Christian Nursing* 15, no. 2 (1998): 9-13.
2. Jürgen Moltmann, "The Liberation and Acceptance of the Handicapped," in his *The Power of the Powerless*, trans. Margaret Kohl (San Francisco: Harper and Row, 1983), p. 142.

with disabilities, which contributed to painful conflict with my daughter. Despite my personal familiarity with disability as a family member, and as a nurse for thousands of patients with functional limitations and physical disabilities, I remained blind to other perspectives surrounding disability. To continue my preparation to carry out God's admonition, I began a doctoral program in disability studies and health-care ethics. It was only through the critical comments of my doctoral committee that I began to look at disability through other lenses. This chapter uses personal stories, excerpts from my research, and findings from the disability studies literature to convey themes associated with disability, life, and God. I share lessons from the transformational journey of my life in hopes that it will enable the reader to improve his or her personal and professional practice.

Promoting Wholeness in Disability

Changing Models for Disability

Disability changes the landscape of life. It commonly invokes public perceptions of suffering and abnormality.[3] The dominant Western medical model focuses on treatment of disease, yet people with disabilities may not be ill. Contemporary perspectives for disability worldwide emphasize a social model that normalizes disability and that focuses on modification of environment barriers (e.g., attitudinal, architectural, sensory, economic) rather than on personal deficits.

The Same, but Different

Commonly, the media paints people with disabilities and their caregivers as heroic and/or tragic figures. People with disabilities quickly refute these images, reframing their experience as simply part of life. Cathy, a young adult who uses a motorized wheel chair, described the "challenges" in her life:

> Sometimes they might be like an obstacle course, but in an obstacle course there is a way to get to the other end. Just have to do it a bit differently — not the conventional means. I have speed bumps, doors and windows, all those different types of metaphors.[4]

3. Robert P. Marinelli and Arthur E. Dell, eds., *The Psychological and Social Impact of Disability,* fourth ed. (New York: Springer, 1999).
4. Quoted in Linda L. Treloar, "Perceptions of Spiritual Beliefs, Response to Disabil-

According to Cathy, others see difficulties or burdens in her life "because it's more than what they have to deal with in their everyday life. Something that might be a struggle in their life might not even be a speed bump in mine."[5]

Although well intentioned, the helping professional's failure to recognize and acknowledge the perspectives of the person with a disability may provoke anger and resentment in the person he or she intends to help. Cathy continues:

> Health care providers who have training of some sort, at whatever level, already have set ideas of how things are supposed to be done. I prefer someone that has no idea what they are supposed to do. . . . They do it exactly how they're being told, to the best of their ability, and they do it like a human being instead of like a robot that's going by a list of instructions.[6]

Personal Reflections

People with disabilities have experienced centuries of bias and stigma. Although I consider myself to be an "insider" and an advocate for people *affected by* disabilities, people *with* disabilities may view me differently. Since I am not disabled, how can I understand their position? As one of my doctoral committee members remarked, "You are guilty until proven innocent." My status as a parent of a person with a disability and a health-care professional promotes "double jeopardy." Although both roles establish familiarity with disability, they fail to guarantee *respect for the perspectives and experience* of the person with a disability. Commonly, both parents of disabled children and helping professionals respond as well-intentioned "experts" who operate as if they know what is best for the person with a disability. In my experience, the person with a disability may view the actions of parents and helping professionals as barriers to running his or her life on an equal level with others.

---

ity, and the Church" (doctoral dissertation, The Union Institute, Cincinnati, Ohio, p. 142), in *Dissertation Abstracts International*, vol./issue 60-02A (University Microfilms International No. AAI9919753) (1999).

5. Quoted in Treloar, "Perceptions of Spiritual Beliefs."

6. Linda L. Treloar and Barbara M. Artinian, "Populations Affected by Disabilities," in *Community Health Nursing: Promoting the Health of Aggregates,* ed. Mary A. Nies and Melanie McEwen (Philadelphia: W. B. Saunders, 2001), pp. 496-525, at p. 521.

Life Lessons

Do not make assumptions about the goals or the experience of persons affected by disability. Helping professionals and others should develop a collaborative partnership that seeks first to understand the other. Different kinds and levels of assistance may be indicated. Personal experience with disability contributes to an "expert" knowledge basis that must be acknowledged and built upon. Following a clear definition of the problem or need, carefully assess the knowledge and skills, motivation, and resources for both the receiver and the helper before establishing goals and interventions.[7]

Impact on the Family

Historically, the birth of a child with severe disabilities has been viewed as an "unquestioned tragedy and lasting hardship for the family of the child."[8] Acute emotional distress, disrupted lives, and marital dysfunction or dissolution are well documented. According to Philip Ferguson and his colleagues, a growing body of more recent literature indicates that the quality of these families' lives resembles that of other families. Parents report numerous benefits to the family and positive outcomes associated with raising children with disabilities. Commonly, the experience is accompanied by joy amidst chronic grieving. Notice these themes and the divergence in perspectives in Peter's description of taking his daughter who has spina bifida to a father-daughter dance:

> Even in the area of disability it doesn't take much effort to find someone who's in a more difficult situation than us. So, at any time, I can say, "I'm thankful, I'm joyful" in the overall situation. There are times when still it breaks my heart. I know it's harder for me to go through a father-daughter dance than it is for Michelle. She has a blast! I look around and say, "What a tragedy that she can't do that." She says, "Come on, let's dance, Dad."[9]

7. See Barbara M. Artinian and Margaret M. Conger, eds., *The Intersystem Model: Integrating Theory and Practice* (Thousand Oaks, Calif.: Sage, 1997); and Treloar and Artinian, "Populations Affected."

8. Philip M. Ferguson, Alan Gartner, and Dorothy K. Lipsky, "The Experience of Disability in Families: A Synthesis of Research and Parent Narratives," in *Prenatal Testing and Disability Rights,* ed. Erik Parens and Adrienne Asch (Washington, D.C.: Georgetown University Press, 2000), pp. 72-94.

9. Treloar, "Perceptions of Spiritual Beliefs," p. 137.

Personal Reflections

Much like Peter and other parents, my husband and I encouraged Joy to participate in activities with her peers. At times, it was agonizing to watch her on the sidelines, but at least she was present! Since Joy uses a motorized wheelchair, Bob or I took her to after-school events and church activities. For overnight trips, we carried a multitude of pillows and a special mattress, in addition to other equipment. Personal care activities related to chronic health-care needs regimented Joy's life. Every morning and evening, she had respiratory treatments to help keep her lungs clear and exercises to maintain joint mobility. Because Joy was "tough," she rarely revealed how she felt or the frustrations she experienced as she grew up with a disability. The sheer monotony of performing the daily routines and the fatigue from getting up at night to turn Joy from side to side, however, contributed to personal exhaustion and marital stress.

Although any parent can be accused of over-protective behaviors, establishing independence remains a daunting task for any young adult and disability complicates the situation. Our daughter rarely allowed anyone to glimpse the disappointment and resentment she felt over limitations in coming and going like other teens. One day Joy erupted in heart-wrenching sobs, angrily conveying the powerlessness she felt in her situation. When I offered to take and pick her up from a prearranged meeting place with her friends, she angrily rejected the option. After all, her friends could come and go as they pleased. More important, they could drive themselves. Joy had parents who were far too involved and a restricted life-style. My attempts to "fade into the woodwork" were not good enough. Her anger toward me grew.

During her freshman year in college, Joy moved into the dormitory but returned home on weekends. One day I came home to find her room barren, with only blue and yellow globs of putty on the walls and ceiling that previously held colorful posters and pictures. With the help of her young adult caregiver, Joy had stripped our home of everything she considered hers. She left behind a five-page single-spaced typed letter that revealed her hurts and established her independence. I could bear the pain of only one reading of that letter before placing it in a secret location. To have a child minimally acknowledge my good intentions as a parent, and to reveal hurts and anger toward me for wrongs associated with disability that she perceived I inflicted, crushed me.

While the manner and the timing of developmental tasks may change for people with disabilities, Joy experienced a "normal" separation as a young adult. During her years at college, conflict between the two of us continued to escalate. Family gatherings became events where I "walked on eggshells." My statements of apology, with acknowledgement that parents are not perfect, and that "God is not done with me yet," did little to improve our relationship.

In my experience, neither adult children with disabilities nor their parents can fully appreciate the position of the other. Like most mothers and health-care professionals, I am quick to offer counsel to others. I learned long ago, however, that Joy would not accept my influence; her strong will rivals my own. My prayers for healing of our relationship intensified. That healing began a few years later when I sought her counsel and assistance during my doctoral studies. Her role as a disability consultant allowed her to be "expert," while I was the learner and seeker of my daughter's help.

It is through my family's struggles that I came to the end of myself. I carry the following in my Bible (reference unknown): "Surrender is a definite, deliberate, and voluntary transfer of control of all we are and hope to be to God." *Much like any parent, my single biggest challenge has been to give my daughter to God.* His care for her surpasses anything I can offer.

Life Lessons

Children with disabilities can assume control of their lives when parents allow them to do so. In the words of one teen, "Parents must be willing to let go of the leash and be an advocate for their child rather than someone directing their lives."[10] The person with a disability should participate in decision-making from an early age, developing skills that promote independence and self-care.

When a family member's disabilities stem from life-threatening illnesses, open communication about the illness and its prognosis create special challenges for families. My daughter believes that I concealed details about her neuromuscular disease, including its grim prognosis. The statistics weren't in her favor: Most children like Joy die in infancy or early in life. I recognized the limitations of statistical averages and feared that this information would stymie her potential, and perhaps lead to an early death. On another level, I was a coward.

When Joy left home to go to college, she assumed responsibility for her health care. During a visit to a neuromuscular disease clinic, imagine her shock and embarrassment when she discovered the limitations of her knowledge specific to her disease and its prognosis. *The fact that children seldom ask*

10. Tara Wood, "Growing up, Staying Healthy and Taking Charge," *Quest* (2001): 32-36, at p. 34.

questions about their disease or its prognosis does not relieve parents of their re-sponsibility to help ensure that children have the information necessary to be fully informed. Helping professionals should facilitate open discussions that include these kinds of issues.

Spiritual Implications of Disability

Irrespective of religious beliefs, we are spiritual beings. We seek meaning for events that affect us from the beginning to the end of life. Although disability may be anticipated with aging and/or chronic illness, its presence may provoke questions about our mortality, the person of God, and our relationship with him. Regardless of the strength of our faith, we may ask, "Why, God? Why me/my family? What did I do to deserve this?" People with developmental disabilities, those present from birth or acquired early in life, develop a self-concept that incorporates disability. Their response to disability may differ dramatically from an adult whose acquired disability challenges his or her experience as able-bodied.

While religious beliefs promote positive coping, they may contribute to spiritual distress and turning away from God. Health-care and religious professionals' failure openly to consider spiritual issues surrounding disability contributes to the problem.[11] Unfortunately, many people within and outside of the church hold the misconception that disability results from divine punishment for sin or inadequate faith. Despite continued progress in welcoming and promoting accessibility for people with disabilities, it appears that the population remains grossly underrepresented in Christian congregations.

Personal Reflections

For Christians, spiritual growth follows experiences of difficulty and trial (James 1:2-4). Upon receiving Joy's diagnosis of a genetic neuromuscular disease when she was about one year of age, I accepted that a special child had been lent to us for however many days God willed. But I begged, "God,

11. Regarding health-care professionals, see Linda L. Treloar, "People with Disabilities — the Same, but Different: Implications for Health Care Practice," *Journal of Transcultural Nursing* 10, no. 4 (1999): 358-64. Regarding religious professionals, see Linda L. Treloar, "Spiritual Beliefs, Response to Disability, and the Church — Part 1," *Journal of Religion, Disability, and Health* 3, no. 4 (1999): 5-32; Linda Treloar, "Spiritual Beliefs, Response to Disability, and the Church — Part 2," *Journal of Religion, Disability, and Health* 4, no. 1 (2000): 5-31.

please take her now rather than let her suffer. I can't bear to watch this. How can I stand to love her and then lose her?" I felt too weak to handle the excruciating pain and sorrow. With maturing of my faith, I learned to ask not that her suffering would be limited, but that we would have the faith and the strength for whatever trials Joy's health presented. A few years later, I began to pray that her faith would be so strong that the trials would be light, not overwhelming.

When living with disability provokes self-pity and resentment that threaten to dampen my spirit, God uses others to increase my awareness of this and to encourage me. While 1 Thessalonians 5:16-18 is easy to memorize, it remains challenging to live out: "Rejoice always; pray without ceasing; in everything give thanks: for this is the will of God in Christ Jesus" (ASV).

Life Lessons

Disability is a unique spiritual experience. Helping professionals can assist people affected by disabilities to establish meaning for the experience of disability. Offering a listening ear and one's presence provide strategies that allow the person to discover his or her own answers. Regardless of religious/spiritual perspective, disability and experiences that cause suffering force us to consider whether there is a God and our relationship to him. Helping professionals should not assume that offers of prayer or other spiritual care interventions will be rejected by people who have previously denied spiritual interest. Recently a woman (a self-described "atheist") remarked that information on the importance of spiritual care for people affected by disability had provoked her to reconsider her spiritual beliefs.

The Church and People Affected by Disabilities

A growing body of literature supports a positive relationship between religion and health.[12] Families who trust God weather the storms of life more readily. A serious disability in a family member creates tremendous demands, leaving little energy for oneself, a marital partner, or other family members.

People affected by disability may benefit from religious support that includes practical, social, emotional, and/or spiritual dimensions. Regardless of personal faith, people who feel unsupported may blame the church and with-

---

12. See Harold G. Koenig, Michael E. McCullough, and David B. Larson, *Handbook of Religion and Health* (Oxford: Oxford University Press, 2001).

draw from fellowship and worship activities. Chuck and his wife, Emily, who is a quadriplegic, withdrew from their large church, well known for its evangelical Christian outreach to people with disabilities. In Chuck's words, "the church failed us" when it knew of the difficulty they were having in recruiting and retaining a licensed practical nurse to provide personal care for Emily on weekday mornings. The main barrier involved limited financial resources. Few options exist for families who do not qualify for federal or state disability social support programs. For those who do, support remains extremely limited and families often exist at poverty level.

Further Reflection

What Would Jesus Do?

What ethical imperatives direct the actions of the church? As "salt" and "light" (Matt. 5:13-16), how are Christians to influence the world? The two greatest biblical commandments direct us to love God and to love our neighbor as ourselves (Matt. 22:37-39). We are to care for widows and orphans, in other words, those who cannot support themselves (Acts 6:1-4; 1 Tim. 5:3-16; James 1:27). A member of a non-Christian religious group that was well known for its emphasis on the family and religious community indicated to Chuck that they had a group of women who "went around meeting the kinds of needs" his wife had. The implication was clear: If he would join their group, he, too, could benefit. Although Chuck recognized the offer as an unholy option, the possibility that other faiths are willing to meet their practical needs fuels his anger at the Christian community.

Personal Reflections

I am struck by the anger I sense from people affected by disabilities when I discuss spirituality, disability, and the role of the church. Not only are people angry with God, they blame the church for failing to meet their needs. In the words of one man who became a quadriplegic at age fifteen, and who subsequently graduated with a master of divinity degree from a conservative mainline Protestant seminary, "I didn't get any answers. I only learned to ask better questions." Although he may deny this, I suspect that he no longer believes that God is good or sovereign. Clearly, he denies that there is any purpose or benefit for disability or suffering, and states angrily that the "church failed to help me to grieve [my disability]."

Life Lessons

In my experience, people expect the church to treat them differently than people in the world treat them. When the body of Christ fails to demonstrate compassion and love for them, they become angry and disillusioned. When governmental social programs fail to meet their practical needs, they expect the church to do so. Although it would be nice to have a pool of available nurses who could meet Emily's needs, this does not exist in my community. Ideally, Chuck and Emily, representatives of their church, social services agencies, and health insurers could work together to create an optimal program of care. Unfortunately, few churches have parish nurses or health ministry programs that can facilitate this kind of collaboration. The church should have elders or a group of designated church leaders who assist pastoral staff in determining how the church's resources can be allocated to take care of those who cannot meet their own needs. A friend shared these thoughts:

> Sometimes, it's easier to blame the Christian community than to seek additional means for receiving care or for accepting a level of care that is fully adequate but "less than acceptable" to the individual. I know of an instance where my church tried to help an individual, but this person expected the church to provide everything for them and to provide the level of financial help that they desired. The church gave from the elders' fund, provided counseling, and offered financial counseling, but it was never "enough" or "what this person wanted it to be." So the person blamed the church. This person then went around seeking funds from individuals, whoever would listen to their complaint — laying guilt here and there to find someone to help support a *desired* lifestyle. . . . Should churches be ready to help? Of course! For there are people with legitimate needs. But as in all things, our idea of the type and the kind of help we need may not be the same as God's.

Ethical Implications of Disability and Health

We live in a complex, postmodern society that is fraught with spiritual and ethical questions related to disability. Having been made in God's image (Gen. 1:26-27) we share personhood, being equipped with different gifts and abilities (Rom. 12:4-8; 1 Cor. 12). Despite this biblical assurance, how do we reconcile the value of a person with a serious intellectual disability (e.g., mental retardation)? Parents with disabled children have much to teach us in this regard.

How can God permit the suffering associated with a serious neurological event, such as a stroke, a head trauma, or spinal cord injury? According to Scripture (Gen. 3:14-19), sin entered the world through Adam and we are destined to earthly difficulties. Is God good? Is God powerful? Does he cause disabilities or simply allow them to occur? The psalmist writes in Psalm 139:13-15,

> For thou didst form my inward parts:
>   Thou didst cover me in my mother's womb.
> I will give thanks unto thee; For I am fearfully and wonderfully made:
>   Wonderful are thy works;
>   And that my soul knoweth right well.
> My frame was not hidden from thee,
>   When I was made in secret,
> And curiously wrought in the lowest parts of the earth.   (ASV)

What is the purpose of disability? Jesus responds in John 9:1-3:

> And as he passed by, he saw a man blind from his birth. And his disciples asked him, saying, Rabbi, who sinned, this man, or his parents, that he should be born blind? Jesus answered, Neither did this man sin, nor his parents: but that the works of God should be made manifest in him. (ASV)

Society continues to grapple with other questions related to disability, including the following: How much and what kind of medical treatment should be offered? Is all possible care indicated? Does the presence of intense suffering, congenital abnormalities, or severe cognitive impairment change the situation? Is physician-assisted suicide ever indicated? How should cost containment, resource allocation, futility of treatment, and quality of life issues be addressed as these relate to disability? How can and how should we care for an aging American population? What about prenatal testing and disability rights? While this chapter will not attempt to address the preceding questions, I suggest that we look to the Bible for direction in responding to issues related to disability.

Life Lessons

The Scriptures offer timeless truths with practical direction for contemporary ethical and social challenges. Men and women who are well grounded in their faith are better prepared to answer tough social and ethical questions

surrounding health and disability. In some cases, the Scriptures apply principles or truths that provide clear direction for our actions. At other times,
there are no easy answers.

Summary

Consistent with the reports of other parents with disabled children, I view my
daughter as my best teacher. Disability impacts every area of my life, refining
my character and increasing my skills. My most important life lesson involves
surrender and relinquishing of control to God. Because I am human, periodically I must relearn this lesson.

Joy is an amazing young woman who teaches a bilingual class of students in an inner-city public school. Her body enslaves her to others for physical care, but her mind and spirit remain unfettered. Although she lives her
life without fear, I cannot attest to living my life with similar assurance.
Learning to pray and to wait on God to work through my family, rather than
rushing ahead, is a continuing lesson. God demonstrates his faithfulness over
and over, drawing our family to him. I take great comfort in knowing that Joy
loves Jesus and has no doubt of her future home in heaven.

Health is not the absence of disease, but the ability to live well in the
presence of disability or other infirmities. Contemporary perspectives for disability focus on environmental modifications, rather than on personal deficits. People affected by disabilities reframe disability as a variation in the human condition. Professionals must seek first to understand the person they
intend to help. They should assist families to establish open communication
that promotes independence and self-care of the person with a disability.

Christians should help their churches welcome people affected by disabilities, and develop a continuing model for caring and support. Since life is
a spiritual journey, we seek meaning for events that seem "bad." A biblical
foundation provides skills that help us to answer tough ethical, societal questions.

In Search of the Philosopher's Clone:
Immortality through Replication

WILLIAM P. CHESHIRE JR., M.D.

An international team of scientists attempted in 1999 to clone the prehistoric woolly mammoth using tissue extracted from a carcass found frozen for twenty-three thousand years in a Siberian ice field. Sustaining their effort as their ice picks chipped away at permafrost was the belief that this forbidding arctic world might be pregnant with its fossil past. The investigators hoped that the frigid conditions of one of the coldest places on Earth might have preserved intact a copy of the mammoth's genetic code in suspended animation. From it might be born the living product of a cloning experiment, the mammoth's much younger twin.

Their plan was to thaw some mammoth cells, insert the DNA into a hollowed-out egg borrowed from an elephant, return the egg become embryo to the elephant's womb, and wait. Such are the extraordinary possibilities offered by modern biotechnology. Since early human hunters may have been responsible for the mammoth's extinction, perhaps human biotechnology might now serve a redemptive purpose.

The ambitious experiment failed. Cloning technology has not yet succeeded in bringing to life an extinct mammal. Even when applied to living mammals, the number of defective clones unable to survive far outnumbers viable progeny. Ian Wilmut's laboratory in Scotland created 277 cloned embryos before producing in 1996 just one healthy sheep. Of the 277 embryos, Wilmut implanted into the uterine horns of recipient ewes all 34 that developed to the morula and blastocyst stage. Ultrasonography one month later revealed 8 fetuses. Following three miscarriages, his ewes gave birth to 5 lambs. Two malformed creatures died within minutes of birth, one died at ten days, and another died later. Only one, named Dolly, survived.[1] Production and duplication of "elite" embryos through cloning has since become a field of active research in veterinary medicine.

Clone Age Tools

At this moment in history the world debates whether to commence cloning human beings. In fact, experiments are already taking place. In the quiet town of Nitro, West Virginia, a secret human cloning laboratory operated by the Raelian cult was recently discovered in an upstairs room of a former high school. Their first client was a politician who wanted to clone his dead child.[2] We have entered the clone age.

Most shudder at the thought of replicating people. Mass production of countless genetically identical copies of made-to-order people seems incompatible with the special dignity all human beings possess as individuals created in the image of God according to Genesis 1:27.

There is a particular category of cloning that deserves careful attention. "Therapeutic" human cloning severs cloning from its troublesome reproductive context to smuggle in the same technology under the more acceptable banner of medical progress. The proposed technique would manufacture a genetically identical copy of a human being — a younger twin — to become a source of undifferentiated precursor cells to treat disease. These stem cells taken from the human embryo have the capacity to differentiate into any cell type. Stem cells are, in a sense, immortal, for they can divide indefinitely when cultured in petri dishes. Some scientists contend that further research will lead to the knowledge of how to coax embryonic stem cells to develop along desired pathways to become specialized tissue types, such as neurons or pancreatic islet cells, or even of how to grow them into transplantable organs to treat a wide range of presently incurable diseases. The recipient's immune system might not reject as foreign these genetically identical, hence histologically compatible, cells.

What of the fate of the young human clone? Therapeutic cloning is

---

1. K. H. Campbell, J. McWhir, W. A. Ritchie, I. Wilmut, "Sheep Cloned by Nuclear Transfer from a Cultured Cell Line," *Nature* 380 (March 7, 1996): 64-66; Ronald M. Green, "Much Ado about Mutton: An Ethical Review of the Cloning Controversy," in *Cloning and the Future of Human Embryo Research,* ed. Paul Lauritzen (Oxford: Oxford University Press, 2001), p. 123.

2. James A. Haught and Tara Tuckwiller, "Cloning Effort Hidden in West Virginia Town," *Charleston Gazette,* 14 August 2001.

hardly therapeutic for the living human embryo, who is destroyed in the lethal harvesting procedure so that his or her stem cells can be, as Aldous Huxley might have put it, "decanted."[3] This fragile human embryo, fully capable of developing into an adult human being unless violated by the dissecting tweezers' pointed pincers, becomes subject to what Chuck Colson has characterized as "clinical vivisection of our own kind."[4] Yet it is unproven whether the sacrifice of tiny human life is even necessary to medical progress.

Considerable political momentum presses for the gates to human embryonic stem cell research to swing wide open. Therapeutic human cloning, now legal in the United Kingdom, has become a topic of debate in the United States. Rumors promising no less than "cures" for a host of devastating disorders such as Alzheimer's disease and Parkinson's disease attract headline attention. Although similar expectations kindled the decision to proceed with human fetal tissue research a decade ago, the actual results have proven tragically disappointing.[5] Once more a case has been made that far exceeds what can reasonably be justified by proven evidence in the scientific and medical literature. It is important to note that embryos are not the only source of stem cells. Impressive data supporting the potential therapeutic value of stem cells derived from adult tissues are too often overlooked.[6] Other ethically noncontroversial sources of stem cells such as umbilical cord blood or placenta have been inadequately explored.

This is not only a debate about science. Something more has captured the public imagination — something larger than fact — and not without danger. Those who look to science for something more than science will inevitably be disappointed by science. Will the "something more" then satisfy humanity's wounded expectations?

3. Aldous Huxley, *Brave New World* (New York: Perennial Classics, 1998 [originally published in 1932]).

4. Charles W. Colson, "A Statement on Stem Cell Research," 5 July 2001, http://www.wilberforce.org.

5. C. R. Freed, P. E. Greene, R. E. Breeze, W.-Y. Tsai, W. DuMouchel, R. Kao, S. Dillon, H. Winfield, S. Culver, J. Q. Trojanowski, D. Eidelberg, S. Fahn, "Transplantation of Embryonic Dopamine Neurons for Severe Parkinson's Disease," *New England Journal of Medicine* 344 (2001): 710-19.

6. For example, Lamya S. Shihabuddin, Philip J. Horner, Jasodhara Ray, and Fred H. Gage, "Adult Spinal Cord Stem Cells Generate Neurons After Transplantation in the Adult Dentate Gyrus," *Journal of Neuroscience* 20 (2000): 8727-35; V. K. Ramiya, M. Maraist, K. E. Arfors, D. A. Schatz, A. B. Peck, and J. G. Cornelius, "Reversal of Insulin-Dependent Diabetes Using Islets Generated In Vitro from Pancreatic Stem Cells," *Nature Medicine* 6 (2000): 278-82. For a periodically updated bibliography by the Do No Harm coalition, see http://www.stemcellresearch.org.

A recent *Scientific American* article surveying progress in stem cell research accurately identified this something more by the title: "Biological Alchemy."[7] Alchemy is the missing variable that begins to explain the allure of permitting destructive research on human embryos when alternative sources of stem cells would do. Cloning technology has resurrected, not an ancient beast, but an ancient philosophy.

And its ethical implications are mammoth.

Alchemy and the Philosopher's Stone

Alchemy is an art of ancient Egyptian origin which has two related aims: the transmutation of base metals into gold, and the prolongation of life. Our word *chemistry*, in fact, derives from the word *alchemy*, which may be traced to the Coptic word *khem* for the black soil of the Nile delta. As understood by alchemy, *khem* refers esoterically to the dark mystery of primordial matter through which all creation manifests.

Alchemy embraces a magical worldview in which Nature is believed to be a living organism undergoing a process of evolution toward perfection. Within this pantheistic framework, the alchemist endeavors to assist nature's "engine" to perfect chaotic matter, whether as expressed in metals, in the cosmos, or in the substance of human souls.

The alchemists of old dreamt of finding the "Philosopher's Stone," a mystical substance believed to embody the power to transmute base metals into gold. Alchemists appreciated gold not only for its scarcity and brilliance, but also for its seeming imperishability. Because gold does not corrode, to the alchemist's logic it had a sympathetic relationship to human immortality. By implication, securing one would confer access to the other. And while the prospect of making gold did not hinder patron funding, purification of metals into the noblest metal, gold, was of secondary importance. If held in solution by wine, the Philosopher's Stone would become the glimmering "elixir of life," the universal cure for all diseases. Producing the Philosopher's Stone was the alchemist's ultimate dream, for it alone was imagined to be capable of prolonging life indefinitely and securing for the alchemist the "virtue" of eternal youth. The laborious task of producing the Philosopher's Stone was termed the *magnum opus*, or Great Work.

Crouched in a dark, cluttered laboratory, the alchemist would tediously follow the steps cryptically encoded in crumbling ancient texts. The alchemist

7. W. Wayt Gibbs, "Biological Alchemy," *Scientific American* (February 2001): 16-17.

labored endlessly, heating first one and then another metal over a flame — silver and mercury, then iron, lead, and copper, each made molten, dissolved, or ground to powder. Gazing upward past pungent swirls of toxic smoke, the alchemist sought spiritual guidance from the stars for the task of controlling, through a sequential chain of purifications, the transformation of the very essence of nature and being. Alchemists believed that their procedures and incantations actually killed and resurrected metals. They were sworn to secrecy in order to protect their hidden knowledge from the eyes of the uninitiated.

Alchemy is mingled with the early history of Western science and medicine. The seventeenth-century fathers of chemistry and physics, Robert Boyle and Isaac Newton, experimented with alchemy.[8] Paracelsus, a sixteenth-century physician, reasoned from his knowledge of alchemy that some diseases might originate from seeds, which today are known as germs. Paracelsus was the first to prescribe mercury compounds, a spin-off from alchemy, in the treatment of syphilis. Mercury remained the standard treatment for syphilis until the discovery of penicillin. Even today gold is used to treat rheumatoid arthritis. The Chinese discovery of gunpowder has also been attributed to alchemy.[9]

The alchemists' quest for gold and immortality inspired early Spanish exploration of the New World. Twenty-five miles from my home, down the Florida coast, is the traditional site of Ponce de Leon's "Fountain of Youth" in St. Augustine. Ponce de Leon, who discovered Florida in 1513, was driven by an obsession to find the legendary Fountain of Youth, rumored to flow amidst a wealth of gold. If he did find it, he has managed to conceal his survival exceptionally well.

Occasionally after melting lead the alchemist was rewarded in his efforts by finding a tiny residue of gold in the bottom of the cauldron. But this was no transmutation. Chemistry now recognizes that lead ore naturally contains traces of gold. Gold, being heavier than lead, once molten merely settles to the bottom.

The eighth-century discovery of an acid that could destroy gold led alchemists to suspect that the ability to create gold would soon follow. But this *aqua regia,* a solution of nitric and hydrochloric acids, only dissolved gold into solution. The search went on for the mysterious Philosopher's Stone.

8. Robert Boyle, a founder of the Royal Society, in 1670 contracted a peripheral neuropathy, the likely result of mercury vapor poisoning from one too many alchemy experiments. See William P. Cheshire, "Robert Boyle and a Corpuscular Model of Tremor," *Neurology* 42 (1992): 455-56, and correspondence, pp. 2058-59.

9. The editors of Time-Life Books, *Secrets of the Alchemists* (Alexandria, Va.: Time-Life Books, 1990).

Despite more than two thousand years of melting metals over flames, no alchemist has ever produced the Philosopher's Stone, that elusive key to changing metals into gold and attaining eternal life. It turned out that metals were not as the alchemists imagined, but in reality something quite different. The findings of modern chemistry have shown that the experiments of alchemy only rearranged the electrons of metals but did not change the protons and neutrons making up the nucleus. Hence alchemy did not alter the fundamental atomic identity of metals. Following a lengthy history, alchemy is no more. Or is it?

Alchemy's Death Exaggerated

Writing about human cloning and genetic engineering in the *Hastings Center Report,* Mary Midgley chose the provocative title "Alchemy Revived."[10] Modern biotechnology has, it seems, conceived a new *magnum opus.* Its catalyst was the initial isolation in 1998 of embryonic stem cells. Alchemy, which regards all metals to be transmutations of primordial dark matter, offers an enchanting philosophical paradigm from which to interpret stem cell science. Announcing the discovery of embryonic stem cells in *Virtual Medical Worlds,* Leslie Verswevveld appealed to this paradigm in the title: "Modern Alchemists Discover Philosopher's Stone with Promise of Eternal Youth."[11]

The list of witnesses to alchemy's rebirth goes on. Commentary in *New Scientist* characterized embryonic stem cells as "the quintessential spare part."[12] "Quintessence," meaning the fifth element, is a term derived from alchemy and refers to the ethereal embodiment of the life force which animates or gives a substance its deepest characteristics. Stuart Orkin, writing in *Nature Medicine* about "Stem Cell Alchemy," concluded that the "extraordinary plasticity of tissue stem cells, such as the ability of blood stem cells to differentiate into liver, would intrigue even the ancient alchemists."[13] Rick Weiss, in a *Washington Post* editorial, portrayed experiments in which stem cells from one tissue were transformed under laboratory conditions into cells of other

10. Midgley, "Alchemy Revived," *Hastings Center Report* 30 (March-April 2000): 41-43.

11. Leslie Verswevveld, "Modern Alchemists Discover Philosopher's Stone with Promise of Eternal Youth," *Virtual Medical Worlds,* 5 November 1998.

12. Arlene Judith Klotzko, "Embryonic Stem Cells . . . Are the Quintessential Spare Part," *New Scientist,* 5 December 1998.

13. Stuart H. Orkin, "Stem Cell Alchemy," *Nature Medicine* 6 (November 2000): 1212-13.

tissues as "feats of biomedical alchemy."[14] Gregg Easterbrook, writing in *The New Republic,* concluded, "Stem cells are the philosopher's stones of biology, magical objects capable of metamorphosing into any component of the body."[15] A webpage forum on human cloning extended the comparison further with the words, "Today, the modern alchemist exercises his assumed divine prerogative by placing in the alembic human genomes cannibalized from aborted babies to serve as the base metals used in genetics research."[16]

What brave new quest is underway? Human cells, as though they were base metals, are now transmuted in the laboratory from one tissue type into another. Embryonic stem cells are hailed as the Philosopher's Stone. Sometimes promoted as "replacement parts" for degenerated or diseased organs, immortal stem cells seem to glisten with the quintessential life force. According to some media claims, science at last has found the elixir of life. Could it be that the cure for aging is at hand? Will death soon become obsolete?

Alchemy has not vanished. Its underlying assumptions and sustaining aspirations have been with us all along, suspended in the fluid of Western culture, brewing over the flames of human disease and suffering. In the biomedical sciences alchemy now takes on a new transmutation that the ancient alchemists would surely have envied. Biotechnology dangles before our eyes alchemy's dual goals. We are assured that stem cells contain a fount of renewable youth. They also promise a potential gold mine of biotech venture stock.[17]

One alternative medicine periodical claimed this about human cloning and stem cell research:

> The mystical quest — the transmutation of matter (flesh) into spiritual gold — goes on. In one way or another, we continue to seek eternal life through reincarnation, cloning, stem cell research, cryonics, etc. Olympic athletes strive for "the gold," strive to become the best that they can be, strive for a moment of immortality achieved through the transmuta-

14. Rick Weiss, "Cell 'Alchemy,' an Alternative to Embryo Studies," *Washington Post,* 24 April 2000.

15. Gregg Easterbrook, "Will Homo Sapiens Become Obsolete?" *New Republic,* 1 March 1990, p. 20.

16. "First Human Embryo Cloned," commentary published at http://www.watchpair.com/clone.html.

17. Stem cells are "viewed as a likely biotechnology gold mine," writes Rick Weiss in "A Crucial Human Cell Is Isolated, Multiplied. Embryonic Building Block's Therapeutic Potential Stirs Debate," *Washington Post,* 6 November 1998. Science is "turning stem cells into therapeutic gold," writes Orkin in "Stem Cell Alchemy," pp. 1212-13.

tion of ordinary flesh and blood into Olympic supermen, into Olympic gold.[18]

Make a Wish

In the tradition of astrology, ancient alchemists looked to the stars for guidance. Today, in an age of science, it is no longer believed that movements in the heavens have anything to do with events on earth. Therefore, when perplexed by human cloning conundrums and stem cell research quandaries, where does the culture now look for ethical guidance? To the stars, naturally, but stars a little lower than the heavens — stars of the silver screen, stars well-versed in the trusted wisdom of the television sit-com.

Five stars testified to Congress in 2000 in support of destructive research on human embryos.[19] Three of these actors suffer from very serious neurologic conditions, and regardless of their views on bioethics, their personal courage in the face of suffering is admirable. The purpose of this chapter is not to criticize these actors' positions. What is remarkable is the degree of confidence the public has placed in their claim to expertise on complex bioethical issues. Just as a spellbound imagination can subconsciously confuse a man with a fictional superhero, so too it can see a human embryo slated for destruction as something other than human. If opposing human deleterious embryonic stem cell research is as difficult as stopping a locomotive, this is because its proponents believe they can leap large moral obstacles in a single bound. Reason, once aroused from slumber, realizes that kryptonite is no precursor to the Philosopher's Stone. A comic book approach to ethical theory simply will not resolve the moral questions.

There is one ageless star whose personal experience in alchemy culminated in a cloning experiment resulting in disaster. In his role as the sorcerer's apprentice in the Disney film *Fantasia,* Mickey Mouse has access to the mysteries of alchemy without the wisdom of application. Through magical incantations offered over a fiery cauldron, Mickey manages to animate, then replicate, his broom. A multitude of mindless marching copies proceed to do his work for him. But he cannot control them. The story illustrates the peril of getting the clones one wishes for.

18. Magzcha Westerman, "Alchemy — the Quest for Gold," *Tampa Bay New Times,* Clearwater, Florida, March/April 2000, published at http://www.altnewtimes.com/eo2mwe.html.

19. The stars were Christopher Reeve, Michael J. Fox, Mary Tyler Moore, Gina Gershon, and Jenifer Estess.

Onward Human Cloners?

The boundary between science fact and fantasy blurs in discussions about human cloning. Consider, for example, the technique of somatic cell nuclear transfer, or therapeutic human cloning, as a means to mass produce human embryonic stem cells.[20] First a somatic cell is removed from the patient's own tissue. This somatic cell might be a skin cell or a white blood cell. The somatic cell nucleus is then extracted and inserted into the hollowed-out egg of a cow. The resulting fused cell, if it survives, is a hybrid embryo composed of cellular parts of two species. It is genetically human, a copy of the patient, but also part cow, even genetically part cow, for the egg contains mitochondrial cow DNA. The cloned embryo is grown in culture for up to fourteen days. Its stem cells are then harvested by breaking the embryo up into individual cells. This procedure invariably annihilates the life of the embryo. The stem cells can then be collected, multiplied, passaged, frozen, shipped, thawed, researched, or transplanted, as if they were any other commodity. The human embryo herself, absent legal protection, is similarly vulnerable to commodification.

Some proponents of therapeutic cloning hold, through some transmutation of reason, that a human embryo, if created in the petri dish rather than in the womb, is not a real human being at all, but only a "potential person." There is, however, no biologic distinction between the embryo inside and the embryo outside the womb. Either will die if denied nourishment, whether this comes from culture media mixed from powder or the vascular lining of the mother's womb. Geography would seem to be an arbitrary basis on which to decide the status of personhood. It took no less than a feat of ethical alchemy to devise the corrosive distinction that categorizes some human embryos, on the basis of location or destiny, as being less than true human beings and unworthy of protection.

Another way of evaluating the ethics of sacrificing human embryos for their stem cells is to appeal to the one who made them. Western civilization through the ages has looked to the Bible when seeking to understand human origins. The same question Jesus asked when shown a denarius coin can be asked about the human embryo: "Whose image and inscription does it have?" (Luke 20:24 NKJV). The image is that of the Creator (Gen. 1:27), who is undeniably the Author of the inscription, the genetic code, the DNA. Science has not replaced, but has magnified, what the psalmist knew long ago:

20. Ian Wilmut, "Cloning for Medicine," *Scientific American* (December 1998).

For you created my inmost being;
    you knit me together in my mother's womb.
I praise you because I am fearfully and wonderfully made;
    your works are wonderful,
    I know that full well.
My frame was not hidden from you
    when I was made in the secret place.
When I was woven together in the depths of the earth,
    your eyes saw my unformed body.
All the days ordained for me
    were written in your book
    before one of them came to be.   (Ps. 139:13-16 NIV)

The prophet Jeremiah records that the Lord God spoke the following words to him: "Before *I formed you* in the womb I knew you" (Jer. 1:5 NKJV, emphasis added). This is not only a statement about divine foreknowledge; the verse says that it was *God* who formed him, not someone other. And Psalm 100 declares, "Know that the LORD, He is God; It is He who has made us, and not we ourselves" (Ps. 100:3 NKJV).

At the dawn of the third millennium the tools of science have opened up previously unimagined possibilities. Human embryos can now be created in a petri dish.[21] Whether for reproductive or research purposes, computer-assisted micromanipulators can now assemble the cellular components to make new human embryos, and freeze them like the woolly mammoth for later use. The human embryo engineered to produce stem cells enters the world with an obligation not, as far as science can discern, to the calling of God, but to the skill of the technician. In a moral sleight of hand, this tiny human is offered not the saving hand of salvation but the grasping latex glove of exploitation. Her very cells are all numbered (cf. Matt. 10:30), as are her days. Both are exceedingly few.

If the conditions under which some human embryos come into being are artificial, what of the product? If laboratory conditions render the embryo somehow artificial, is it valid to reason that such an embryo is not truly human? If so, then the interests of the human embryo can be dismissed as having no compelling bearing on the ethical decision of whether to create and destroy them to be a source of living stem cells for the treatment of diseases in others.

21. Rick Weiss, "Firm Aims to Clone Embryos for Stem Cells," *Washington Post,* 12 July 2001; Sheryl G. Stolberg, "Scientists Create Scores of Embryos to Harvest Cells," *New York Times,* 11 July 2001.

Science begs the question ever more strongly: who made the embryo? If one believes God to be creator, then the next question is whether God intends human embryos to be subjected to research entailing their destruction. Might the Creator have a greater purpose in mind for human beings?

If instead one believes humanity to be its own creator, then humanity would seem to possess the moral authority to create and destroy human life at will, according to the standard of utility society chooses to set for the purpose of maximizing happiness for the greatest number. Armed with technology, and regarding human embryos as material products of technology, a naturalistic appraisal of human life evades the moral objection to deleterious embryonic stem cell research. To be artificial is, perhaps, to be dispensable.

Behold the Homunculus

The alchemists were here first. Less than twenty years after Martin Luther nailed his ninety-five theses to the church door at Wittenberg, the Swiss physician and noted alchemist Paracelsus published a recipe for creating a tiny artificial human being — a "homunculus" — by means of an alchemical process. Paracelsus's 1572 recipe entailed the following:

> Let the semen of a man putrefy by itself in a sealed cucurbite [gourd] with the highest putrefaction of venter equinus [horse manure] for forty days, or until it begins to live, move, and be agitated, which can easily be seen. At this time it will be in some degree like a human being, but, nevertheless, transparent and without a body. If now, after this, it be every day nourished and fed cautiously with the arcanum of human blood, and kept for forty weeks in the perpetual and equal heat of venter equinus, it becomes thencefold a true living infant, having all the members of a child that is born from a woman, but much smaller. This we call a homunculus.[22]

There is no evidence that Paracelsus ever succeeded in creating a homunculus, but his recipe did inspire a number of artists. In one nineteenth-century engraving a Faustian alchemist sits in a shadowy corner, peering through spectacles past billowing smoke into his flaming alembic,

22. Aureolus Philippus Theophrastus Bombast von Hohenheim (Paracelsus), *De Natura Rerum* (1572), cited by Clara Pinto-Correia, "Honunculus: Historiographic Misunderstandings of Preformationist Terminology," published at http://zygote.swarthmore.edu/fert1b.html.

where he has concocted a miniature human form.[23] The tiny homunculus grasps at the enclosing glass wall. The distorted figure of another forlorn homunculus staggers at the edge of a sixteenth-century triptych by Hierony-mus Bosch.[24] Interestingly, some contemporaries speculated that homunculi, once grown, tended to turn on their creators.

The advent of microscopes a century later gave rise to preformationist theories of reproduction. Some of these were stirred by a 1694 drawing by Niklaas Hartsoeker, who depicted what he thought he saw under the micro-scope — a homunculus, or fully formed tiny man tightly curled up within a sperm cell. Preformationist theories postulated that all generations of hu-manity were sequentially encased in miniature within previous generations, much like a Russian nested doll. There were also the "ovists," who challenged the findings of the "spermists," maintaining that successive generations of humanity were enfolded instead within the maternal egg. Better microscopes eventually proved both versions false.

Each of these theories of the homunculus demonstrates that, when it comes to understanding what it means to be human, one may see only what one expects to find. It is not surprising, then, that a view of the human em-bryo premised on naturalistic philosophy finds under the lens of the micro-scope a collection of cells, an arrangement of molecules, a mechanism — nothing more.

Alchemists and preformationists who reported seeing homunculi saw human beings where there were none. Modern proponents of destructive hu-man embryo research see no human being where there is one. Both are de-ceived.

The Philosopher's Clone

This discussion has explored several strata of philosophy, some ancient, some futuristic. From frozen arctic ice fields to the alchemist's blazing furnace, from the long extinct to the newly living, from the enormous woolly mam-moth to microscopic human life, science continues to seek to understand the world, the place of humanity in it, and what it means to be human. Increas-ingly able through technology to subdue the world, scientifically elevated hu-

23. Jean-Loup Charmet Archive, Paris, reproduced in Editors of Time-Life Books, *Secrets of the Alchemists*, p. 68.
24. The Granger Collection, Luisa Ricciarini, Milan, reproduced in Editors of Time-Life Books, *Secrets of the Alchemists*, p. 69.

manity next wrestles with whether and how to revise not only its place in the world but also the meaning of human life. Biotechnology in particular is introducing afresh these old questions in entirely new terms. The genome has been penetrated. To examine now the essence of humanity under the lens of science is to gaze down the winding staircase of the genetic double helix. Like the alchemist of old, the biotechnologist of today manipulates successive transmutations of cellular differentiation and rearranges snippets of genetic code in the great work of conquering the forces of life and nature in order to overcome disease, extend youth, and turn out wealth.

Having failed to produce the Philosopher's Stone, the biomedical alchemist proposes to settle for creating the "Philosopher's Clone." The Philosopher's Clone is that human embryo created solely to be harvested for his or her stem cells. These embryonic stem cells seemingly embody the elixir of life in their anticipated capacity to replace degenerated cells and extend the lives of others. Intoxicated by the age-old fantasy of abolishing aging, the biomedical alchemist comes face-to-face once more with the apparition of the homunculus, that synthetic human being supposedly having no soul.

Biomedical alchemy is not the only new alchemical subspecialty. The bioethical alchemist now steps forward to clarify the place of the Philosopher's Clone in society by conjuring a novel category of life at the margin of humanity. This putative twilight class exists somewhere between person and property. In language befitting a cryptic alchemical text, the Human Embryo Research Panel of the National Institutes of Health appealed to this vague category by concluding that the human embryo subjected to lethal research ought to be treated with "profound respect."[25] With quintessential ambiguity, John Polkinghorne expounded that "Embryos are entitled to profound respect, but not the same respect as is accorded to a full human being."[26] Daniel Callahan offered the following golden comment in reply: "I have always felt a nagging uneasiness at trying to rationalize killing something for which I claim to have a profound respect."[27]

A remarkable transmutation of logic appeared in the 1984 Warnock Report, which addressed the ethical problems of reproductive technology in the United Kingdom. The Warnock Committee deliberately bypassed the question of whether the early embryo is to be regarded as a human life and ad-

25. National Institutes of Health, report of the Human Embryo Research Panel, 27 September 1994.

26. Quoted in "Vatican Leads Chorus Objecting to Human Cloning," *CNN.com*, 18 August 2000.

27. Daniel Callahan, "The Puzzle of Profound Respect," *Hastings Center Report* 25, no. 1 (1995): 39-40.

dressed instead the practical question of "how it is right to treat the human embryo."[28] The report did not explain, as Nigel Cameron has pointed out,[29] how it is possible to decide how it is right to treat something without first considering what that thing is.

Harold Shapiro, during his tenure as chair of the National Bioethics Advisory Commission, held that society's moral obligation to the human embryo is only "symbolic."[30] From his point of view the human embryo is a representation of humanity, an abstraction, not a real human being. The homunculus has crept into his thinking.

Peter Singer has descended even further into the murky depths of moral skepticism. Devaluing human life by use of cursory imagery, he wrote, "Looking at embryos in glass dishes on laboratory benches makes it more difficult to cling to the belief that all human life is equally precious from the moment of conception."[31] Writing with ink more caustic than *aqua regia*, Singer reached the stark conclusion that in the end there is nothing "so special about the fact that a life is human."[32] If Singer had been looking at cultures of smallpox virus in those glass dishes, he would have been mistaken to think them harmless on the basis of their size or their ordinary outward shape. His error is all the greater when denying the humanity of tiny human beings on the basis of his prejudices concerning superficial appearance. Not even the alchemists regarded the stars to be mere points of light.

Those who pursue the Philosopher's Clone strain to see clearly past the veil of ethical smog emanating from the biotechnical *magnum opus* that vainly snatches at immortality. The moral boundaries that separate the Philosopher's Clone from the rest of humanity are as hazy as the edges of the alembic, ever enshrouded by noxious clouds sputtering from the alchemist's stove. Those who inhale deeply these curls of rhetorical smoke may imagine the young human being to be composed of primordial dark matter, her stem cells biologic base metal to be taken to pieces and reprocessed to serve a supposedly nobler purpose.

The progress of science has brought not less but greater urgency to the

---

28. "Report of the Committee of Inquiry into Human Fertilisation and Embryology (Cmnd. 9314)" (London: HMSO, 1984), p. 60.

29. Nigel M. de S. Cameron, *The New Medicine: Life and Death After Hippocrates* (Wheaton, Ill.: Crossway, 1991), p. 106.

30. Quoted in R. Weiss, "Presidential Ethics Panel Supports Some Research on Human Embryos," *Washington Post*, 23 May 1999.

31. Peter Singer, *Rethinking Life and Death: The Collapse of Our Traditional Ethics* (New York: St. Martin's Griffin, 1994), p. 97.

32. Singer, *Rethinking Life and Death*, p. 105.

timeless questions that still haunt us: "Who is my neighbor?" (Luke 10:29 after Lev. 19:18) and "Am I my brother's keeper?" (Gen. 4:9). How medical science will exercise its stewardship of human embryos will depend on to what authority humanity believes it is accountable. Alchemy answers to a self-contained, organic yet impersonal nature subject to human control. Those who believe in the authority of the Bible as God's revealed Word for humanity answer to nature's transcendent Author, the living God and King of the universe.

Regression to the Core

As one proceeds to unwrap the moral questions and peel away the biologic layers of human identity, one's task resembles that of the alchemist of old, coaxing scraps of metal through a graded progression toward the highest level of purity and nobility. The alchemist seeks to distill the essence of things, to render them comprehensible, tangible, containable, as liquid condensing out of vapor. Yet the human spiritual essence cannot be so distilled. The soul is inaccessible to direct scientific observation or manipulation, as intimated by the psalmist's question, "What can man do to me?" (Pss. 56:11; 118:6).

The image of a Russian nested doll again comes to mind. Drawing from the analogy of the *matrioshka,* what Winston Churchill said of Russia in 1939 could also be said of the human embryo, indeed of the politics of human embryonic stem cell research: "I cannot forecast you the actions of Russia. It is a riddle wrapped in a mystery inside an enigma."[33]

Discoveries in the field of nuclear physics have, in the years since Churchill, penetrated past the layers of the classical molecular models to the deepest subatomic level. Incredibly, or perhaps not, through modern science the alchemists' age-old dream of transforming base metal into gold has become a reality. In the 1960s physicist Judith Temperley bombarded mercury, an element having eighty protons, with a beam of high-energy neutrons from a powerful cyclotron. A single neutron entering the nucleus of a mercury atom dislodged a proton, taking with it one electron. The result was an atom with only seventy-nine protons — by definition an atom of gold, containing just a few extra neutrons.[34]

How efficiently can the *magnum opus* proceed assisted by nuclear phys-

33. Winston Churchill, radio broadcast, 1 October 1939.
34. Ruth Kassinger, "Alchemy: Then and Now," *Washington Post,* 22 March 1999, published at http://www.crystalinks.com/alchemy3.html.

ics? Physicists estimate that the time it would take to accumulate a penny's worth of gold by this method is 10^{24} years.[35] That number is a one followed by twenty-four zeros. One million billion billion years' work for one penny's worth of gold. The quest of alchemy is just as futile when it comes to efforts to secure human immortality.

For Thy Sake

The quest for the Philosopher's Clone appears to be headed down the same worthless path already trodden by countless alchemists who found no pot of gold but only a dead end. Unlike the metallurgical alchemist who left behind scraps of metal, the biomedical alchemist leaves behind a trail of shelled human embryos. The crossroads, however, are still near. There is still the opportunity to pause and reason together what kind of perfection we should seek, what kind of vision we should follow, at what cost, and to what purpose.

The problem alchemy seeks to repair is, alas, our fallen human condition. All human beings as mortals disobedient to God are fundamentally flawed — biologically, genetically, and spiritually. Thus science can forestall death only a little while. No utilitarian reallocation of stem cell assets can reverse the aging process. No magical transmutation from alchemy can renew us. The tree of knowledge cannot be genetically engineered to produce the fruit of the tree of life. Only God himself can restore us.

Bear in mind, not all ancient sages looked to the same stars for guidance. Certain wise men from the East followed a single bright star that pointed them to something more wondrous than the alchemists could have imagined. In Bethlehem in a manger they found the child Jesus, the Messiah of the Jews (Matt. 2:1-2). God himself entered this world, not as a simulated human being, but truly as one of us, to live and die as we do, yet without sin. The Word became flesh, first as a human embryo, and dwelt among us (Matt. 1:18-23; John 1:14). By his incarnation God affirmed the dignity of the human being at every stage of development.

Psalm 19 declares that "The judgments of the LORD are true and righteous altogether. More to be desired are they than gold, Yea, than much fine gold" (vv. 9-10 NKJV). No homunculus, no artificial humanlike entity, no philosopher's clone can remove the taint of sin, the penalty of which is death. Being less than human, they cannot substitute for humanity. But Je-

35. Kassinger, "Alchemy: Then and Now."

sus Christ, being in very nature God yet also fully human (Phil. 2:6-8), suffered execution (Ps. 22; Isa. 53), and in his death took upon himself the penalty for the sins of humanity (Rom. 6:5-11). In his great love, God has not abandoned humanity to its futile state. By his atoning sacrifice and resurrection he has reconciled us to himself so that we may have eternal life in fellowship with him. In Jesus Christ humanity has access to the precious gift of eternal life (John 3:16; 6:54; 10:28; 11:25-27; 17:2-3; Rom. 6:23; 2 Cor. 4; 1 John 5:11-13). You might poetically say that we must look to his cross to shed our dross.

In his 1633 poem "The Elixir," George Herbert draws from the language of alchemy to express the Christian belief that dignifies all experience. This elixir is to do everything in life for God, "for Thy sake":

> Teach me, my God and King,
> In all things Thee to see,
> And what I do in anything
> To do it as for Thee.
>
> Not rudely, as a beast,
> To run into an action;
> But still to make Thee prepossest,
> And give it his perfection.
>
> A man that looks on glass,
> On it may stay his eye;
> Or if he pleaseth, through it pass,
> And then the heav'n espy.
>
> All may of Thee partake:
> Nothing can be so mean,
> Which with his tincture — "for Thy sake" —
> Will not grow bright and clean.
>
> A servant with this clause
> Makes drudgery divine:
> Who sweeps a room as for Thy laws,
> Makes that and th' action fine.
>
> This is the famous stone
> That turneth all to gold;

For that which God doth touch and own
Cannot for less be told.[36]

Perfection of fallen people in a broken world cannot be achieved through the alchemist's crucible but has been decisively accomplished by Christ crucified. "Therefore, if anyone is in Christ, he is a new creation; old things have passed away; behold, all things have become new" (2 Cor. 5:17 NKJV).

36. George Herbert, "The Elixir," in *The Temple. Sacred Poems and Private Ejaculations,* ed. N. Ferrer (Cambridge: T. Buck and R. Daniel, 1633). Further commentary on this poem may be found in Nigel M. de S. Cameron, *Complete in Christ: Rediscovering Jesus and Ourselves* (London: Paternoster, 1989), pp. 44-45.

Index

Advance medical directives, 22, 30, 49-50

Age-based rationing of life-sustaining health care, 58-74; and biblical alternative, 64-66, 73-74; and Christian perspective, 72-74; and cultural differences/alternative perspectives, 63-64, 73; and economic impact of aging population, 61-62; equal opportunity justification, 68, 69-70; and ethical allocation of resources, 58-61; funding issues, 58-60, 67, 68; medical benefit justification, 67-69; natural life-span justification, 68, 70-71; non-utilitarian justifications for, 67-72; and other hidden injustices, 73-74; prudence justification, 69, 71-72; and quality-of-life criterion, 71; and sinfulness of the world, 73; and utilitarian orientation, 62-63; weakness and protection, 65-66, 73; wisdom and respect, 65-66, 73; and women, 73-74

Aging American population: American culture and views of, 62-63, 108; and demographic shifts in aging, 46, 61-62, 76-77, 109-10, 155; demographics of dementia, 76-77; and economic impacts, 61-62; and intergenerational church communities, 109-10; and longevity trends, 154-55

Aging with Grace (Snowdon), 159-60

Akamba people (Kenya), 63-64, 73

Alchemy: defining worldview of, 178-80; and embryonic stem cell research, 178, 180-82, 187; and modern cloning biotechnology, 178-82, 185-86, 189-92; and the philosopher's stone, 178-80, 181, 182. *See also* Biotechnology

Alexopoulos, G. S., 123

Allen, Woody, 154

Allshorne, Florence, 14

Alzheimer's dementia: and aesthetic and spiritual well-being, 93-94; and assisted oral feeding, 101-3; and caregivers' spirituality, 97-98, 99; in Chinese/Japanese culture, 90; clergy and diagnosis, 94, 95; comfort care and the avoidance of hospitalization, 101; coping with diagnosis, 94-99; diagnosing of, 79; and emotional and relational well-being, 92-93; and health-care professionals, 94-95, 98; and hope, 94; and hospice care, 101-2; "hypercognitive" values and the narrowing of "personhood" in, 89-92; and life extension treatments, 100, 101-3; and longitudinal study of nuns, 159-60; and love, altruistic, 87-89; love and overcoming of exclusion, 92; medical interventions and advanced stage,